F

N

International Textbooks in Art and Art Education

ITALO L. DE FRANCESCO
Consulting Editor

Source Book
for Art Teachers

Source Book for Art Teachers

KATHERINE C. LA MANCUSA

INTERNATIONAL TEXTBOOK COMPANY

Scranton, Pennsylvania

TO MY PARENTS:

Catherine *and* Joseph La Mancusa

Editor's Preface

This book is a *tool* in the best sense of the word. It deals with terms often used by artists and art teachers and refers primarily to materials used in the performance of the creative act.

When the author first broached the idea of a "Dictionary" of art terms for use by art teachers and elementary teachers who teach in self-contained classrooms, it seemed a very plausible project. We believe she is rendering a worthwhile service to the practice of art teaching.

It may be pointed out that *all terms* are not included.

And yet, textbooks on any subject do not pretend to be complete in every sense. What seems important is that a good beginning has been made.

In addition to listing and defining art terms, the author often gives the teacher related information on the subject covered. This is worthwhile.

In presenting the volume, it is hoped that a handy reference tool will have been made available to professional art teachers and to those who work under their direction.

I. L. de Francesco

Foreword

The author believes that the one common need of teachers lies in the area of economy of reference, for teachers do not have time to read preambles when they are looking for specifics.

This source book presents a concise organization of terms, materials, and processes. It was developed by a teacher for the classroom teacher of art. The terms, materials, and processes described are presented with a glossary format for the sake of economy. The crossfile references which run throughout purport to show relatedness within the classroom learning laboratory.

This source book is not complete, nor was it intended to be complete. When a new process is discovered, new terms and materials will accompany the process. When new materials are developed, the old process might well be simplified, modified, or extended.

Hopefully, this book is presented not as a philosophical tome but rather as a springboard toward understanding and communication and as a catalyst toward experimentation and further research.

Katherine C. La Mancusa

Acknowledgments

Gratitude is expressed to the following persons for their invaluable help in the preparation of this manuscript:

To International Textbook Company, particularly to Dr. Italo de Francesco for his criticisms and suggestions; to Mr. Kenneth Gromlich for his steadfast communications and his comprehensive guidelines; and to Mr. Kay Chamberlain for his initial interest in the publication of this source book.

To Michael Finnegan for his line drawings; and to Linda Paccagnella for her illustrations on the alphabet.

To Albert Dorsa, Jr., George Paige, and Paul Finnegan for their help in photography; and to professional colleagues Paul Finnegan, Harry Green, Clare Jordan, Marjorie Livingston, Alma McConnell, and John Moyer for their cooperation in making it possible to photograph students' work.

To Marjorie Livingston for allowing me to photograph her weaving and stitchery; and to Ralph Putzker for allowing me to use his line sketches for this publication.

To students and teachers at Frederic Burk Laboratory Demonstration School, Francisco Junior High, Galileo High, and San Francisco State College for their cooperation in providing many of the subjects for photography and illustration.

To the proprietor and employees of Fasts Camera Shop in San Francisco for their patience and help in teaching the author the intricate workings of an often perplexing German camera.

To my family and my friends who provided the interest and the incentive to get the job done.

And finally to the task itself which began, developed, and grew into a three-year challenge. Toward those who helped, I express my deepest gratitude.

Katherine C. La Mancusa

Contents

List of Illustrations

* Both the Art Department and the Frederic Burk Laboratory-Demonstration School are part of San Francisco State College, San Francisco, Calif.

Figure	Description or Content	Institution*	Credit	Photographer
B-16	Facing inside of back cover		Michael Finnegan	
B-17	Completed booklet		Michael Finnegan	
B-18	Border example		Author	
B-19	Rubber roller brayer		Author	
B-20	Brush		Michael Finnegan	
B-21	Different types of brushes		Author	
B-22	Speedball steel brushes		Hunt Manufacturing Co.	
B-23	Science bulletin board	Frederic Burk School	First grade class	George Paige
C-1	Chinese calligraphy		Audrey Lum	
C-2	A campanile		Michael Finnegan	
C-3	Candles		Author	
C-4	A caricature		Author	
C-5	Aggregate carved sculpture	Art Department	Student	Paul Finnegan
C-6	Plaster-of-paris sculpture	Art Department	Student	Author
C-7	Sand casting utilizing driftwood	Art Department	Student	Author
C-8	Ceramics		Author	
C-9	Cutting a slab pot pattern		Author	
C-10	A kiln showing stacking of ceramic pieces		Author	
C-11	View of Parthenon showing classical orders			Albert Dorsa, Jr.
C-12	Collage utilizing textured papers, paints, chalk, and crayon resist	Art Department	Student	Author
C-13	Color wheel		Author	
C-14	Sculpture construction created with scraps of wood		Ralph Putzker	Author
C-15	Copper enameling		LaClairs	Author
C-16	A poster using the principle of counterchange	Art Department	Student	Author
C-17	A melted-crayon design	Art Department	Student	Author
D-1	Decorative paper done with chalk + starch + press	Art Department	Student	Author
D-2	Crackled paper	Art Department	Student	Author
D-3	Crayon engraving	Art Department	Student	Author
D-4	Crayon laminations with thread	Art Department	Student	Author
D-5	Colored tissue lamination	Art Department	Student	Author
D-6	Confetti lamination	Art Department	Student	Author
D-7	Crayon resist	Art Department	Student	Author

* Both the Art Department and the Frederic Burk Laboratory-Demonstration School are part of San Francisco State College, San Francisco, Calif.

* Both the Art Department and the Frederic Burk Laboratory-Demonstration School are part of San Francisco State College, San Francisco, Calif.

Figure	Description or Content	Institution*	Credit	Photographer
K-1	A school-type ceramic kiln		Author	
K-2	Copper enameling kilns		Author	
L-1	Onion skins laminated with waxed paper	Art Department	Student	Author
L-2	Laminated paper sculpture	Art Department	Student	Author
L-3	Horizontal spacing of letters		Michael Finnegan	
L-4	Initial fold for cut-paper letters		Author	
L-5	Paper folded in accordion fashion for cut-paper letters		Author	
L-6	Letter guide		Author	
L-7	Plastic letters used as captions for bulletin-board displays	Frederic Burk School	Fifth grade classroom	George Paige
M-1	Magnesite sculpture	Art Department	Student	Author
M-2	Manzanita branch		Author	
M-3	Egg tree		Author	
M-4	Outline map	Frederic Burk School	Elementary grade student	George Paige
M-5	Mitered corner		Author	
M-6	Mobile		Michael Finnegan	
M-7	Mat		Author	
M-8	Mount		Author	
M-9	Paper movie		Author	
M-10	Mural painted by preschool children	Frederic Burk School	Classroom for the deaf	Author
M-11	Mixed media mural	Art Department	College students	Author
N-1	Potato print notan	Art Department	Student	Author
O-1	Oil painting	Art Department	Student	Author
P-1	Kindergarten tempera painting	Frederic Burk School	Kindergarten class	Author
P-2	Watercolor painting	Art Department	Student	Author
P-3	Paper cutter		Author	
P-4	Paper sculpture form	Art Department	Student	Author
P-5	Papier-mâché animal	Art Department	Student	Author
P-6	Papier-mâché mask	Frederic Burk School	Sixth grade student	Author
P-7	Wooden dowel stand		Author	
P-8	Standard types of repeat patterns		Michael Finnegan	

* Both the Art Department and the Frederic Burk Laboratory-Demonstration School are part of San Francisco State College, San Francisco, Calif.

Figure	Description or Content	Institution*	Credit	Photographer
P-9	Extension of experimentation with repeat patterns	Art Department	Student	Author
P-10	Peep show		Author	
P-11	One-point perspective		Author	
P-12	Two-point perspective		Author	
P-13	Lithograph: "Le Tir a L'Arc"		Georges Braque	Author
P-14	A poster	Art Department	Student	Author
P-15	Block print		Michael Finnegan	Author
P-16	Bottle print	Art Department	Student	Author
P-17	Brayer print	Art Department	Student	Author
P-18	Brayer relief print	Francisco Junior High School, San Francisco, Calif.	Student	Author
P-19	Brayer string print	Art Department	Student	Author
P-20	Fish print	Art Department	Student	Author
P-21	Gadget print	Art Department	Student	Author
P-22	Gum eraser print	Art Department	Student	Author
P-23	Leaf print	Art Department	Student	Author
P-24	Monoprint	Art Department	Student	Author
P-25	Potato print	Art Department	Student	Author
P-26	Rubber tube print	Art Department	Student	Author
P-27	Sandpaper print	Art Department	Student	Author
P-28	Silk screen print	Art Department	Student	Author
P-29	Spatter print	Art Department	Student	Author
P-30	Stencil print	Art Department	Student	Author
P-31	Stencil with bridge		Author	
P-32	String print	Art Department	Student	Author
P-33	Tagboard print	Galileo High School, San Francisco, Calif.	Student	Author
P-34	Onion print	Art Department	Student	Author
P-35	Woodcut: "Coronation of the Virgin"		Albrecht Dürer	Author
R-1	Examples of rubbings		Author	
S-1	Toothpick and Saran wrap sculpture	Art Department	Student	Paul Finnegan
S-2	Turtle constructed from scrap materials	Art Department	Student	Author
S-3	Sculpture		Ralph Putzker	Author

* Both the Art Department and the Frederic Burk Laboratory-Demonstration School are part of San Francisco State College, San Francisco, Calif.

Figure	Description or Content	Institution*	Credit	Photographer
S-4	Miniature silhouette		Property of Mary Dorsa	
S-5	Silk screen print	Art Department	Student	Paul Finnegan
S-6	Side A—back of silk screen		Author	
S-7	Side B—front of silk screen		Author	
S-8	Squeegee		Author	
S-9	Stabile		Ralph Putzker	Author
S-10	Stained glass window	Art Department	Student	James McManus
S-11	Staple gun		Author	
S-12	Stitchery	Art Department	Marjorie Livingston	Author
T-1	Template		Author	
T-2	Tie-dye	Art Department	Student	Author
T-3	Torn-paper collage	Art Department	Student	Author
U-1	Undercuts		Author	
W-1	Woven wall hanging	Art Department	Student	Author
W-2	Apple box loom		Michael Finnegan	
W-3	Examples of cursive and manuscript writing		Author	

* Both the Art Department and the Frederic Burk Laboratory-Demonstration School are part of San Francisco State College, San Francisco, Calif.

Source Book
for Art Teachers

ABRASIVES

Materials which are used for purposes of grinding, smoothing, cleaning, and polishing. Sand, emery, chalk, and pumice represent some of the natural forms of abrasives. Other types include forms of scouring pads, steel wool, and household cleansing agents. Abrasives commonly used in school art programs include the following:

Carborundum Stone: For smoothing rough edges on mosaic tile and copper pieces in copper enameling (see also COPPER ENAMELING and MOSAICS).

Crystolon Stone: For smoothing rough edges on cut tiles; generally used under running water for safety purposes (see also MOSAICS).

Emery Cloth: For smoothing filed edges on metal, cleaning copper pieces in the copper-enameling process, and removing rust. It is available in individual sheets or in packages of assorted grits from coarse to fine (see also COPPER ENAMELING).

Household Cleansing Powders: Effective in removing dried grout from mosaic tile surfaces (see also MOSAICS).

Pumice Powder: For rubbing over plastic, stone, or wood to achieve a smooth surface (see also LACQUER, LINSEED OIL, PLASTICS, SHELLAC, and VARNISH).

Sandpaper: For multipurpose craft program; available in individual sheets or in packages of assorted grits from coarse to fine (see also CERAMICS, DRIFTWOOD, MANZANITA, PRINTMAKING, and WOODWORKING).

Steel Wool: For smoothing and cleaning copper and driftwood, and removing grout from mosaics; available in varied gauges (see also COPPER ENAMELING, DRIFTWOOD, MOSAICS, and WOODWORKING).

Tripoli: Used for buffing metals; available in 1-pound cakes.

ABSTRACT

Quality of not being imitative of nature; capturing the essence of the subject without being wholly dependent upon it. Abstract art may be called a subjective new vision, in design or composition, which has been refined through the artist's personal interpretation. This may include distortion, modification, or rearrangement of the elements of design (see also DESIGN ELEMENTS). Figure A-1 shows in a) a realistic portrayal and in b) an abstract portrayal of an ink bottle. Cubistic art forms are considered to be the earliest examples of abstract art [see also ABSTRACT-EXPRESSIONISM, CUBISM, HISTORY (ART), MODERN ART, and NONOBJECTIVE ART].

EXAMPLE: "Lower Manhattan," by John Marin.

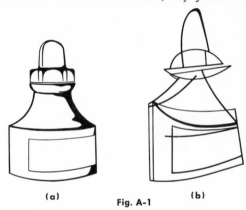

(a)   Fig. A-1   (b)

ABSTRACT-EXPRESSIONISM

Contemporary twentieth-century art movement which is qualitatively both abstract and expressionistic; also called Action Painting and Tachisme (see also ABSTRACT and EXPRESSIONISM). Abstract-expressionism may be considered as intuitive in approach rather than deliberate and planned. It avoids the geometric forms of nonobjective art and the often recognizable forms of synthetic cubism. Allowing for latitudes of expression in the graphic arts, for example, paint is often dripped or splashed on large canvases. Brush strokes are characteristically bold and free [see also CUBISM, HISTORY (ART), MODERN ART, and NONOBJECTIVE ART].

EXAMPLE: "Number 1, 1949," by Jackson Pollack.

A

ACADEMIC

To rely upon tradition in one's approach to art rather than on experimentation and exploration. The academic teacher of art might be considered one who is process-oriented in approach. The nonacademic teacher does not feel restricted by learning a process but considers the process as a jumping-off place toward further experimentation and discovery in the development of a highly personalistic statement—the contemporary art education approach.

ACCENT

Additional significance which is given to an area of design through skillful manipulation and rendering of one or more of the elements (see also COMPOSITION, DESIGN, and DESIGN ELEMENTS).

ACETATE COLORS

Water-soluble colors for use on acetate, cellophane, foils, and like materials of slick surfaces (see also ACETATE SHEETING, FOILS, PAPERS, and PLASTICS). Acetate colors are used with a brush and will not crack, chip, peel, or crawl on slick surfaces. These colors are used extensively by motion picture studios and designers [see also MOVIES (FILM)]. They are useful in classroom activities relating to the making of acetate overlay maps (see also MAPMAKING). They are available in a wide range of colors in 2-ounce containers for the classroom [see also ACETATE INKS and SUPPLIES (VENDORS)].

ACETATE INKS

See INKS.

ACETATE PAINTS

See ACETATE COLORS.

ACETATE PRINTS

Acetate printing plates are sometimes used by the professional printmaker in place of the more traditional zinc and copper plates in the intaglio processes [see also ACETATE SHEETING, INTAGLIO, and PRINTMAKING (PROFESSIONAL)]. Oil-base printing ink is rubbed into tool-incised lines and the print is taken on a printing press. This printmaking process has been adapted for school children by utilizing pressure, in a rubbing fashion, from the back of a tablespoon instead of from a printing press [see also PRINTMAKING and PRINTMAKING (PROFESSIONAL)].

ACETATE SHEETING

Also called cellulose acetate; similar in appearance to celluloid; available in varied thicknesses in clear or transparent, frosted or matte, and in colors (see also MATTE and PLASTICS). It is available in sheets: 20″ x 25″, 25″ x 40″, and 20″ x 50″ and may be purchased by single sheets, dozens, or by 100 lots. It is also available in rolls and may be purchased by the yard in 60″ widths. Acetate sheeting is used in classroom printmaking processes, in the rendering of overlay maps, and as a protective covering for charts (see also ACETATE PRINTS, LAMINATED RESIN, and MAPMAKING).

ACETIC ACID

Organic acid which results from the oxidation of alcohol; a 28 percent acetic acid is used for mordants in the setting of dyes for wool and silk fabrics (see also MORDANTS). Because acetic acid is considered a dangerous acid, it is never recommended for use in the elementary grades. Salt mordants are best suited for classroom experiences in dyeing (see also BATIK and TIE-DYE).

ACETONE

Colorless, inflammable liquid; used in the manufacturing of varnishes, lacquers, plastics, and rubber cement. Acetone may be used to remove print from 16-millimeter film when such film is being used in the production of classroom movies [see also MOVIES (FILM)]. It is also used as a solvent for Duco cement (see also ADHESIVES and SOLVENTS).

ACROPOLIS

Highest elevation of a Greek city; often its citadel. This was sometimes fortified and contained temples. In Greece, there was, for example, the acropolis at Mycenae, as well as the acropolis at Athens which contained the magnificent structure of the Parthenon (see also BALANCE, CLASSIC, and CLASSICISM).

ACTION PAINTING

See ABSTRACT-EXPRESSIONISM.

ADHERING SOLUTION

See SILK SCREENING.

ADHESIVES

Any material which will paste, glue, adhere, bond, weld, or cement. Some of the adhesives used in school art programs include the following:

Duco Cement: Fast drying cement; used for wood, leather, glass, metal, paper, or fabric (see also MOBILES, PRINTMAKING, and STABILES).

Epoxy Resin: Outstanding bonding power; often used to replace soldering in jewelry-making processes; will set in less than a minute and dry completely in 3 hours. Epoxy is sold with an accompanying tube of hardening agent. Both must be mixed together for bonding (see also COPPER ENAMELING).

Gum Tragacanth: For adhering enamel powder to copper pieces in the copper-enameling processes; also called gum solution (see also COPPER ENAMELING).

Higgins Vegetable Glue: For booklet making, bookbinding, and heavy paper work; may be diluted with water for economy and easier application (see also BOOKLET MAKING).

Kling-Kote Liquid Cloth: New adhesive for mending cloth, glass, china, crockery, plastic, leather, metal, wood, rubber, or canvas. When dry, it is flexible, clear, waterproof, weatherproof, and fracture proof; is not affected by heat and cold; and will wash and dry-clean.

NOTE: Available from L. A. Kling Enterprises, Inc., 701 Washington Street, Evanston, Illinois.

Lacquer (Clear): For overlays of colored tissue in paper collage techniques (see also COLLAGE).

Lepages Glue: For heavy materials such as wood, chipboard, and leather. It is also used as a blocking-out substance in tusche silk screening (see also SILK SCREENING).

Liquid Starch: For overlays of colored tissue in paper collage techniques, when diluted with water (see also COLLAGE). It is also used as a substitute for wheat paste in the strip- and pulp-papier-mâché processes (see also PAPIER-MÂCHÉ).

Lucite Cement: For all lucite welding (see also LUCITE and PLASTICS).

Mastic Tile Adhesive: For large wall mosaics; for bonding tile to plaster, cement blocks, cement stepping stones, or wood (see also MOSAICS).

Mazola Oil: Used to adhere colored tissue cutouts to windows in the techniques for stained glass windows [see also STAINED GLASS WINDOWS and TISSUE (COLORED)].

Rabbit-Skin Glue: For the sizing and coating of canvas; used also as a binder in the preparation of gesso (see also CANVAS and GESSO).

Rez-N-Glue Cement: For welding of styrofoam (see also STYROFOAM).

Rubber Cement: For adhering material to paper, plastics such as acetate sheeting and vinylite sheeting, glass, or metal. It may be rubbed off with the fingers or removed with an art gum eraser; may be thinned with rubber-cement thinner. It will not penetrate, wrinkle, or stain papers (see also ACETATE SHEETING, DECORATIVE PAPERS, ERASERS, PLASTICS, PRINTMAKING, and SOLVENTS).

Silicone Rubber Sealants: Tube-rubber silicone preparation which is used extensively in the construction of missiles and space capsules. Available under the trade name of "Bathtub Seal," it is a General Electric product. This preparation is flexible and waterproof when dry. It will not shrink or crack and will act as a seal and bond for ten years. It sets up to a firm rubber in 3 hours and will continue to improve as it ages. "Bathtub Seal" dries white and is recommended for the caulking and bonding of bathtubs, shower stalls, sinks, tiles, and bathroom fixtures. It is used for ceramic, porcelain, glass, metal, and plastics. It is also available as "Metal Seal" which is recommended for metal sealing and bonding and dries aluminum colored; "Clear Seal" which is recommended for the repair of rubber goods, fabrics, leather, appliances, and electrical insulation and dries colorless; and "Auto Seal" which is recommended for sealing leaky windshields, door gaskets, and convertible tops.

Spray Glue: Pressurized spray can of glue; used for wood, china, paper, and glass (see also SPRAYS).

Testor's Cement for Plastics: For welding of all common plastics (see also PLASTICS).

Wheat Paste: For papier-mâché processes; used commonly as a binder in the preparation of some modeling materials such as asbestos and sawdust (see also MODELING MATERIALS, WHEAT PASTE, and PAPIER-MÂCHÉ).

White Resin Glue: Versatile glue which dries colorless; can bond wood, glass, and paper; used in stitchery and booklet making. It is also used as an adhesive in mosaics for adhering tile to plywood, walls, or cement blocks. It is sold under trade names of Elmer's Glue, Wilhold Glue, and others (see also CHEESECLOTH, MOSAICS, PAINT SUBSTITUTES, STAINED GLASS WINDOWS, and STITCHERY).

White School Paste: Most commonly used in classroom art programs in the elementary grades for all work relating to paper [see also SUPPLIES (CLASSROOM) and SUPPLIES (VENDORS)].

ADOBE

Crude, unrefined earth clay which was used extensively in California and Mexico during the early Spanish Mission period. Adobe clay was dug from the ground, mixed with straw, put into brick molds, and dried in the sun. Abobe brick constructions were protected from the elements with a coating of white limestone. Figure A-2 illustrates a reproduction of an early Californian adobe mission created by fourth-grade students (see also CERAMICS, CLAY, and LIMESTONE).

ADVANCING COLOR

See COLOR.

AEGEAN ART

Pre-Hellenic art of antiquity, 4500-200 B.C.; also called Cretan Art and Minoan Art. The Aegean civilization was located in the area of the Aegean Sea at Mycenae, Tiryns, Crete, and Cyprus. Art forms were advanced in their degree of development, particularly in ceramics [see also ANTIQUITY, CERAMICS, HISTORY (ART), PRE-HELLENIC, and WESTERN ART].

AERIAL PERSPECTIVE

See PERSPECTIVE.

Fig. A-2

AESTHETIC

Pertaining to the study of aesthetics; the science or theory of the beautiful.

AESTHETIC-DISTANCE

That distance which the viewer voluntarily puts between himself and the art form being viewed in order to see it with maximum satisfaction and appreciation.

AGGREGATES

Collection of materials which have been combined into a common medium for building, carving, or sculpture (see also CARVING MATERIALS).

ALABASTER

Semitransparent stone which is usually white, easily cut, and capable of a high polish (see also LAPIDARY).

ALLOVER PATTERNS

See PATTERNS.

ALPHABET

The word alphabet is derived from the first and second letters of the Greek alphabet: alpha (A) and beta (B). The four basic styles of the alphabet are shown in Fig. A-3: a) Italic, b) Gothic, c) Roman, and d) Text. The Gothic style is most commonly used in the classrooms in

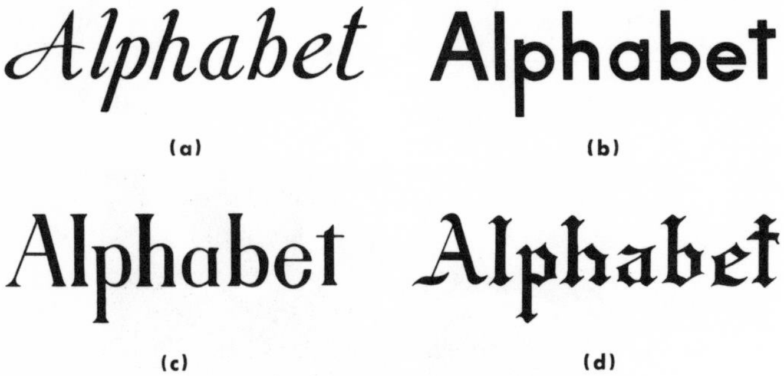

Alphabet **Alphabet**

(a)   (b)

Alphabet Alphabet

(c)   (d)

Fig. A-3

both the upper-case letters (capitals) and the lower-case letters (small letters). The terms upper-case and lower-case come from the early trade vernacular of the linotype operators who used to set type by hand. They stored their capital letters in an upper case, above their working area; and the small letters in a lower case, below their working area [see also LETTERING, LETTERS (CUT-PAPER), LETTERS (PLASTIC), POSTERS, and WRITING].

ALPHATONE PAPER

See PAPERS.

ALTAMIRA

Caves located in the Cantabrian mountains of northern Spain where prehistoric drawings of bison and other images exist. These drawings on the walls of the caves have been traced to the Paleolithic period. The caves at Altamira were discovered in 1879. Similar Paleolithic drawings and paintings exist on the walls of the rock shelters of southwestern France at Lascaux (see also LASCAUX and PALEOLITHIC).

ALUMINUM FOIL

See FOIL.

ALUMINUM WIRE

See WIRES.

AMERICAN BLACK WALNUT

See WOODS.

ANALOGOUS COLORS

See COLOR.

ANALYTICAL CUBISM

See CUBISM.

ANIMALS

See ARMATURES, CARVING MATERIALS, CERAMICS, MODELING MATERIALS, and PAPIER-MÂCHÉ.

ANTIQUE WHITE PINE

See WOODS.

ANTIQUITY

The arts of antiquity include: Chaldean-Sumerian, Babylonian, Egyptian, Aegean—Cretan or Minoan, Early Chinese, Hittite, Etruscan, Phoenician, Assyrian, Early Indian, Early Greek-Hellenic, Early Persian, and Roman [see also HISTORY (ART)].

A

APPLIED DESIGN

Essentially the Bauhaus approach to the design of utilitarian forms. The Bauhaus held as its educational concept that there should be no division between design as related to the fine arts and design as related to pure utilitarian forms. As a result of this philosophy, utilitarian objects today, such as kitchen utensils, tools, and machinery, have reached the apex of development in terms of design of form relating to function (see also BAUHAUS).

APPLIQUÉ

Method of sewing or gluing cloth, felt, cotton roving, yarn, or other like materials to a ground of fabric; used extensively in stitchery. An example of appliqué is shown in Fig. A-4 (see also GROUND and STITCHERY).

Fig. A-4

AQUATINT

See INTAGLIO and PRINTMAKING (PROFESSIONAL).

ARCHITECTURE

Art of designing and constructing buildings. Among the contemporary architects who have made monumental contributions to the field of architecture are Frank Lloyd Wright, Pier Luigi Nervi, and Le Corbusier.

EXAMPLES: Civic Center for Marin County, California, designed by Frank Lloyd Wright; UNESCO Headquarters in Paris, designed by Pier Luigi Nervi; and High Court Building, Chandigarh, India, designed by Le Corbusier.

ARMATURES

Basic skeletal form which will support clay, papier-mâché, plaster, or any of the other modeling or sculpturing media. Depending entirely upon the weight of the material it will support, an armature is made of wood, steel, wire (see also WIRES), folded paper, or tin foil. Figure A-5

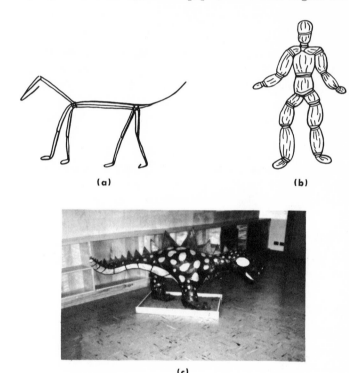

(a) (b)

(c)

Fig. A-5

shows a) a wire armature, b) a crushed newspaper armature, and c) a papier-mâché animal built over a wooden armature. In school art experiences relating to modeling and sculpture, armatures most generally support coverings of papier-mâché in either the pulp or the strip form (see also PAPIER-MÂCHÉ). Modeling materials such as asbestos, sawdust, structolite, and magnesite can also be used over armature supports (see also MAGNESITE and MODELING MATERIALS).

An excellent ready-made armature is the sawhorse. With added appendages of wood for the neck and head, one has the beginning skeletal form for a four-legged papier-mâché animal. Wrap the sawhorse armature with newspaper, padding it generously, and tie it in place with string. Cover this with four or five layers of strip papier-mâché. Paint it with tempera, shellac it, and add decorative details. Children can ride this animal (see also PAPIER-MÂCHÉ).

ARMORY SHOW

First significant showing of so-called Modern Art; held in 1913 at New York in the Armory of the 69th Cavalry Regiment. Among those exhibiting were: Matisse, Picasso, Braque, Kandinsky, Brancusi, and Duchamp. It was at this showing that Marcel Duchamp's "Nude Descending a Staircase" was exhibited (see also FUTURISM). Although the exhibit was ridiculed, it received a great amount of publicity and public interest. From the time of this Armory Show in 1913, the contemporary art movement enjoyed both controversy and popularity.

ARRANGEMENT

Manner in which things are placed, such as a room arrangement, a flower arrangement, or a still life.

ART BRUSHES

See BRUSHES, BRUSHES (CARE AND CLEANING), BRUSHES (STEEL), BRUSH STROKES, and SUPPLIES (CLASSROOM).

ART FILMS AND FILMSTRIPS

See FILMS AND FILMSTRIPS (ART).

ART GUM ERASERS

See ERASERS.

ART HISTORY

See HISTORY (ART).

ARTISTS

The following represents a listing of some of the better known painters, sculptors, and architects and the countries with which they were associated:

America: *(18th and 19th centuries)* John Copley, Charles Willson Peale, Thomas Jefferson, John James Audubon, and Henry Richardson. *(19th and 20th centuries)* Albert Bierstadt, James Abbott Whistler, Thomas Eakins, Louis Sullivan, John Singer Sargent, Mary Cassatt, Frank Lloyd Wright, Ben Shahn, Jackson Pollack, Willem de Kooning, Franz Kline, Stuart Davis, and Georgia O'Keeffe.

England: *(16th, 17th, and 18th centuries)* Inigo Jones, Christopher Wren, William Hogarth, Thomas Gainsborough, Joshua Reynolds, Thomas Chippendale, and Robert Adam. *(19th and 20th centuries)* William Blake, John Constable, Joseph Turner, Jacob Epstein, and Henry Moore.

Italy: *(13th and 14th centuries)* Giovanni Cimabue, Duccio di Buoninsegna, Giotto di Bondone, and Simone Martini. *(15th and 16th centuries)* Filippo Brunelleschi, Lorenzo Ghiberti, Donatello, Fra Angelico, Tommaso Masaccio, Piero della Francesca, Leonardo da Vinci, Piero and Antonio Pollaiuolo, Benvenuto Cellini, Sandro Botticelli, Donato Brámante, Raphael Sanzio, Tiziano Vecelli (Titian), Michelangelo Buonarroti, Antonio Correggio, Andrea de Pietro Palladio, Jacopo Robusti (Il Tintoretto), and Paolo Veronese. *(17th, 18th, and 19th centuries)* Michelangelo Caravaggio, Carlo Maderna, Giovanni Bernini, Francesco Borromini, Giovanni Tiepolo, Bernardo Caneletto, Francesco Guardi, Umberto Boccioni, and Gino Severini. *(20th century)* Pier Luigi Nervi.

The Netherlands and Belgium: *(15th, 16th, and 17th centuries)* Jan van Eyck, Rogire van der Weyden, Hugo van der Goes, Pieter Breughel, Peter Paul Rubens, Frans Hals, Anthony Van Dyck, Harmensz van Rijn Rembrandt, Jacob van Ruysdael, and Jan Vermeer. *(18th, 19th, and 20th centuries)* Vincent van Gogh, James Ensor, Piet Mondrian, and Josef Albers.

France: *(15th and 16th centuries)* Claus Sluter, Pol de Limbourg, Jean Fouquet, and Jean Clouet. *(17th and 18th centuries)* Nicolas Poussin, Claude Lorrain, Charles Le Brun, Jean Antoine Watteau, Jean Baptiste Chardin, François Boucher, Jean Fragonard, and Jacques Louis David.

A

(19th and 20th centuries) Jean Baptiste Corot, Honoré Daumier, Jean Louis Théodore Géricault, Jean Ingres, Eugène Delacroix, Gustave Courbet, Edouard Manet, Edgar Degas, Auguste Rodin, Claude Monet, Henri de Toulouse-Lautrec, Paul Gauguin, Paul Cézanne, Georges Seurat, Henri Matisse, Georges Braque, Fernand Léger, Marcel Duchamp, Marc Chagall, and Charles Edouard Le Corbusier.

Germany: *(14th, 15th, and 16th centuries)* Conrad Witz, Albrecht Dürer, and Hans Holbein. *(17th, 18th, 19th, and 20th centuries)* Lucas Von Hildebrandt, Johann Neumann, Franz Marc, Ernst Barlach, Paul Klee (Switzerland), Wassily Kandinsky (Russia), Ludwig Mies Van der Rohe, Walter Gropius, Emil Nolde, and Max Beckman.

Spain: *(16th and 17th centuries)* Domenico Teotocopulo (El Greco), Francisco de Zurbarán, Diego de Velásquez, and Bartolomé Murillo. *(18th, 19th, and 20th centuries)* Francisco Goya, Pablo Picasso, Joan Miró and Salvador Dali.

ART MAGAZINES

See MAGAZINES (ART).

ART PAPER

See PAPERS.

ART (POP)

See POP ART.

ART REPRODUCTIONS

See REPRODUCTIONS (ART).

ART SLIDES

See FILMS and FILMSTRIPS (ART).

ART SMOCKS

See SMOCKS (ART).

ART SUPPLIES

See SUPPLIES (CLASSROOM).

ART VENDORS

See SUPPLIES (VENDORS).

ASBESTOS

Also called asbestos powder and asbestos shorts; used for modeling experiences (Fig. A-6) in elementary and secondary classrooms. Gray asbestos powder will hold its shape when mixed with water only, with wheat paste, or with diluted mucilage or glue (see also ADHESIVES and MODELING MATERIALS). It is an inexpensive material which can be ordered from building supply houses such as Johns-

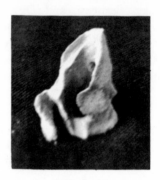

Fig. A-6

Manville, in 100-pound sacks. Asbestos powder may be used with or without an armature support for modeling experiences and sculpture (see also ARMATURES and SCULPTURE). It is a useful material in fashioning puppet heads (see also PUPPETS). It may also be used as a material to build relief maps and to fashion beads (see also BEAD-MAKING and MAPMAKING).

ASBESTOS PAD

Protects working surfaces from heat in batik and copper-enameling processes (see also BATIK and COPPER ENAMELING).

ASH

See WOODS.

ASHCAN SCHOOL

Significant group of early twentieth-century painters who were also known as "The Eight"; could best be described as painters of realism (see also REALISM). The painters of the Ashcan School centered their activities in New York and distinguished themselves by finding inspiration for their canvases through subject matter which had social impact.

EXAMPLE: "Forty-Two Kids," by George Bellows.

ASPHALTUM

Acid-resisting compound which is used in the etching process; more properly called an "etching ground" [see also GROUND, INTAGLIO, and PRINTMAKING (PROFESSIONAL)].

ASSEMBLAGE

Creation of art forms, for example, collage and sculpture, from "found objects" (see also FOUND OBJECT).

ASSYRIAN ART

One of the Eastern arts of antiquity, 1500-612 B.C.; derived from the Assyrian culture located in the valley of the Tigris River. Assyrian contributions in art forms were highly stylized and stiff, and included carvings in relief, sculpture, architecture, engraved ivories, and textiles [see also ANTIQUITY, HISTORY (ART), EASTERN ART, and SCULPTURE].

ASYMMETRICAL BALANCE

See BALANCE.

ASYMMETRY

See BALANCE.

ATELIER

Studio for painter or sculptor.

ATOMIZER

Metal mouth-type tool (Fig. A-7) which is used for the spraying of fixatives on drawings of charcoal, pencil, pastels, or colored chalk. The application of fixatives with

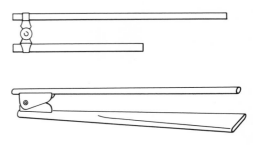

Fig. A-7

an atomizer will prevent smearing. Although commercial atomizers may be purchased inexpensively, teachers often prefer to use household spray cans or to buy one of the pressurized spray-can fixatives [see also FIXATIVES, FIXATIVE SUBSTITUTES, KRYLON, SPRAYS, and SUPPLIES (VENDORS)].

AUGER BITS

See WOODWORKING.

AWL

See WOODWORKING.

AXIS

Imaginary line in the graphic and plastic arts around which the component elements of design are arranged and balanced (see also BALANCE, DESIGN ELEMENTS, GRAPHIC ARTS, and PLASTIC ARTS).

AZTEC ART

See HISTORY (ART).

BABYLONIA

One of the great empires of the ancient world, 6000 to 500 B.C.; the country through which the Tigris and Euphrates rivers flowed; once called Mesopotamia, now Iraq. Babylonians, who were contemporaries of the early Egyptians, were skilled in relief carvings of limestone, wood, and bone; metal sculpture; and small mosaics [see also ANTIQUITY, EGYPTIANS, HISTORY (ART), LIMESTONE, MOSAICS, RELIEF, and SCULPTURE].

BALANCE

There are basically three kinds of balance in the rendering of designs both in the graphic and plastic arts (see also GRAPHIC ARTS and PLASTIC ARTS).

Asymmetrical Balance: Unequal distribution of parts of a design around a central axis causing balance to be achieved through skillful manipulation of the elements and tension (Fig. B-1). Asymmetrical balance is contemporary in style

Fig. B-1

and informal in character (see also AXIS and TENSION).

EXAMPLE: "Animals in the Underbrush," by Paul Klee.

Radial Balance: Purposeful equalization of attraction from a central point as in the wheel (Fig. B-2).

EXAMPLE: Rose windows in Gothic cathedrals.

Symmetrical Balance: Purposeful visual equilibrium of parts of a design through like distribution of weight around

Fig. B-2

a central axis as shown in Fig. B-3. Symmetrical design is classic in style and formal in character.

EXAMPLE (architecture): Parthenon, in Athens, Greece.

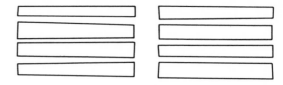

Fig. B-3

BALLOON CRAFT

Balloons can be used as bases for interesting forms which can hang from ceilings as mobiles or as part of a decorative motif for holidays and special events (see also HOLIDAYS and SPECIAL EVENTS). After the balloon has been blown up and tied securely, colored yarn which has been dipped in liquid starch may be wrapped around it. Allow the balloon to hang suspended from a line until the yarn is thoroughly dry, about four days. The balloon is easily removed and the shape of the balloon remains in linear form. This same technique can be applied with yarn, string, or cotton roving which has been dipped into a mixture of plaster of paris (see also PLASTER OF PARIS and YARNS AND STRINGS). Balloons may also be used as forms or armatures in the papier-mâché process in mask making (see also PAPIER-MÂCHÉ).

NOTE: If the balloon leaks air during the drying period, the basic linear form will become distorted. To insure against air leakage, tie the balloon securely and then put a few drops of white resin glue in the neck at the closure point (see also ADHESIVES).

BALLOONS (WEATHER)

Old weather balloons can be used as an armature over which students may build a world globe. Weather balloons are available at surplus stores (see also ARMATURES and PAPIER-MÂCHÉ).

BALSA WOOD

Light porous wood from Peru; useful in classroom activities relating to model building, carving, mobiles, and stabiles (see also CARVING, MOBILES, and STABILES). Totem poles and Kachina dolls are rendered successfully in balsa wood [see also DOLLS (KATCHINA) and TOTEM POLES]. When ordering from supply houses, the following sizes may be considered as standard: 1″ x 1″ x 36″, 2″ x 2″ x 36″, and 3″ x 3″ x 36″.

BAMBOO PENS

See PENS.

BAMBOO STICKS

Excellent kind of scrap material which can be obtained from curtain and drapery departments of local stores (see also SCRAP MATERIALS). Bamboo sticks represent the discarded trimmings when bamboo shades are cut to size; trimmings come in wide ranges of colors and lengths. When these sticks are bonded together with Duco cement from a common triangular base, they become stabiles (Fig. B-4) (see also STABILES). They may also be used in the rendering of mobiles (Fig. B-5) (see also MOBILES). When bamboo sticks are dipped into black ink, they became drawing tools for linear compositions. This is especially effective when the lines are rendered on wet paper (see also DRAWING and INKS).

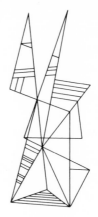

Fig. B-4

BANAK WOOD

See WOODS.

BARBIZON SCHOOL

Group of nineteenth-century artists who lived and painted in the area of a French village called Barbizon. They created a movement to paint outdoors because they saw nature as a subject unto itself; this movement preceded Impressionism (see also IMPRESSIONISM).

EXAMPLE: "The Oak of the Rocks," by Theodore Rousseau.

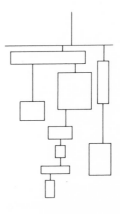

Fig. B-5

B

BAROQUE

Period in art history which originated in Italy and spread throughout Europe; flourished from the sixteenth to the eighteenth century, reaching its highest peak of development during the seventeenth century [see also HISTORY (ART)].

EXAMPLE (painting): "Burial of St. Petronilla," by Guercino.

EXAMPLES (architecture): The Church of San Carlo alle Quatro Fontaine in Rome, designed by Francesco Borromini; and the Chapel of St. Teresa in the Church of Santa Maria della Vittoria, designed by Gian Lorenzo Bernini.

BASILICA

Architectural structure which was adopted by the early Christians as a place of worship (see also CATACOMBS, CHRISTIAN ART, and MEDIEVAL ART).

BASKET BASES

Commercially made basket bases for the craft of basketry are made of 3-ply wood with holes bored through the bases for the purpose of inserting spoke reed. Holes generally correspond with spoke reed size 4 or 5. Basket bases are available in rectangular, round, and oval shapes and in the following sizes: rectangular, 4″ x 6″, 5″ x 8″, 6″ x 10″, 8″ x 12″, 12″ x 18″; round (diameter), 3″, 4″, 5″, 6″, 8″, 10″; and oval, 4″ x 6″, 5″ x 8″, 6″ x 10″, 8″ x 12″ [see also BASKET REED, BASKETRY, and SUPPLIES (VENDORS)].

BASKET REED

Reed is the dry stalks of grass which grow in marshes and is used in basket weaving. It is available under two classifications: spoke reed for basket spokes and weaver reed for horizontal weaving. Commercial basket bases will often take either size 4 or 5 spoke reed; generally spoke reed should be two sizes larger than the weaver reed. In smaller baskets, there may be a difference of only one size. Reed is sold by the pound. Purchase two pounds of spoke reed and two pounds of weaver reed per 24 children. Sizes of reed are: 0, 1, 2, 3, 4, 5, 6, 7, ¼″, ½″ (round), and ⅜″ (flat) [see also BASKET BASES, BASKETRY, and SUPPLIES (VENDORS)].

BASKETRY

One of the easier methods of weaving baskets is to begin with one of the precut commercial basket bases (see also BASKET BASES). However, as one grows in his experience in basketry, basket bases can be made in the classroom from 3-ply wood and holes can be fashioned for the spoke reed with hand drills (see also WOODWORKING). Commercial basket bases already have the spoke reed holes drilled in them, and these holes will generally correspond to sizes 4 and 5 spoke reed. It is important when ordering supplies to indicate the size of the spoke reed hole and to correspond the spoke reed to it (see also BASKET BASES). Order enough basket bases for the number of students in the classroom and order both the spoke reed and the weaver reed (see also BASKET REED).

Basket reed in its natural state is brittle. It is necessary to soak all reed in water for approximately 30 minutes. Add a teaspoon of glycerine to the water to increase the elasticity of the reed (see also GLYCERINE).

Procedure: Cut the spoke reed into 16″ lengths, cutting as many lengths as there are holes in the basket base. Insert the reed into the basket base, extending them out about 2½″ through the bottom of the base. Weave these bottom spokes together, underneath the base of the basket, in the following manner: Weave spoke 1 around the outside of base spoke 2 and tuck under base spoke 3. Take base spoke 2 around the outside of base spoke 3 and tuck it under base spoke 4. Continue around the bottom of the basket base in this fashion to both finish and secure the bottom spokes underneath the basket base.

Begin weaving the top of the basket with long lengths of weaver reed, beginning at the base of the basket. Weave with an under-one, over-one weaving pattern. Continue weaving in this fashion until the weaver reed is finished. Make sure that the weaver reed ends inside the spoke of the basket. If it is too long, cut it off. Insert another length of weaver reed in back of the spoke where the first weaver reed ended. Continue weaving, adjusting the shape of the basket as one weaves up. If a low flat basket is desired, pull the spoke reeds out as you work; if a high vertical basket is desired, keep the spokes almost perpendicular to the basket base. Continue weaving until approximately 3″ of spoke reed remain.

In finishing the basket, take each of the spokes and stick them into the basket in a fluted fashion, inserting them adjacent to the next spoke reed. Apply two or three coats of clear shellac to the finished basket (Fig. B-6). For

Fig. B-6

other kinds of baskets, particularly those without wooden bases, consult sources relating to basketry (see also WEAVING).

BAS-RELIEF

Also called low relief (see also PRINTMAKING, RELIEF, and RUBBINGS).

BASSWOOD

See WOODS.

BATIK

Wax-resist textile process wherein melted wax is applied to fabric to block out areas of fabric or color. Once the wax is applied, the fabric is dipped into a dye bath. The areas that contain the melted wax will resist color. The process of painting on wax, or applying it with a batik spoonlike tool called a tjanting, and dyeing is repeated several times.

Indonesians who practice this native craft apply melted wax to cloth with elaborate hand, wrought-iron stamping tools, and they removed the wax in boiling water. Professional batik artists use beeswax and remove the wax with carbon tetrachloride.

A simplified batik process has been perfected for school experiences. It involves the use of paraffin instead of bees-

wax; the wax is removed with an ironing process using a household iron.

Materials needed: 3 packages of dry dye in the primary colors, brilliant yellow, scarlet red, and royal blue (see also DYES); 6 enamel pans; 3 cakes of paraffin; 3 medium size easel brushes; an electric plate; an empty 2-pound coffee tin; cooking pot; ironing board; iron; bucket; Glauber's salt; newspaper; newsprint; and old white sheeting.

Selection of fabric for dyeing: Use old sheeting which has been torn into rectangles or squares; 12″ x 14″ is a good size for a beginning experience. If new material is used, wash and iron it to remove the sizing from the fabric.

Preparation of dye: It is best to prepare the dye the evening before it is to be used in the classroom. Pour the three colors of dry dye into three mason jars. Add about 1½ cups of boiling water to each jar. Stir the dye mixture with a spoon and allow the mixture to set in the mason jars until thoroughly cool. When the dye has cooled sufficiently, place lids tightly on the mason jars.

NOTE: There will be some residue of dye left in the jars even after the dye has been stirred. Leave it in the jars until the next day when the dye is poured into the enamel pans. At that time, stretch a nylon stocking over the mouth of the jars and strain the residue of dry dye from the concentrated dye solution.

Melting the wax: This step is done by the teacher in all instances. Never allow students to participate in this part of the process, particularly in the elementary grades. Never allow the students to transport the melted wax from the electric plate to the working area. Fill the cooking pot about ⅓ full of water. Place the paraffin in the coffee tin and then place the coffee tin inside the pot of water. Place the electric heating unit on the plate at "medium." When the wax begins to melt, the electric plate may then be turned down to "low."

Setting up the working area for painting with wax: Set up the work area on a low table which has been covered with newspapers. In the center of the table, place an asbestos pad on which to set the hot coffee tin containing the melted wax. Lay out the brushes at this work center.

Setting up the working area for dyeing: A large, long table which has been covered with newspapers will serve

B

best as a working area for dyeing. Pour the concentrated dye solutions into 3 of the 6 enamel pans. Add 1½ quarts of cold water to each pan. Stir the dye solution into the cold water. Arrange the pans about two feet apart so that from left to right there is a pan of yellow dye, a pan of red dye, and a pan of blue dye. Next to each dye pan, place another enamel pan half full of cold, clear water. This clear water will be used for rinsing between each dye bath. It is necessary that each dye have its own rinsing water

Setting up the ironing area: This area should be adjacent to the dyeing table as the students will travel between the dyeing table and the ironing area. Cover the ironing board with about 30 sheets of plain newsprint. On a small table next to the ironing board, place another pile of 12″ x 18″ plain newsprint.

Procedure: Allow the students to work two or three at a time under supervision. The process begins by painting a design directly on the piece of sheeting with liquid wax and brush. Allow the wax to cool on the fabric; then dip the fabric into the yellow dye bath. Allow the fabric to remain in the dye bath for at least three minutes. The longer the fabric remains in the dye bath the more intense the colors become. Take the fabric out of the yellow dye bath allowing the excess dye to run off into the enamel pan. Pat and press off the excess dye. Do not wring the fabric.

Place the fabric into a clear water bath. Allow the rinse water to remove the remaining excess dye; this takes about one minute. Lift the fabric out and place it on a paper towel or a sheet of newsprint and bring it to the ironing board. Place the fabric on top of the pile of newsprint which is lying on the ironing board. The batik fabric should be wax side up. Over the batik, place two sheets of plain newsprint. The heat of the iron will melt the wax readily. As the wax melts and comes through the newsprint, peel off the top sheets of newsprint as well as the bottom wax-stained ones. Place clean newsprint on top again and proceed to iron as before until most of the wax is ironed out. Not all of the wax will come out with the ironing. It is all right to begin the next step with a semistiff batik fabric. You will note that after this step all of the areas that were blocked out with wax remained white, while the background was dyed yellow.

Repeat the painting with wax again on the same fabric. If some of the white area is to be "saved" from the next dye bath in red, block it out with wax. If one wishes to save some of the yellow area, block this out with wax also. Dip into the red dye bath, rinse in clear water, and iron. The areas of white fabric which were blocked out by the wax remain white; the areas of yellow which were blocked out by the wax remain yellow; but with the addition of red dye to the exposed yellow, the background will now be orange. If some of the white had been left exposed to the second dye bath of red, it would have been dyed red. At this step it is possible to have areas of white, yellow, red, and orange.

Repeat the blocking-out process with wax, saving some of the white, some of the yellow, and some of the orange and red. Dip into the third dye bath of blue. Rinse in clear water and iron out. Where the white, yellow, red, and orange have been left exposed to the blue dye bath, changes in color will occur. The white will turn blue, the yellow will turn green, the red will turn purple, and the orange will turn brown. In addition, where other colors have been "saved" or blocked out with wax consistently, there will be additional areas of white, red, yellow, and orange. It is possible by continually "saving color," or blocking it out with wax, to achieve seven different hues plus white.

Obtaining a crackle effect: To obtain a "crackle" effect, one can stop at either the yellow dye bath and crackle with red, or one can stop at the red dye bath and crackle with blue. One must achieve all crackle effects with a darker color. It is quite possible to go through the three dyeing steps to the blue dye bath and then to prepare an additional dye bath of black for the crackle effect.

After the fabric has been ironed out and is thoroughly dry, lay it flat upon a table and paint the entire surface with melted wax. Dip the entire fabric into cold, clear water. Bring the fabric together with the fist in a gentle manner to crack the wax. Bring the fabric to the dyeing table and open it, taking care not to break off the wax. Flatten the fabric as best you can, and then brush a darker dye over the entire surface of the batik fabric. For the crackle effect, it is best to brush the dye over the fabric rather than dipping it into the dye; the crackle effects become more subtle. Bring the fabric to the ironing table and iron the wax out as described earlier.

Alternate Batik Method: Instead of dyeing the fabric in dye baths, the dye can be painted on the fabric with large stiff-bristle easel brushes or 2-inch varnish brushes (see also BRUSHES). Mix dyes in a concentrated formula of one package of dye (yellow, red, and blue) to two cups of water. Put these mixtures into three one-quart mason jars. Arrange tables for batik as previously described, except that pans of rinse water are not needed. Paint the colored dye directly on the fabric between wax applications. In this process there is no need to paint the entire area with dye, nor is it necessary to rinse the fabric between dye applications. The wax is ironed out as before. This is a particularly successful technique in the lower grades. Figure B-7

Fig. B-7

illustrates the utilization of this technique by a third-grade child.

Permanency of color: To insure permanency of color, the fabrics should be placed overnight in a mordant solution of Glauber's salt (see also MORDANTS).

Additional suggestions: Try rubbing cakes of paraffin over heavily textured areas or surfaces in order to pick up some interesting detail for batiks. Try scratching through areas of wax for some fine linear effects. Try using colored, permanent drawing inks instead of dry dye.

NOTE: For those who are interested in exploring the possibilities of using natural dyes in the batik process, the following source is offered: Superintendent of Documents, *Home Dyeing With Natural Dyes* (Washington, D. C.: U. S. Government Printing Office).

BAUHAUS

School of design which had as its educational concept the idea of linking all of the arts, from the applied arts to the fine arts. The Bauhaus was founded by Walter Gropius in Germany in 1919 and was later closed by Hitler. On its teaching staff were some of the most reknown names in art history: Paul Klee, Lionel Feininger, Oskar Schlemmer, Wassily Kandinsky, and Ladislaus Moholy-Nagy (see also APPLIED DESIGN).

BEAD MAKING

Asbestos Beads: Mix powdered asbestos with water and dry wheat paste until a modeling consistency is reached. Diluted mucilage or plain water may be substituted for the wheat paste. Form beads by rolling the asbestos modeling material in the palms of the hands. Beads may be pressed, elongated, or retained in round shape. Push toothpicks through the beads in order to maintain holes for stringing. Allow to dry on the toothpicks. Paint the dry beads with tempera, and either spray with plastic, such as Krylon, or paint with a coat of clear shellac (see also ASBESTOS, KRYLON, MODELING MATERIALS, SHELLAC, and WHEAT PASTE).

Ceramic Beads: Roll clay in palms to create round forms. Or vary this with the slab method, cutting beads into shapes of circles, ovals, or other geometric forms as shown in Fig. B-8 (see also CERAMICS). Make certain that

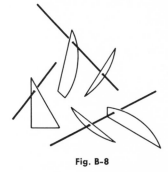

Fig. B-8

the holes are large enough for stringing. Round beads may be dried on toothpicks or cocktail picks to ensure against shrinkage. Glaze the beads and fire them [see also CLAY (KITCHEN-OVEN FIRING) and CLAY (NONFIRING)].

Macaroni Beads: Holes for stringing can be made with needles which have been heated over a candle flame. Hold the needle with a pair of pliers. When the needle is sufficiently hot, it will bore a hole through the hard macaroni effortlessly. Macaroni beads may be painted with tempera and given a final coating of clear plastic spray (see also KRYLON).

Natural Material Beads: Soak natural materials such as dried beans, peas, and cloves in water overnight. Color may be added to white beans for example, by soaking them in a dye solution for 48 hours (see also DYES). When these dried natural materials have been softened sufficiently through soaking, they may be strung effortlessly by pushing a threaded needle through them. Beads may be finished with a matte-finish plastic spray (see also KRYLON).

Pulp Papier-Mâché Beads (see also PAPIER-MÂCHÉ): String the beads with nylon cord, raffia, or yarn (see also NEEDLES, RAFFIA, and YARN AND STRINGS).

Salt and Flour Beads: Roll beads in the palm of the hands with a salt-flour modeling material (see also MODELING MATERIALS). String the beads on a wire to dry or dry them individually on small toothpicks. Paint the beads with tempera, and spray with clear plastic (see also KRYLON).

NOTE: Inexpensive commercial beads may be used as interesting color accents which would either complement or relate to the hand-hewn painted beads. The use of clasps is optional. It is important that the toothpicks be stuck through the modeled beads. When modeling material is pressed around the toothpicks, it is difficult to remove the beads when they have dried. To hasten drying, beads from modeling materials may be put in a warm oven.

BEESWAX

See WAX.

BENZINE

Not to be confused with benzene. Benzine is a colorless liquid which is highly inflammable; is commonly used as a solvent for oil printing inks and Duco cement (see also INKS, PRINTING INK SUBSTITUTES, and SOLVENTS).

BIAS-JOIN

See CERAMICS.

BICYCLE PUMP

May be used as a type of siphon to extract liquids from heavy immovable containers. Once the liquid is taken up through one pumping motion, lift the tubing and place it through the neck of a container such as a mason jar. The liquid will empty out when the tubing is turned in a down position. Bicycle pumps are particularly effective when extracting magnesium chloride from heavy five gallon containers (see also MAGNESITE and MAGNESIUM CHLORIDE).

BINDER

Binding agent which is used in the manufacturing of paints to hold the pigment together. Glue is most commonly used as a binding agent in paints today (see also PAINT, PIGMENT, and VEHICLE). Egg was used as a binder in early fresco painting (see also FRESCO).

BIOMORPHIC

Term which is used in relation to contemporary art which relates itself in design to life or living organisms. Biomorphic art forms can be seen in kidney-shaped swimming pools, furniture design, architecture, and painting.

BIRCH WOOD

See WOODS.

BISCUIT

See CERAMICS.

BISQUE

See CERAMICS.

BISQUE FIRING

See CERAMICS.

BIT AND BRACE

See WOODWORKING.

BLACK WALNUT

See woods.

BLACK WILLOW

See woods.

BLEEDING

When two or more colors run together in painting, either intentionally or unintentionally (see also PAINTING).

BLOCKING IN

Initial plan of sketching in general planes and shapes onto a ground as illustrated in Fig. B-9 (see also GROUND).

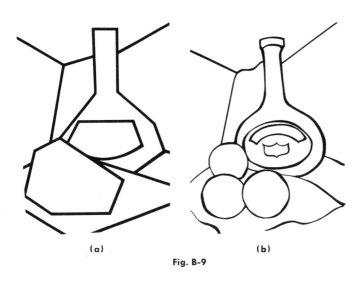

(a)   (b)

Fig. B-9

BLOCK-OUT SOLUTION

See SILK SCREENING.

BLOCK PLANE

See WOODWORKING.

BLOCK PRINTING

See PRINTMAKING and RELIEF.

BLOTTING PAPER

Provides an excellent ground for prints in the printmaking processes (see also PRINTMAKING). It provides a tool for picking up excess paint or water in watercolor painting (see also PAINTING). It is also used in textile designing, being placed underneath fabrics to catch excess textile colors (see also PAPERS, SILK SCREENING, and TEXTILE DESIGN).

BLOW PAINTING

An interesting introductory lesson in the pigment theory of color. Spoon some liquid tempera paint of different colors onto a sheet of 12″ x 18″ white drawing paper. Using a beverage straw, blow the paint in the direction you wish it to go. The more colors that are put on the paper, the more possibilities there will be for color discoveries (see also COLOR). A blow painting in black and white is shown in Fig. B-10.

Fig. B-10

BOGUS PAPER

See PAPERS.

B

BOOKLET MAKING

Cutting the booklet from chipboard: See Fig. B-11.

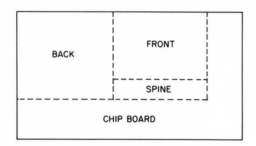

BACK

FRONT

SPINE

CHIP BOARD

Fig. B-11

Attaching spine to the front of the booklet using 1½″ mystic tape: See Fig. B-12.

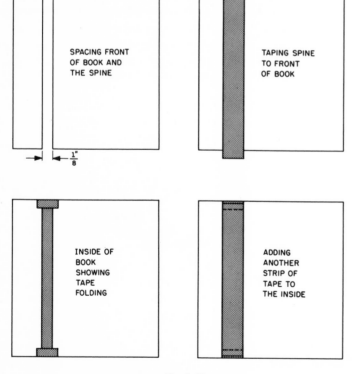

SPACING FRONT OF BOOK AND THE SPINE

$\frac{1}{8}$"

TAPING SPINE TO FRONT OF BOOK

INSIDE OF BOOK SHOWING TAPE FOLDING

ADDING ANOTHER STRIP OF TAPE TO THE INSIDE

Fig. B-12

Covering the front of the booklet with a decorative paper and adhesive: See Fig. B-13.

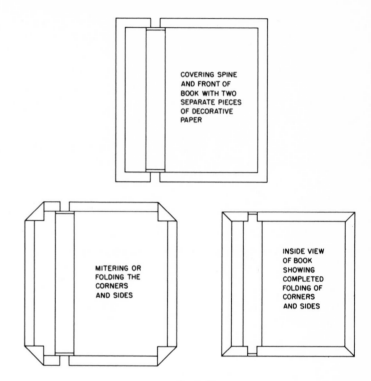

COVERING SPINE AND FRONT OF BOOK WITH TWO SEPARATE PIECES OF DECORATIVE PAPER

MITERING OR FOLDING THE CORNERS AND SIDES

INSIDE VIEW OF BOOK SHOWING COMPLETED FOLDING OF CORNERS AND SIDES

Fig. B-13

Facing the "inside" of the front cover of the booklet with contrasting paper: See Fig. B-14.

FACING THE INSIDE FRONT COVER OF THE BOOK WITH A CONTRASTING COLORED PAPER

Fig. B-14

Covering the back of the booklet with decorative paper and adhesive: See Fig. B-15.

Facing the "inside" of the back of the booklet with contrasting paper: See Fig. B-16.

Completing booklet with eyelets and twine: See Fig. B-17 (see also DECORATIVE PAPERS, EYELET PUNCH, EYELETS, PAPERS, and TAPES).

BORDERS

Horizontal or vertical repetition of a motif; a continual design which carries the eye across the page from left to right or down the page from top to bottom (Fig. B-18). Borders can be created in a freehand manner using crayon, colored chalk, felt pens, paint, or mixed media (see also MIXED MEDIA). They can also be effectively rendered with some of the classroom printmaking processes such as potato prints, stencils, or eraser prints (see also PRINTMAKING).

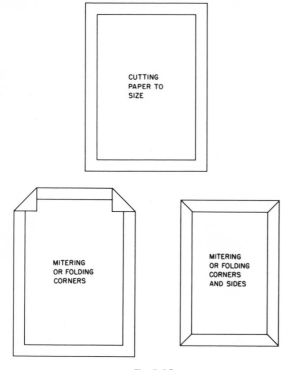

Fig. B-15

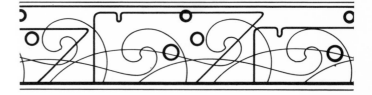

Fig. B-18

BORIC ACID

See PRESERVATIVES.

BOTTLE PRINTS

See PRINTMAKING.

BOXES

See TOTEM POLES.

BOX TOPS

Try painting, drawing, or creating paper mosaics or collages inside cardboard box tops. Hatbox tops, shoebox tops, and general gift-box tops provide an array of interesting shapes and sizes. When the design is completed, it is already framed and ready for a three-dimensional display (see also COLLAGE and MOSAICS). Box tops also provide handy, quick devices for elementary techniques in silk screen printing (see also PRINTMAKING).

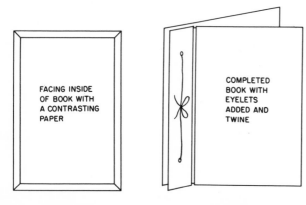

Fig. B-16   Fig. B-17

B

BRAYER

Rubber roller with a handle (Fig. B-19) which is used in printmaking processes. It applies ink evenly to incised or excised relief areas on the plate's surface (see also EX-

BRAYER

Fig. B-19

CISED and INCISED). In the classroom, brayers are most commonly used in linoleum block printing, brayer prints, brayer relief prints, brayer string prints, and monoprints (see also PRINTMAKING). Brayers are available in three basic sizes for classroom use: 4″, 6″, and 8″ rubber rollers.

NOTE: Homemade brayers may be made by slipping a rubber bicycle tube (balloon tire type), over a 2″ or 2½″ length of wood doweling (see also DOWELING). Conventional commercial brayers tend to lose their elasticity and become hard after an extended period of use. These can be repaired by slipping small bicycle tire tubes over the roller portion.

BRAYER PRINTS

See PRINTMAKING.

BRAYER RELIEF PRINTS

See PRINTMAKING.

BRAYER STRING PRINTS

See PRINTMAKING.

BRIDGE

See PRINTMAKING.

BRISTOL BOARD

See PAPERS.

BROKEN COLOR

In painting, the introduction of one or more colors which do not touch each other; a method of mixing colors visually, for example, red dots and orange dots will achieve the illusion of red-orange. The technique of broken color was popularized by the Impressionists and Neoimpressionists (see also IMPRESSIONISM and NEOIMPRESSIONISM). Broken color is also used effectively as a technique in the rendering of mosaics (see also MOSAICS).

BRONZE AGE

An age around 3500 B.C. when copper and bronze were used; chiefly in Egypt and in Mesopotamia, following the Stone Age [see also BABYLONIA, EGYPT, HISTORY (ART), IRON AGE, and STONE AGE].

BRUSH

Instrument for painting which has three basic parts: bristles, metal ferrule, and handle (Fig. B-20) [see also

Fig. B-20

BRUSHES, BRUSHES (CARE AND CLEANING), and BRUSH STROKES].

BRUSHES

For classroom art programs, there should be ample supplies of brushes both in type and size [see also SUPPLIES

(CLASSROOM)]. Brushes are available for specific art experiences. There are easel brushes for easel painting, oil brushes for oil painting, watercolor brushes for watercolor painting, lettering brushes for lettering, stencil brushes for stenciling, enamel and varnish brushes for household painting, and paste brushes for pasting. Each type of brush comes not only in a variety of sizes, but in varied degrees of quality as well. When ordering, it is best to look for the "school art brushes"; these will do the job without being excessively expensive.

It is impossible to give information relative to the number or size of a brush and its corresponding length, width, and diameter. Each brush manufacturer codes his brushes numerically, but the number on a brush will not correspond with the bristle sizes of other brush manufacturers. For example, a size 10 easel brush for one manufacturer might have a bristle measurement of 9/16″ in width, while a size 10 easel brush of another manufacturer might measure 12/16″ in width. The best advice is to consult an art-supply or school-supply catalog where specific manufacturer's brush sizes are indicated both numerically and by width and/or diameter of the bristles. Generally, it can be stated that the smaller the coded number on a brush, the smaller the brush bristles will be, in both width and diameter.

For purposes of planning a school program, the following brushes and general brush sizes are recommended [see also SUPPLIES (CLASSROOM)].

Kindergarten–Primary Grades:
1. Easel brushes: Flat, large and small; round, large and small
2. Enamel or varnish brushes: large, medium, and small
3. Paste brushes: Optional

Intermediate–Upper Grades:
1. Easel brushes: Flat, large and small; round, large and small
2. Enamel or varnish brushes: Large, medium, and small
3. Paste brushes: Optional
4. Stencil brushes: Large and small
5. Watercolor brushes: Large, medium, and small

Secondary Schools (Junior High and High School):

1. Easel brushes: Flat, large and small; round, large and small
2. Enamel and varnish brushes: Large, medium, and small
3. Lettering brushes: Large and small
4. Oil brushes (high school only): Round, large and small; bright, medium and large; and flat, medium-large and extra-large
5. Paste brushes: Optional
6. Stencil brushes: Large and small
7. Watercolor brushes: Large, medium, and small

Brush Characteristics:

Easel brushes: Long handles with stiff bristles; round and flat (Fig. B-21a).

Enamel brushes or varnish brushes: Short handles with semistiff bristles; flat (Fig. B-21b).

Lettering brushes: Medium handle with soft bristles; flat (Fig. B-21c).

Oil brushes: Long handles with soft sable or stiff bristles; bright, flat, and round (Fig. B-21d).

Paste brushes: Short handle; stiff bristles (Fig. B-21e).

Stencil brushes: Medium short handle; stiff bristles in round ferrule (Fig. B-21f).

Watercolor brushes: Medium handles; soft pointed bristles (Fig. B-21g).

BRUSHES (CARE AND CLEANING)

Clean brushes immediately after using them. Before allowing the brush to dry, straighten the bristles into their natural shape. Allow the brushes to dry in a jar with the handles down and the bristles up. If you have an excess of brushes which necessitate storage over a long period of time, store these brushes flat. Soft bristle brushes, such as watercolor and sable oil brushes, may be rendered moth-proof by sprinkling moth crystals around them.

Cleaning brushes thoroughly and properly is not only important from an economic standpoint but from a creative standpoint as well. No child or student will paint well when bristles have curled from improper drying or have matted or broken at the ferrule from improper cleaning. The rules for good brush housekeeping are simple; the rest is habit.

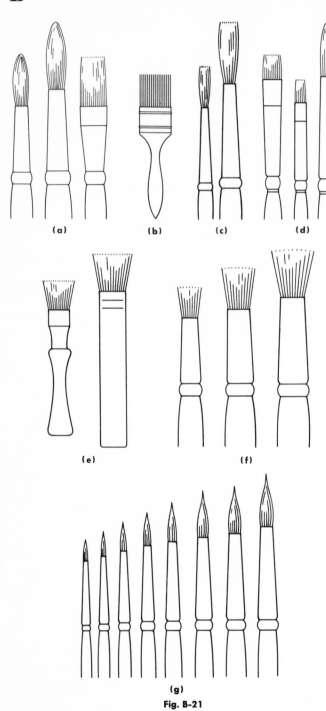

(a) (b) (c) (d)

(e) (f)

(g)

Fig. B-21

Oil-Base Paints: Clean these brushes by first wiping off the excess paint with a paper towel or a bit of cloth. Dip the brush into thinner or turpentine (see also SOLVENTS). Work the solvent around the bristles, particularly in and around the ferrule. Lather the brush with mild soap and water; rinse in clear water.

Water-Base Paints: Clean these brushes by first wiping off the excess paint with a paper towel. Repeated washing in cold water will remove the paint or ink. A little mild liquid soap may be used if necessary.

NOTE: For additional solvents relating to the cleaning of brushes which have been used in wax, textile colors, varnish, shellac, and lacquer (see also SOLVENTS).

BRUSHES (STEEL)

Speedball steel brushes, as shown in Fig. B-22, are useful in lettering and as auxiliary brushes for watercolor and

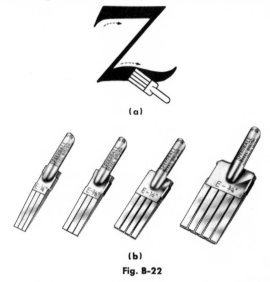

(a)

(b)

Fig. B-22

oil painting. Steel brushes fit into common pen holders and are available in sizes ⅜″, ½″, and ¾″ (see also LETTERING, LETTERS, and PAINTING).

BRUSH STROKES

Techniques with brush strokes in watercolor or tempera painting:

Wet Brush: Bristles are fully charged with paint and the design is rendered on a dry ground (see also CHARGE and GROUND).

Dry Brush: Excess paint on bristles have been "painted off" on a paper towel. The brush is used almost dry. This technique is usually combined with the wet-brush technique.

Wet Brush-Wet Paper: Bristles are fully charged with paint and the design is rendered on wet paper (see also PAINTING).

Rules of thumb for watercolor and easel brush strokes:

1. Use flat, large brushes for watercolor washes, large areas, and planes (see also WASH).

2. Use small brushes for detail work.

3. Render vertical planes with vertical strokes, horizontal planes with horizontal strokes, and contours with curved lines to enhance the feeling of dimension.

4. Paint with a light stroke; avoid scrubbing.

Rules of thumb for stencil brushes:

1. Use stencil brushes with a rapid up-and-down stippling motion. Never sweep the stencil brush across the stencil design.

2. Use very little paint or ink on a stencil brush. Heavy color is built up in stencil work through several light applications (see also PRINTMAKING, STENCIL, STIPPLE, and TEXTILE DESIGN).

BRUSH SUBSTITUTES

Use small rectangles of sponges or foam rubber which have been adhered to the mouth of a spring-type clothespin. Try painting with various sizes of sponges. Use large ones for mural work in rendering sky and grass and smaller ones for detail work. Additional details may be added with pen and ink or brush and ink.

BULLETIN BOARD

Ideally, a bulletin-board area should be more than an end product in terms of display. It should provide opportunity for seeing, reading, thinking, touching, and learning. Figure B-23 shows a first-grade science bulletin board. Titles should extend beyond the area of mere labeling of subject matter. They should provoke thought, interest, and

challenge. Instead of "telling all" they might ask a question, for example, "What IS a Balanced Aquarium?" or "WHY Practice Conservation?" Beware of the trap of establishing too many bulletin-board areas. Just as the eye is neutralized when it beholds a picture with too much going on, the student's eye might suffer like neutralization and fatigue. Allow for areas of space where the eye might rest and find repose. This is called negative space (see also DESIGN ELEMENTS). The effective use of negative space will allow for contrast and render bulletin-board displays more dominant and effective.

Fig. B-23

Setting up an effective bulletin board:

1. Establish the subject of the bulletin board.

2. Establish the title.

3. Gather the materials to be used.

4. Plan the color (see also COLOR).

5. Plan the arrangement. Is the board to be symmetrical or asymmetrical? Are captions to be used (see also BALANCE)?

Check points:

1. Is the subject appropriate for the grade level in terms of curriculum, interest, and need?

2. Are the display materials arranged for seeing, if they are to be seen? Are the materials arranged for reading, if they are to be read? Are they arranged for touching, if they were meant to be touched? Might an extension of a table from the bulletin-board area give more possibilities for integration of related three-dimensional materials and realia?

3. Are the captions arranged according to the grade level of the child who is looking at the bulletin board? Are primary captions at a small child's eye level and not up high where he cannot read them?

4. Do the captions read from left to right? Or are they going off in an "arty" diagonal or vertical direction? Do not confuse children who are just beginning to read with "clever" arrangements of letters. Remember that function is still the mainstay of good design.

5. Is the title a thought-provoking one? Does it invite further looking, reading, or examination?

6. Are the colors appropriate to the materials being displayed?

7. Is there unity within the bulletin-board display? Does it hold together?

8. Are all of the straight lines really straight? If your eye is faulty, use a ruler and be on the safe side.

9. Are you using pins instead of thumb tacks? Thumb tacks tend to distract from the display—too big, too shiny.

10. Finally, did you spell all of the words correctly? If you did not, it has happened before; teachers refer to this bothersome quirk as "bulletin-board blindness." Keep it interesting, but not with your spelling.

Use variations. Use both large and small areas; group smaller like areas together. Use contrasting textures, both visual and tactile (see also DESIGN ELEMENTS). Introduce a three-dimensional aspect to your display. Pin papier-mâché masks, grass skirts, leis, egg-cartons, etc. to the board. How about a three-dimensional bulletin-board display using liquid measurement in arithmetical concepts as the theme? Use cardboard cartons in the half-pint, pint, and quart sizes. Pin these to the wall. Experiment with that versatile new material called bulletin-board wax. When it is rolled into the size of a marble, it will adhere a hammer to the wall. Try it (see also WAX).

BULLETIN-BOARD LETTERS

See LETTERS (CUT PAPER) and LETTERS (PLASTIC).

BULLETIN-BOARD WAX

See WAX.

BURIN

See INTAGLIO.

BURLAP

Inexpensive material which lends itself to numerous art areas and activities. It is used as a textured ground for displays and bulletin boards (see also BULLETIN BOARD and GROUND), to achieve texture in pottery making (see also CERAMICS), as a texture in rendering a collage (see also COLLAGE), as a ground for stitchery and murals, and as a fabric on which to render textile designs (see also MURALS, STITCHERY, and TEXTILE DESIGN). Burlap is available by the single yard, 12 yards, or 25 yards in the following colors: red, rust, blue, green, yellow, natural, eggshell, white, black, and brown.

BURR

See INTAGLIO.

BUTCHER PAPER

See PAPERS.

BUTTERING

See MOSAICS.

BUTT-JOIN

See CERAMICS.

BUTTONS

Use buttons as tesserae in mosaic work (see also MOSAICS). Try making your own buttons out of ceramic clay by rolling out the clay with a rolling pin in slab fashion. Cut out the shape of the buttons with a knife or a mold press such as the top of a small jar. Decorate the buttons with any of the known glaze techniques (see also CERAMICS).

BUTTRESS

Relates to architecture; a compensatory projection and/or support for walls to offset the structural pressure of vaulting (domes or arched ceilings of cathedrals). The buttress was used extensively in Gothic architecture, as well as in Roman and Romanesque (see also GOTHIC, ROMAN ART, ROMANESQUE, and VAULTING).

BYZANTINE

Relates to the Byzantine Empire or the Eastern Roman Empire in that period of history from A.D. 395 to 1453 (see also CHRISTIAN ART). The Byzantine Empire made monumental contributions to art in the forms of mosaics, illuminations, carved ivory, and cloisonné. Its art forms were a blend between the oriental and the classic [see also CLOISONNÉ, HISTORY (ART), ILLUMINATIONS, MOSAICS, and PARCHMENT].

EXAMPLES: Throne of Maximinius, carving in wood and ivory, and mosaics depicting Justinian at San Vitale, Ravenna; and mosaics in the church of Hagia Sophia in Istanbul.

CADO FLO-MASTER PENS

See PENS.

CALLIGRAPHY

Relates to beautiful writing and fine brush work; particularly applicable to Chinese and Japanese calligraphic work (see also WRITING). Figure C-1 illustrates Chinese calligraphy (translation: "Within the sea, we are all good friends.") A form of calligraphy relating to brush strokes might be introduced in the classroom by encouraging students to render linear compositions over watercolor washes [see also BRUSH STROKES, HISTORY (ART), PAINTING, and WASH].

CAMPANILE

Tower for bells (Fig. C-2). The original campanile was designed by Giotto in Florence during the thirteenth

Fig. C-2

century. Contemporary counterparts are found all over the world; the most famous perhaps is the campanile tower at the University of California in Berkeley, California.

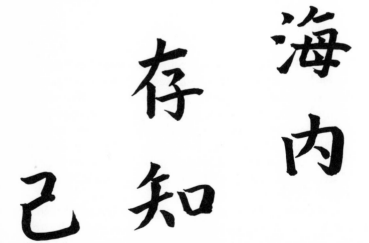

Fig. C-1

C

CANDLE

Cylinder of tallow or wax formed around a wick composed of linen or cotton thread. The finer candles are made of beeswax (see also CANDLEMAKING, TALLOW, WAX, and WICKING).

CANDLEMAKING

One of the easiest methods of making candles is to purchase sheets of commercial comb-textured beeswax. These sheets are extremely supple and can be rolled around a wick. Sheets of comb-textured beeswax are available in a wide range of colors and can be purchased from American Handicrafts Company [see also SUPPLIES (VENDORS)]. American Handicrafts Company also carries related materials such as candlewicking in 30′ lengths, candle kits, and a honeycomb candle instruction book entitled *Making Honeycomb Candles From Beeswax Foundations,* by Sidney Dubin. The honeycomb candle is particularly applicable in the kindergarten-primary grades where, with smaller children, the problem of heating wax for candlemaking is particularly acute from a safety standpoint (see also WICKING).

Dipped Candles:

Materials needed: Paraffin or old candles, dry dye for color, two 2-pound empty coffee tins, 12″ lengths of candlewicking, and waxed paper (see also DYES and PAPERS).

Procedure: Melt paraffin or old wax candles in a 2-pound coffee tin. Take the melted paraffin off the stove and set it next to another coffee tin filled with cold water. Dip a 12″ length of candlewicking in the melted paraffin; then dip it into the can of cold water. Repeat this process of dipping the wick first into melted paraffin and then into cold water until a fair-sized candle is formed. When the candles are finished, they may be placed on sheets of waxed paper or, more authentically, tied to a wire which has been strung across the room (see also DRYING).

NOTE: In all of the candlemaking processes involving the melting of wax at a stove, there is always the danger of spilling some of the wax on the stove and causing a fire. There is also the danger of burns from the hot wax. For this reason, it is always a good idea for the teacher to handle the wax melting at the stove, particularly in the elementary grades. In other grades, wax melting must always be done under close supervision.

Molded Candles:

Materials needed: Paraffin, dry dye (Tintex or Rit, etc.), string for wicking, pencil or small dowel, 2-pound empty coffee can, and a cooking pot (see also DOWELING).

Molds for candles: Use milk cartons, small tin cans, paper cups, or flower pots. (See Fig. C-3.)

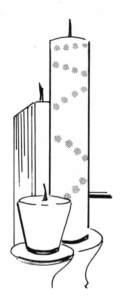

Fig. C-3

Melting the wax: Place coffee can into a cooking pot which has been half-filled with water. Never place paraffin directly on the heat. About 1½ pounds of paraffin will fill a quart milk carton. Each pound of paraffin requires about 2 teaspoons of dry-powder dye for coloring. Stir the dye into the melted paraffin. Remove from the heat and stir for several minutes. Old wax crayons may be used in place of dry dye and stumps of candles of the same color will add color (see also CRAYONS).

Securing wick in can or carton: Punch a small hole in the bottom of the carton or can. Run a piece of string through the hole and secure it to the bottom of the mold with a bit of tape. Bring the string to the top of the mold and tie it around a pencil or a piece of doweling. Lay the pencil or dowel across the top of the mold.

Pouring wax into molds: After the wax has been heated and colored, pour it directly into the mold. Allow the candle to harden. If a hollow area appears around the candlewick when the wax has hardened, melt a little bit more of the wax and fill up the hole.

Taking candle from the mold: If the mold is cardboard, tear it away from the candle. If the mold is metal, glass, or another kind of material which cannot be torn away, dip it in hot water several times and then shake it out of the container.

Decorative effects: Felt cutouts, glitter, and sequins may be added with a white resin adhesive (see also ADHESIVES). Decorative effects in relief may be added with a linoleum cutting tool (see also GLITTER, LINOLEUM BLOCK CUTTERS, and RELIEF).

Snow effect: Allow plain paraffin to cool after melting. Begin to whip it with a fork as soon as a film appears on the surface. Apply "snow" directly to the candle.

CANNED MILK

See FIXATIVES, FIXATIVE SUBSTITUTES, and PAINT SUBSTITUTES.

CANTILEVER

Structural projection in architecture and engineering from either wall to space as in balconies or from land to sea as in bridges.

EXAMPLE (architecture): Kauffmann House, Bear Run, Pennsylvania, designed by Frank Lloyd Wright.

EXAMPLE (engineering): Golden Gate Bridge, between San Francisco and Marin County, California.

CANVAS

The ground or surface on which the oil colorist paints (see also GROUND). The standard size of a canvas is 40″ x 50″; however, contemporary artists of the abstract-expressionistic school use canvases which are much larger.

Canvas is sometimes pressed on a canvas board; at other times, it is tightened across a wooden frame which is called a stretcher.

Canvas stretching: When the artist makes his own canvas, first he constructs the frame and then stretches and tacks the canvas to it.

Priming the canvas: After the canvas is stretched, it is sized with glue. When the glue is dry, several coats of flat-white undercoat paint are applied (see also ADHESIVES and PAINTING).

CANVASETTE

Packaged sheet replacement for canvas board in oil and casein painting (see also CANVAS, CANVAS SUBSTITUTES, PAINTING, and PAPERS).

CANVAS SUBSTITUTES

Thick chipboard, 3-ply wood, or masonite may be used as canvas substitutes. It is necessary that canvas substitutes be primed before using (see also CANVAS). Roll-type window shades also make excellent canvas substitutes.

CAPITAL

Uppermost part of a column where decorative detail lies in relief (see also CLASSICAL ORDERS and RELIEF).

CARBON PAPER

See PAPERS.

CARBON TETRACHLORIDE

A solvent which is sometimes used for the cleaning of oil-base printing inks by professional artists; it is also used by the professional batik artist to remove wax from fabrics in the batik process. When carbon tetrachloride is used, safety precautions are needed in terms of proper ventilation to prevent prolonged inhalation of fumes. In school situations where substitutions are sought for safety reasons, oil-base inks my be cleaned from surfaces with benzine or

C

turpentine; in the batik process, wax may be removed by ironing it out of the fabric (see also BATIK, PRINTMAKING, and SOLVENTS).

CARBORUNDUM STONE

See ABRASIVES, COPPER ENAMELING, and MOSAICS.

CARDBOARDS

See PAPERS.

CARICATURE

Satirical pictures in which marked resemblances of personalities are brought about through exaggeration of features, as shown in Fig. C-4 (see also DRAWING). An excel-

Fig. C-4

lent kind of drawing problem for intermediate and upper-grade children where political figures and other widely known personalities might be selected for caricaturing. Aside from the conventional pencil or ink drawings, caricatures could be rendered in yarn or roving. The caricature would, of course, first be drawn with pencil. A trail of white resin glue would be laid down along the lines of the drawing (see also ADHESIVES). Yarn or cotton roving would then be placed on the trailing of glue. A variation of size and color would be desirable and textural effects such as hair might be achieved through manipulation of the yarn by loops, knots, or small pieces (see also COTTON

ROVING and YARNS AND STRINGS). Use heavy chipboard as a ground (see also GROUND and PAPERS).

CARPET WARP

See YARNS AND STRINGS.

CARTOON

Full-scale drawing or one drawn to scale which would serve as a plan or guide for a fresco, mural, mosaic, or stitchery panel (see also FRESCO, MOSAICS, MURALS, and STITCHERY). A secondary meaning in our culture relates to comical drawings.

CARVING

The hewing or cutting of a material into a desired form. There are a variety of carving materials available for experiences in carving and sculpture. In the elementary grades, of course, it would be desirable to limit these experiences to softer materials such as soap, wax, dried clay, balsa wood, and some of the softer aggregate mixtures (see also CARVING MATERIALS).

CARVING MATERIALS

Aggregate: Mixture of sand, cement, zonolite, and plaster; often called Ciro Stone. To the best of the author's knowledge, Larry Argiro brought cement carving mixtures to the attention of art education instructors when he published an article relating to aggregate mixtures in the *School Arts* magazine in November, 1953. Aggregates are interesting for carving experiences because they have the appearance of heavy stone (see the plaster and vermiculite sculpture in Fig. C-5); yet, because of the addition of zonolite, they are lightweight and easy materials from which to carve. Vermiculite can be substituted for zonolite and can be purchased in 30-pound sacks at hardware stores or nursery establishments for approximately $2.00 (see also VERMICULITE and ZONOLITE).

Any combination of these materials will work if one remembers that a binding agent of either cement or plaster must be present in the mixture. One should also remember that the softness or hardness of the carving mixture

Fig. C-5

can be controlled. The more cement or plaster that a mixture contains, the harder it will be to carve. The more zonolite (or vermiculite) a mixture contains, the softer and easier it will be to carve. Here are some carving mixtures to try:

2 parts sand, 1 part cement, 1 part zonolite
1 part sand, 3 parts zonolite, 2 parts plaster
1 part sand, 1 part zonolite, 1 part plaster
1 part sand, 3 parts zonolite, 2 parts plaster
1 part sand, 3 parts cement, 2 parts zonolite

Mix dry ingredients together and add enough water to produce a heavy, pastelike consistency. Pour into cardboard molds such as shoeboxes, milk cartons, cream cartons, and salt boxes. Always be exceedingly careful when adding water. Do not add too much. This is particularly important in the zonolite mixtures. When too much water is added to the dry ingredients, the zonolite will float to the top and will cease to act as a grog for the carving mixture.

After the mixture is poured into a mold, allow it to set for several days until it is dry. Rip the paper molds from the hardened mixtures and the aggregate is ready to be carved. Use carving tools of old spoons, kitchen knives, forks, coping saws, and wood rasps. Finish with sandpaper and steel wool.

NOTE: If zonolite is used in any of the aggregate carving mixtures, mix all of the dry ingredients *except* the zonolite, together first. Then add the dry zonolite to the mixture, mix thoroughly, and add water.

Dried Clay: Here is the answer for using one of those dried out chunks of clay which has lain idle in the clay bin! Allow the shape of the dried clay to help dictate the possibilities for carving. Use wood rasps, kitchen knives, and spoons for carving. Smooth down with sandpaper; then use a wet sponge for final finishing.

NOTE: Some of the softer building stones, such as limestone, marble, and standstone, might be explored as possibilities for carving or sculpture. Use a chisel and hammer, and then abrasives for smoothing (see also ALABASTER).

Foam Glass: See FOAM GLASS.

Magnesite: See MAGNESITE.

Plaster of Paris: Mix 2 cups of plaster to 1¼ cups of water. Sift the plaster into a bowl containing the water and mix with a spoon or by hand. When the plaster mixture reaches the consistency of thick cream, pour into a mold of a half-pint milk carton. Allow 2 days for drying. Carve with kitchen knives or rasps and finish with sandpaper. A plaster-of-paris sculpture is shown in Fig. C-6.

Fig. C-6

Soap: Use one of the softer household soaps such as Ivory for carving experiences.

Structolite: Structolite is a builder's material. Add white structolite to water until a heavy, pastelike mixture is formed. Pour into molds. If you wish to carve this material without the use of molds, add less water and knead the material until it has the consistency of biscuit dough. Allow balls of the material to dry and harden on wax paper; then carve.

C

Styrofoam: See STYROFOAM.

Wax: Melt paraffin and pour into half-pint or pint milk cartons. When wax has hardened, tear away the cardboard carton. Wax may be colored by adding crayons or dry dye. Use 2 teaspoons of dry dye to 1 pound of wax.

Wax-Plaster Mixture: Shred paraffin with a grater and mix with plaster of paris in equal proportions. Add 4 cups of this mixture to 2 cups of water. Mix with a spoon until the mixture begins to thicken slightly and pour into a mold such as a half-pint milk carton. Allow 2 days for drying [see also CLAY (NONFIRING)].

CASEIN

See PAINTING.

CASTING

Duplication of sculpture or pottery by the utilization of molds (see also CERAMICS, MOLDS, and SCULPTURE).

CASTING PLASTER

See PLASTER OF PARIS.

CASTING (SAND)

Sand casting represents in its finished state (Fig. C-7) a type of bas-relief plaster plaque (see also RELIEF).

Fig. C-7

Materials needed: Sand, plaster, and some implements such as gears, sticks, spoons, spools, and forks with which to imprint shapes and lines into the wet sand.

Procedure: Either secure a wooden box from the store or make one with the approximate dimensions of 9″ in width, 7″ in depth, and 14″ in length. The sand should fill about 5″ of the 7″ depth of the box. Wet the sand. Grease the remaining 2″ of the wall of the box which protrudes above the sand. Press shapes and lines into the sand to create a design. Pour a mixture of plaster on top of the sand and design (see also PLASTER OF PARIS).

Before the plaster has hardened, insert a U-shaped wire or coffee key into the back of the plaster plaque for hanging. Remove the plaque from the box when the plaster has hardened. Brush off the excess sand with a soft bristle brush; leave some on if a texture is desired.

NOTE: Sand casting may be done on the beach. Create a depression in the sand to catch the plaster when it is poured. Render the design at the base of the depression with fingers or shells, building up other areas with sand. Pour in the wet plaster.

CATACOMBS

Tunnels which ran underneath the city of Rome during the time of Christian persecution; Christianity, by necessity, was then a secret religious group. Early Christians held religious services and buried their dead there. The walls of the catacombs were decorated with paintings and symbols of Christianity [see also CHRISTIAN ART (EARLY)].

EXAMPLES: "The Baptism in the Jordan," Calixtus Catacomb in Rome, fourth century; and "The Church," mural painting in the Priscillian Catacombs in Rome, third century.

CAVE PAINTINGS

See ALTAMIRA and LASCAUX.

CEDAR

See WOODS.

CELADON

Relates to the hue of green; more specifically and generally to the green glaze which is associated with Chinese pottery.

CELLOPHANE PAPER

See PAPERS.

CELLOPHANE TAPE

See TAPES.

CELLULOSE ACETATE

See ACETATE SHEETING.

CEMENT

See ADHESIVES, CARVING MIXTURES, and CONCRETE.

CENTER OF INTEREST

Area of a composition which is of prime importance and/or attraction.

CERAMIC CRAYON

See CERAMICS.

CERAMICS

Refers commonly to pottery or pots and sculpture (Fig. C-8) which have been fashioned from earth clay. Usually

Fig. C-8

this process involves the application of glazes and the firing of pots or sculpture in a kiln (see also KILNS).

Ceramic Vocabulary:

Pots: All clay pieces except sculpture.

Potting: Hand-built pottery; creating pots by hand.

Throwing: Creating pots on the potter's wheel.

Thrown pots: Pots which have been fashioned on the potter's wheel.

Wedging: Kneading clay to rid it of air bubbles and to make it the correct consistency for potting or throwing.

Slab: Clay which has been rolled or pressed flat.

Coil: Rolled ropes of clay.

Slip: Type of potter's glue which is used for adhering appendages, coils, and slabs together. Slip consists of clay which has been watered down to the consistency of thick cream.

Joining: Method of roughing up the smooth surfaces of flat edges which must be joined together, for example, two pieces of clay slabs, two ropes of coil, or an appendage of an arm to a body in sculpture. This process of joining entails the use of slip on the scratched surfaces.

Butt-join: Incorrect method of joining two ends of coils together in a vertical or up-and-down cut.

Bias-join: Correct method of joining two ends of coils together in a bias or diagonal cut.

Leather-hard: Clay which is not completely dry, yet dry enough to handle the object without misshaping it.

Greenware: Pot or sculpture which is air dried.

Engobe: Colored slip which is used for decorative purposes on ceramic ware; applied on pots and sculpture which are leather-hard.

Sgraffito: Scratching and/or incising a design through the engobe application when a clay pot is leather-hard.

Bisque firing or first firing: Firing of greenware in a kiln.

Bisque ware: Also called biscuit ware; clay pieces which have been fired once. Bisque ware is not water soluble like greenware, yet it is porous and less susceptible to breakage than greenware.

Glaze: Liquid, opaque covering which is applied to bisque ware for decoration and waterproofing. When glazed pieces are fired in a kiln, the glaze becomes mature with color and gloss and renders the fired piece waterproof as well as decorated.

Underglaze: Applied like watercolors on unfired or bisque ware pieces.

Underglaze crayons: Also called ceramic crayons; used on bisque ware and give an effect somewhat like colored chalks, as colors can be blended with fingers.

Underglaze pencils: For decoration or marking of bisque ware.

Glaze firing or second firing: The final firing of bisque ware which has been decorated with glaze.

Kiln: Insulated potter's oven which fires pieces at high and constant temperatures (see also KILNS).

Kiln wash: Applied to sides and bottom of kiln before each glaze firing; keeps glaze from sticking to kiln (see also KILN WASH).

Cone: Also called pyrometric cone; somewhat the shape of a golfer's tee and used for gauging the firing time for clay pieces in both the bisque and glaze firings. Cones are used both when the clay pieces are fired in the bisque firing and during the second firing or glaze firing in order to determine when the glazes have matured.

Clay: Ceramic clay comes in two forms for school art programs: prepared, moist, low-firing clay and clay powder. In the elementary grades where high-firing kilns are not used, it is necessary to be specific when ordering clay and to specify *low-firing clay.*

1. Prepared, moist, low-firing clay is available in plastic containers of 25, 50, and 100 pounds and in gray, white, and terra-cotta (red). This clay is prepared, wedged, and ready for classroom use.

2. Clay powder needs to be mixed with water and wedged before using; it is available in sacks of 25, 50, and 100 pounds. Mix the clay powder in a galvanized garbage pail; a ten-gallon garbage pail will hold 100 pounds of clay. Mix the clay a little at a time using 4 parts of clay flour to 1 part of water. Mix it thoroughly; allow several weeks for "aging." Clay powder mixtures can never be used right away. Clay should be the consistency of putty when it is ready for potting and modeling experiences.

Storing clay: Clay should always be stored in a clay bin or in a galvanized garbage pail with a tight cover. It is highly important that lids be secured tightly during storage to prevent drying out. If clay begins to dry out, cover it with a wet cloth before securing the lid.

Preparing clay for classroom use: It will save time if clay is rolled into small baseball sizes for student use. These could be stored in the clay bin and covered with a damp cloth. The baseball size is recommended as it contains enough clay for a satisfying experience in modeling and potting. Since the moist, prepared, low-firing clay is already wedged, it is ready for use. There is no need to knead it or pound it to rid it of air bubbles. However, if the clay has been mixed from clay powder, there is a need for wedging, for if air bubbles exist in the clay when it is put into the kiln, the clay pot or sculpture will explode. It is always a tragedy when a piece shatters in the kiln firing; but the tragedy is compounded when one shattering pot chips and shatters those around it. The most effective way of wedging clay is to put some clay into an old flour sack or cloth bag. Knead it while it is in the sack then pick up the end of the sack and pound it hard 10 or 12 times on a firm surface.

Reconstituting dried clay: Dried clay, broken pots, and sculpture of greenware are still water soluble, and when water is added, they will be restored for classroom use. Break the dried clay into small pieces and put them into a flour or cloth sack of some kind. Place the sack containing the broken pieces of clay into a container with enough water to cover it. When the clay in the sack has absorbed enough water to make it pliable, knead it and pound it on a hard surface as indicated in the preceding section.

Materials needed: Children will need art smocks [see also SMOCKS (ART)], a plaster bat or similar working surface, clay tools, sponges, cloth for wiping hands and covering clay pieces, brushes for applying slip and glazes, slip, tin cans for covering clay pieces, and some glazes.

Plaster bat: This is a type of working surface which is sufficiently porous to keep the clay piece damp while still in the modeling stage. Plaster bats may be made by mixing plaster of paris with water and pouring this mixture into a pie tin (see also PLASTER OF PARIS). Tap the plaster bat out of the pie tin when it has hardened. An alternate working surface is a piece of plywood with the approximate dimensions of 10″ x 10″. Cover this with the fabric side of oilcloth. The advantage of working on a mobile working surface is that the clay piece may be picked up without having to handle it while it is still in the wet and plastic stage.

Clay tools: These may be purchased and are available in sets of four labeled "School Modeling Tools." However, substitute modeling tools can be used such as popsicle sticks, tongue depressors, kitchen knives, forks, nutpicks, and knitting needles.

Sponges: Use soft, small sponges or Aegean silk sponges.

Cloth: Old sheets provide ample cloths for the wiping of hands and the cleaning of working stations. Each student should have a damp cloth of approximately 14″ x 14″. When the art period is over, this same cloth may be used to cover the clay piece when it is put away for storage. One should always make provision for retarding the drying of clay objects, particularly if one wishes to work on the same piece the next day. A satisfactory method is to dampen a piece of cloth and cover the piece with it; over this, place a large coffee tin.

Slip: May be purchased or may be made in the classroom by simply adding water to clay. Fill a bowl about half full of water and add prepared clay or clay powder to the water, working it well with the hands. Strain through a sieve to remove the lumps. Keep the mixture at the consistency of thick cream. Put the mixture into a mason jar under ¼″ of water. Stir when needed.

Brushes for slip application: Use bristle or easel brushes to apply slip to parts which will be joined together.

Brushes for glaze application: Use a soft sable brush or a watercolor brush for glaze application. For the application of engobes or glazes in detail work, use the smaller, pointed brushes.

Glazes: Seek advice from supply house vendors in obtaining glazes that will mature at the same temperature in the kiln. In this manner, clay pieces may be fired at the same time. Glazes that mature at different firing temperatures will necessitate two or three different, or separate, firings. Glazes are available in either the matte (dull) finish or the high-gloss (shiny) finish. While matte and high-gloss glazes are available in colors, clear glaze is colorless and simply allows the color of the pot to show through a clear glasslike finish. Clear glaze is used effectively over pots of terra-cotta clay.

Clear glaze is available in either the matte or high-gloss finish and is used over engobes, underglazes, underglaze crayons, and underglaze pencils.

It is important to keep lids on glaze containers tightly secured. Wipe each lid and bottle top with a damp cloth before tightening the jar. This will insure keeping the glazes at a thick cream consistency. When glazes dry out, they become thick and need to be thinned down with water.

Clay Construction:

Figure or animal: The nature of clay demands that the material be respected and used in a simple and direct manner. Encourage students to exaggerate legs by making them thick and short; appendages such as arms and legs can be either pulled out of the clay or joined with slip. When the sculpture is leather-hard, hollow the inside with a spoon or a tool. It will not be possible to hollow out arms and heads of figures, but do hollow out the body. Try for a ½″ uniform thickness all around the shell. It is difficult to set up a hard and fast rule for hollowing out clay-sculptured pieces. It is generally safe to assume that legs that are thicker than a man's thumb should be hollowed out to some degree. It is sometimes possible to only hollow out 1″ or so, and in the larger bulkier pieces, the hollowed area might extend as far as 3″ or 4″. It depends wholly upon the size of the clay piece.

Clay Pots:

Pinch pot: This is perhaps the easiest and most satisfying experience in potting for beginners. Roll a ball of clay into a form which is slightly smaller than a tennis ball. Hold this mass so that the thumbs are free to press into the center of it. Rotate this form and press out the inner hollow so that the shape is gradually deepened. Keep the walls of the pot at a uniform thickness of about ½″. If small cracks develop, smooth these out with the fingers.

When the pot is dry, a firm base may be established by rubbing the bottom over some sandpaper. Smooth and finish with a damp sponge after it has dried. If a rough-textured piece is preferred, omit the smoothing and finishing with a damp sponge.

Coil method: Roll out a slab of clay about ½″ thick and cut a disk from this slab which will serve as the bottom of the clay pot. Roll out a coil of clay with the fingertips to about a ½″ uniform thickness. Cut the coil so that it is equal to the circumference of the outside edge of the slab disk. When the coils are cut, both ends should be cut on the diagonal, or bias-cut, so that the edges may be easily welded together. Scratch or rough up the outside edge of the clay disk as well as the coil which will be joined to it.

C

Add slip to each surface and weld both together with a slight pressure.

Place the second coil on top of the first. Rough and add slip to the surfaces which will be joined together. Avoid putting the bias-joins on top of each other as the coil pot is being built up. If you prefer a smooth pot, smooth the inside and outside of the coils as you work, waiting until you have three coils before you start smoothing. Use a template to achieve symmetry of form (see also TEMPLATE). If you prefer to allow the coils to show and not to have a smooth pot, take a pencil and carefully work the pencil point between the coils inside and out, giving the piece added welding as you build. Make the coil pot as deep or as shallow as desired.

Slab method: Prepared working surface should consist of a table which has been covered with the fabric side of a piece of oilcloth. Set a ball of clay in the center of the working surface. On either side of the clay ball, place two vertical lathe strips of wood about 12″ long and about ¼″ wide. The lathe strips will guide the rolling pin and will insure uniformity of the slab when it is rolled flat. Place a paper pattern on top of the clay slab. This pattern will be of a predetermined, planned shape, either rectangular or square. The pattern will consist of five pieces, the bottom and four sides as shown in Fig. C-9.

Fig. C-9

When cutting the clay from the pattern with either a household knife or a clay fettling knife, make certain that the cut is straight up and down and not on the bias. This will insure proper welding when the sides are joined to the bottom and to each other. Begin to build the slab pot by welding the sides around the bottom piece. In all clay welding, be sure to roughen the edges which will be joined together before adding slip. When the slab box is completed, roll out a long, small coil of clay about ⅛″ in diameter. Place this coil inside the pot along the bottom. The coil should be resting on the bottom of the slab box and touching the sides. This step should be repeated at each corner where the sides touch each other. This final step of coil welding keeps the bottom adhered to the sides and the sides adhered to each other.

The slab method can be used in many ways aside from making the traditional slab pot. Try draping slabs over supports to achieve interesting, sculptural forms. Animals can be draped over tin cans to support a slab with four legs, head, and tail. There are, of course, infinite possibilities for ceramic design using the slab method.

Hammock method: Place a piece of cheesecloth or burlap over a wooden working surface. Place the clay ball on top of this surface and roll it out as described in the slab method. When the slab has been rolled out to a uniform thickness, cut a free form from it with a knife (see also FREE FORM). Remove the scraps and lift up the cheesecloth or burlap from the working area and suspend it over the top of a cardboard or wooden box. The cheesecloth or burlap hammock may be either taped or tacked into place around the box. Allow the free form to dry suspended.

When it has dried, remove it from the hammock. A firm base may be established by rubbing the bottom of the hammock pot over a piece of rough sandpaper. The cheesecloth or burlap hammock will have produced an interesting, textural effect on the outside of the pot. Smooth off the edges of the pot with sandpaper and a wet sponge.

Drying Time: Pots and sculpture will take from 1 to 3 weeks to dry, depending entirely on the degree of room temperature and the size of the object. Oftentimes, too rapid drying will crack the pot. On extremely hot days, drying can be retarded by draping a damp cloth over the ceramic piece. It is extremely important, of course, that all ceramic pieces be thoroughly dry before placing them into a kiln.

If you are in doubt as to whether or not a piece is dry, hold it up to your cheek. If it feels cold and damp, it is not dry. An added precaution in kiln firing is to leave the peephole plug out of the kiln for the first hour of firing, should there be any doubt as to whether or not some pieces are thoroughly dry.

Cracking of Greenware: Usually there is nothing that can be done for greenware pots or sculpture which have been broken or cracked. However, sometimes it is possible to put the cracked pieces together in the following ways:

1. When applying glaze, put the broken sections together and apply a liberal coating of glaze over the cracked section. When the pot is fired, often the glaze will mature and "glue" the two sections together.

2. Make a paste of sodium silicate and pulverized dry ceramic clay, and "glue" the broken pieces together (see also SODIUM SILICATE).

Firing of greenware: During the first firing of greenware, there is no necessity either to keep the pots from touching one another or to place the pots on stilts. Greenware may be placed one on top of another in the kiln. If you are in a school where the kiln is used often and the same kind of clay is used consistently, a teacher who is familiar with the firing time of the kiln will tell you how long it will take in terms of hours for the first kiln-firing of greenware. Kilns vary in terms of firing time, but it can be generally stated that the first firing of greenware in a small school kiln will take from 6 to 8 hours.

If the firing time is not available to you from another source, you will need to use a pyrometric cone which will correspond to the kind of clay you are using. A description of the clay to any ceramic supply house will give you the information you will need in terms of the kind of cone that should be used. It will be necessary to put the pyrometric cone into a lump of clay at a 45° angle and to allow the clay support to dry thoroughly. During the firing, line the lump of clay which contains the pyrometric cone on a shelf in the kiln so that it can be seen from the peephole outside the kiln. Observe the cone during what appears to be the end of the firing cycle, and when the cone bends over, the firing cycle is completed, the clay objects have matured, and the kiln may be shut off. There-

after, it will not be necessary to use a cone if the same kind of clay is used. Once the firing time is established, one can either set the thermostat firing timer on the kiln to the desired hours or shut the kiln off manually when the desired hours have elapsed.

When the firing cycle is completed, do not open the kiln immediately. The rush of cold air into a hot kiln will shatter the pieces. Allow the kiln to remain closed until the following morning, and then remove the pieces when they are sufficiently cool to the touch. Use gloves if necessary. When the clay pieces are removed from the kiln, they are called bisque ware; they are no longer water-soluble greenware. However, bisque ware is still porous and will not hold water. It is the glazing that makes them non-porous as well as decorative.

NOTE: The peephole in the kiln is left open during the first hour of firing if there is some doubt as to whether or not the pots or sculpture are thoroughly dry. Thereafter, the plug is placed in the peephole and remains there during the entire firing cycle. It is removed only to check the pyrometric cone.

Glaze Application: Basically there are four methods of applying glaze to pottery: spraying, dipping, pouring, and brushing. In the schools, the most common and practical method is that of brushing. Before the bisque ware is ready for glazing, the piece should be sponged off to remove dust and other foreign particles which may cause imperfections on the glazed surface. Read the directions for glaze application on the bottle in which the glaze is contained. Some glazes recommend two applications, while others require more. Stir the glaze before using and add water if it appears too thick.

Glaze should be applied with a soft sable brush using a gliding motion. Allow the first coat to dry before the second coat is applied and avoid heavy application. Two glaze applications should build up to about 1⁄16″. When the glaze has dried, the sheen will disappear. Apply glaze to all desired areas except the bottom. Avoid handling glazed areas as fingerprints will show. If glaze is needed inside of a high, small-necked pot, fill the pot with glaze and then empty the glaze back into the glaze container. Remember that when the inside of the pot is glazed, it will be water-

C

proof. There is no necessity to glaze the bottom of the pot, or the outside of the pot for that matter.

Engobe or colored-slip application: Engobe is applied to greenware, not bisque ware. For best effects, apply engobe to the greenware when it is leather-hard. The popular sgraffito effect is accomplished by scratching through an engobe application with a sharp tool or instrument. The greenware with engobe decoration can be fired with other greenware pieces during the first firing. When the first firing is completed, an application of clear glaze can then be brushed over the engobe. The resulting effect, after the second firing, will give the ceramic piece a clear, transparent, glasslike glaze, allowing the color of the engobe to show through. This is especially effective in using terracotta clays, where the natural body of the red clay is allowed to show through the clear glaze as well as the engobe color decorative effects. Do not be confused by the clear glaze as it appears in the jar. Clear glaze as it is applied on the ceramic piece will be opaque (nontransparent) until it is fired; then its natural form of transparency is achieved.

Experimentation in glaze application: With experience, students will make discoveries of their own relative to glaze and engobe applications. They will find that glazes may be dripped on or combined in different layers of color. They will make observations relative to interesting effects that can be achieved when glazed surfaces are combined with unglazed surfaces. They may wish to glaze only the inside of the pot, only the outside of the pot, or to leave some of the pot in its natural clay state. They may wish to experiment with underglazes, underglaze crayons, or underglaze pencils.

Students might want to try the resist process with wax crayons or with the commercial wax-resist compounds which are available from ceramic supply houses. By applying wax crayons to clay pots or sculpture in the bisque form, adding a coating of clear glaze, and firing, the waxed areas will resist the glaze in an interesting manner. Further experimentation can be made by dropping small glass marbles or colored bits of glass on the bottom of the bisque pot.

NOTE: Glazes as they appear in bottles never give the true color of the final firing. Glazes in their raw state appear opaque, muddy, and gray in color. It would be well to work from a color chart which is available from ceramic supply houses or to fire small tiles of glaze samples so that students might make more accurate glaze selections. Remember, too, that from a safety standpoint all glazes are toxic. Students should exercise extreme caution when using them, and keep their hands from their eyes and mouth area. Hands should be thoroughly washed after glazing experiences.

Glaze Firing:

Stacking the kiln: In glaze firing, it is important that the pieces do not touch each other. Each object should be at least ¼" apart. If glazed pieces touch one another, they will be welded together in the firing process. There is the added risk that glazes will jump from one piece to another when they are set too closely together in the kiln.

Note the firing temperatures of the glazes which are given on the glaze bottles. Some glazes fire at longer periods of time and under more intense heat, for example, red. Clay pieces of the same firing temperature should be fired at the same time. Set the recommended pyrometric cone number in the kiln as was previously described under Firing of Greenware. The number of the pyrometric cone will depend on the type of glaze that is used, and this number will be indicated on the label of the glaze bottle.

Taller pieces are placed on the bottom of the kiln. If more room is needed, set up some shelf supports on the floor of the kiln and lay a shelf across the supports. These supports and shelves are supplied with the kiln and are especially designed to resist heat. Other pieces may be placed on the shelf. If additional space is needed, set up additional shelf supports on the first shelf and lay another shelf across them. Generally, the kiln stacking is as follows: taller pieces on the bottom, medium size pieces on the next shelf, and small, flat pieces on the top shelf, as shown in Fig. C-10. If there are clay pots or sculpture with glazed areas on the bottom, these will necessitate the use of steel-point stilts. These stilts are easily loosened from the glaze and leave only pin-point markings. They may be used over and over again and are available from ceramic supply houses.

After the glaze firing cycle is completed, the kiln is shut off and the door of the kiln is left shut until the following day. It should be stressed that pyrometric cones

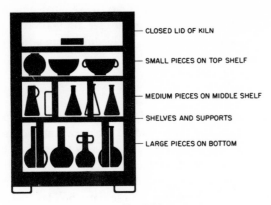

— CLOSED LID OF KILN

— SMALL PIECES ON TOP SHELF

— MEDIUM PIECES ON MIDDLE SHELF

— SHELVES AND SUPPORTS

— LARGE PIECES ON BOTTOM

Fig. C-10

are only used initially to establish firing cycles for clay and glazes. Careful notes should be taken by teachers with reference to establishing firing times for both bisque and glaze firings. When these firing times have been established, the further use of pyrometric cones will not be necessary. A chart might be made and hung next to the kiln so that teachers might read it for easy reference. Small children can be taught to stack kilns, thus relieving teachers of a purely mechanical chore.

Kiln wash: The use of a kiln wash before each glaze firing is recommended (see also KILN WASH). Apply kiln wash to shelves, sides, and floor of the kiln.

Kiln cement: Used to mend loose firing bricks in kilns (see also KILN CEMENT).

NOTE: Two suggested source books for teachers include: Josephine R. Krum, *Hand-Built Pottery* (Scranton, Pa.: International Textbook Company); and Lois Culver Long, *Ceramic Decoration* (Indianapolis, Ind.: The American Clay Company).

CERAMIC SCULPTURE

See CERAMICS.

CHALK (COLORED)

Although colored chalks resemble pastels, they are less costly and more durable.

Large, soft, colored chalks: These are 4″ long and 1″

in diameter and are used in the kindergarten-primary grades. They are available in boxes of 12, 36, and 72 sticks.

Medium size colored chalks: These are 3¼″ long and ⅝″ in diameter and are used in the intermediate grades. They are available in boxes of 48 sticks (assorted).

Small colored chalks: These are of regulation chalk size and are available in boxes of 12, 24, and 144 sticks.

Students should be encouraged to experiment with colored chalks, using them on their sides for broad stroke effects and varying the pressure to achieve gradations of color. Rubbing and blending of colors as well as color overlays should be encouraged as these are all part of the colored chalk technique.

As colored chalks come in large box assortments for the most part, it is best that each child have his own individual set. Put individual sets of colored chalks into half-pint milk cartons and place the milk-carton containers on a large tray for easy storage and distribution. Larger boxes of chalk can be used efficiently by groups of children while making a mural (see also MURALS). Colored chalk techniques are numerous: Try dry chalk on dry paper, wet chalk on dry paper, wet chalk on wet paper, and dry chalk on wet paper.

Give each student a half-pint milk carton filled with water to facilitate chalk dipping for wet-chalk techniques. Colored chalk drawings will smear, so they should be sprayed with fixative (see also FIXATIVES and FIXATIVE SUBSTITUTES). From the standpoint of "fixing" drawings while working, try the sugar-dipping technique. With an electric blender, mix 2 parts water with 1 part sugar. Allow the mixture to set overnight. Shake the mixture before using and pour a little into individual pans or milk cartons for dipping with colored chalks. Colored chalk drawings will be rendered "smearless," and the colors will be intensified as well.

CHALK MARBLING

See DECORATIVE PAPERS.

CHALK (OILS)

The trade name for this chalk-oil medium is "Sketcho." These chalks appear to be crayons, yet they have a heavier oil base and are more intense in color. They are applied heavily to the paper as one would use crayons. The colors may be blended with a brush dipped in turpentine, or the chalk-oil medium may be dipped directly into the turpentine and used as an interesting drawing medium (see also DRAWING).

CHALK + STARCH + PRESS PAPER

See DECORATIVE PAPERS.

CHAMOIS SKIN

Used for blending and erasing charcoal and pastel drawings (see also CHARCOAL and PASTELS). It is also used for finishing and smoothing greenware and as a polishing cloth for glass and metals (see also CERAMICS).

CHARCOAL

Charcoal is available in three basic types: vine charcoal (burnt twigs), compressed charcoal (synthetic), and the charcoal pencil (see also PENCILS). This medium is limited to black and shades of gray which are achieved through direct application of line and mass, rubbing, and shading. In charcoal rendering, one rubs directly with the fingers, a chamois cloth, or a gray-paper stomp [see also CHAMOIS SKIN and STOMPS (GRAY PAPER)].

Line delineation is achieved through contrast of values (see also CHIAROSCURO and DESIGN ELEMENTS). Line and texture may be rendered with the use of a rubber kneaded eraser which is soft and pliable and can be molded into a point for fine detail work (see also ERASERS). Charcoal is an excellent medium for intermediate and uppergrade students for general drawing and sketching experiences (see also DRAWING and PAPERS).

CHARCOAL PAPER

See PAPERS.

CHARGE

Term which is used in watercolor painting with reference to dipping the brush in water to load it with water. The term also applies when a brush is rolled around in a cake of paint to load it with paint (see also PAINTING). The term is also applied to brayers, as loading them with printing ink (see also PRINTMAKING).

CHEESECLOTH

Cheesecloth can be used as a sieve to strain lumps from wheat paste (see also MODELING MATERIALS, PAPIER-MÂCHÉ, and WHEAT PASTE). It can also be used as a hammock in the hammock method of pottery making (see also CERAMICS). It has decorative possibilities such as draping it from walls or ceilings for appropriate holiday décor (see also HOLIDAYS and SPECIAL EVENTS). Cheesecloth has possibilities for sculpture when it is dipped into a mixture of plaster of paris or white resin glue and water and then draped over armature supports until it is dry and will hold its shape (see also ADHESIVES, ARMATURES, PLASTER OF PARIS, and SCULPTURE).

There are ways of making cheesecloth Christmas trees for holiday decorations (see also HOLIDAYS and SPECIAL EVENTS). Start with a chicken wire cone-shaped armature. Pack the inside with cheesecloth and pull it through the chicken wire. Or wrap cheesecloth which has been dipped in plaster of paris around a chicken wire cone-shaped armature. Add ornaments before the plaster has hardened.

CHERRY WOOD

See WOODS.

CHEVRON WEAVE

Type of weaving pattern (see also WEAVING).

CHIAROSCURO

From the Italian words "chiaro" (light) and "oscuro" (dark); the use of light and shade rather than line; particularly applicable in charcoal rendering and in some of the intaglio process (see also CHARCOAL and INTAGLIO). It was also used extensively in painting by sixteenth-century Italian painters.

EXAMPLE: "Death of the Virgin," by Caravaggio.

CHINA

Ceramic ware which is of medium weight (see also CHINA PAINTING).

CHINA PAINTING

Hand-painted china is rendered with brush and china paints directly on the finished ware. It differs from machine-made decorated china where decorative effects are achieved with decals under glaze. True china painting is done with specially formulated china paints, also called overglaze colors, which mature in a kiln at a lower firing temperature than the glazed china being decorated.

Although china painting is considered to be one of the lost arts, there has been a recent surge of interest in the craft. Materials for china painting may be obtained from vendors dealing in general ceramic supplies. Besides the special china colors, one would need sable brushes, covered palette, ground-glass slab for grinding paints, palette knife, tracing paper, plate divider, black drawing ink, and a china marking pencil. A type of china decoration medium can mature in an ordinary kitchen oven (see also DEC-ALL COLORS).

CHINESE ART

One of the most important of the Oriental arts, 3000 B.C.—A.D. 1800. The Chinese influence in art in the Far East was considered as the counterpart of the Greek influence in art in the West. Chinese contributions included calligraphy in painting, sculpture, bronze castings; and they were considered among the most skilled in pottery making [see also CALLIGRAPHY, HISTORY (ART), and EASTERN ART].

CHINESE INK STICKS

Black drawing ink in the solid form which is ground and dissolved, as needed, to the desired consistency (see also INKS).

CHIPBOARD

See PAPERS.

CHISEL

See WOODWORKING.

CHRISTIAN ART

Christian Art included Early Christian, Byzantine, Romanesque, and Renaissance Art [see also BYZANTINE, CHRISTIAN ART (EARLY), HISTORY (ART), RENAISSANCE, and ROMANESQUE ART].

CHRISTIAN ART (EARLY)

One of the arts of antiquity A.D. 100 to A.D. 800 (see also ANTIQUITY). Early Christian art began as frescos on the walls of the catacombs in Rome between the second and fourth centuries (see also CATACOMBS). When Christianity became the official religion of Rome in the first quarter of the fourth century, Christian art took the form of mosaics, Coptic painting, sculpture, illuminations, and architecture (see also BYZANTINE, COPTIC ART, and EGYPTIAN ART). By the sixth century, the arts of the antiquity had reached their apex, and Medieval Art or the art of the Middle Ages followed [see also HISTORY (ART) and MEDIEVAL ART].

CHRISTMAS TREES

See CHEESECLOTH, MANZANITA, and PAPER SCULPTURE.

CHROMA

See COLOR.

CHROMATIC

See COLOR.

CLAMPS

See WOODWORKING.

CLASSIC

Belonging to the arts of antiquity; specifically, to the culture and art forms of the ancient Greeks and Romans (see also ANTIQUITY, GREEK ART, and ROMAN ART). It also relates to established excellence and harmony, for example, as in the High Renaissance (see also RENAISSANCE).

C

CLASSICAL ORDERS

Refers to the uppermost part of a column or capital which may be classified as either Greek (see Fig. C-11) or

Fig. C-11

Roman. Orders for both include Ionic, Doric, and Corinthian (see also CAPITAL, COLUMN, CORNICE, ENTABLATURE, GREEK ART, and ROMAN ART).

CLASSICISM

Classicism strove to recapture simplicity and restraint as exemplified in the art forms of classic antiquity, specifically that of the Romans and the Greeks [see also ANTIQUITY, GREEK ART, HISTORY (ART), and ROMAN ART]. A movement to return to the classic principles in art was led by Jacques David about the end of the eighteenth century. This movement, known as the Classic Revival or Neoclassicism, followed the French Revolution and was, in effect, a reac-

tion against the frivolity of the Rococo period (see also ROCOCO).

EXAMPLE: "Oath of Horatii," by Jacques Louis David.

CLASSIC REVIVAL

See CLASSICISM.

CLAY (FIRING)

See CERAMICS.

CLAY (KITCHEN-OVEN FIRING)

Available under trade names of Seramo and KO Modeling Clays, among others. This type of clay is thoroughly air dried and then placed into a kitchen oven at 250° F. Special glazes are sold by the manufacturers of the clay. Glazes give modeled pots and sculpture a high finish and render the pieces waterproof [see also CERAMICS, CLAY (NONFIRING), and CLAY (PLASTIC)].

CLAY (NONFIRING)

Some of the self-hardening clays, which are suitable for schools because they do not require firing kilns, include:

Marbelex: Gray clay in moist form which is ready for use; no kiln or oven firing is necessary for permanent pots or sculpture. Air-dried pieces are hard but not waterproof. It is available in 5-pound packages.

Mexican Pottery Clay: Air-dried pieces are durable and hard without kiln firing, but are not waterproof. Mexican pottery clay is red in color (terra-cotta), available in powder form, and is mixed with water in a plastic mixing bag which is supplied with each package.

Perma-Kraft: Powdered self-hardening clay which is mixed with water and hardens like stone. It may be sanded or carved when dry.

Play-Doh: Soft, pliable material which is ready for use; available in primary colors and in containers of 8 ounces or one-quart cans. One quart of Play-Doh is equal to 2½ pounds and the volume is the same as 5 pounds of modeling clay. It can be sanded, filed, or carved when hard (see also CARVING MATERIALS).

CLAY (PLASTIC)

Smooth, plastic, waterproof modeling clay which can be used over and over again; available in solid or assorted colors in boxes of 4 individual packages of ¼ pound. It is sold under commercial trade names of: Clayola, Clayrite, Modeline, Permoplast, Plastecine, and Plasteline, among others [see also PAPIER-MÂCHÉ and SUPPLIES (CLASSROOM)].

CLAY (PLASTIC) SUBSTITUTE

Add some glycerine to prepared, moist, low-firing ceramic clay or to powdered clay to achieve a kind of plastic clay which will not harden [see also CERAMICS and CLAY (PLASTIC)].

CLEANER (PENS)

See PENS (CLEANER).

CLEANING SOLVENTS

See SOLVENTS.

CLOISONNÉ

Enameling on metal distinguished by delicate metal dividers on the surface (see also BYZANTINE).

CLOROX

Household bleach which is used as a technique in watercolor painting. By brushing clorox over watercolor washes, the ground or paper will be defined through a bleaching process (see also PAINTING). Try brushing clorox on construction paper which is in the low value ranges of dark blue, dark green, or dark red. Clorox will bleach out the brush strokes in an interesting manner. Apply detail with black drawing ink, using either brush or pen (see also INKS, PAPERS, and PENS). Clorox is also effective in removing dye stains from the hands in both the batik and tie-dye processes (see also BATIK and TIE-DYE).

NOTE: Safety precautions in the use of Clorox are somewhat obvious but would bear repeating in terms of its use in the elementary grades. Children should wear protective coverings when using this material as it bleaches clothing as readily as paper. In addition, teachers should caution children against getting Clorox on hands, face, mouth, or near the eyes.

CLOSED-EYE DRAWING

See DRAWING.

COIL

See CERAMICS.

COLLAGE

From the French words papiers collés (glued papers); a method of pasting pieces of paper, newspaper, illustrations, and other textured or patterned materials to a heavy ground such as chipboard, as shown in Fig. C-12 [see also

Fig. C-12

MONTAGE, PAPERS, RUBBINGS, SCRAP MATERIALS, and TISSUE (COLORED)]. Line is often added to textured compositions of the collage. The collage was essentially a development of the French Cubists around 1907, growing from synthetic cubism (see also CUBISM). The collage was imported to America by Moholy-Nagy who was vitally involved in textural experiments (see also BAUHAUS). Max Ernst, Georges Braque, Pablo Picasso, Kurt Schwitters, and Jean Arp were among those who utilized texture and line in rendering the collage.

A collage technique which is used successfully in the schools from elementary through secondary grades involves the use of colored tissues. Interesting color is achieved through overlapping the colored tissues on a stiff paper ground. Liquid starch or clear lacquer may be used as an adhesive (see also ADHESIVES). The adhesive is applied to the ground and each shape and color is laid down (see also GROUND). Since the colored tissue is transparent, the colored tissue underneath shows through and mixes, yielding a new visual dimension. This technique is used over line pen-and-ink drawings or used alone as experience in rendering nonobjective designs. Line may be added on top of the colored tissue collage if desired. Colored tissue can be torn and laid down as well as cut.

NOTE: Do not apply adhesive of either lacquer or liquid starch to the backing of colored tissue and then attempt to transfer colored tissue to a ground. Tissue is fragile, and it will be impossible to lift once adhesive is applied. A more successful method would be to place the tissue down on the ground, and brush adhesive on top of it. The tissue is highly absorbent and will allow the adhesive to penetrate and make immediate contact with the ground underneath. Additional overlays may be applied in the same manner (see also ADHESIVES and GROUND).

Colored tissue may be purchased in mixed colors which are beautiful and intense, including tints, shades, tones, black, gray, and brown. The size of the paper is 20″ x 30″ and it may be purchased by the ream with 20 quires to the ream. Samples of available colors may be requested (see also PAPERS).

NOTE: One of the vendors for colored tissue is Austens of New York [see also SUPPLIES (VENDORS)].

EXAMPLE: "Collage in Blue and White," by Kurt Schwitters.

COLONNADE

Line of columns supporting horizontal lintels or arched structures (see also COLUMNS and LINTELS).

EXAMPLE: Colonnade at St. Peter's Square in Rome, designed by Giovanni Bernini.

COLOR

Color Vocabulary:

Hue: Refers to the color itself such as blue, red, or green.

Chroma: See following entry on Intensity.

Intensity: Refers to the pureness of a color; colors which are high in intensity would be relatively pure in color, while colors which are low in intensity would indicate that the colors have been rendered less intense by the addition of another color.

Saturation: See preceding entry on Intensity.

Value: Refers to the modification of a color with reference to its being light, medium, or dark. For example, light blue would be light in value, medium blue would be medium in value, and dark blue would be dark in value. In terms of light, one could find a value change by looking at a cylinder or a vase of the same color. The value change would occur in terms of where the light strikes the object. Where the object is struck by light directly, the object and color would be light in value, where the object is neither struck directly by light nor obscured directly from the light, the object and color would be medium in value; and where the object is obscured by light, the object and color would be dark in value.

High key colors: Colors to which white has been added.

Low key colors: Colors to which black has been added.

Middle key colors: Colors which are high in intensity or pure untampered colors.

Tint: Color plus white; sometimes erroneously called a pastel.

Shade: Color plus black.

Tone: Color plus gray.

Cool colors: Colors which lie adjacent to each other on the color wheel and are cool in feeling such as yellow-green, green, blue-green, blue, blue-violet, and violet.

Warm colors: Colors which lie adjacent to each other on the color wheel and are warm in feeling such as yellow, yellow-orange, orange, red-orange, red, and red-violet.

Receding colors: Cool colors are receding colors as they appear to recede from the picture plane; used to make a room look larger and to create the illusion of distance in aerial perspective (see also PERSPECTIVE).

Advancing colors: Warm colors are advancing colors as they appear to advance from the picture plane; used to make a room appear smaller and are frequently used as a foreground color in aerial perspective (see also PERSPECTIVE).

Color Theories: Basically there are two theories on color: the light theory which relates to light and the pigment theory which relates to paint.

Light theory: The light theory, or the Newtonian theory, is the more complex of the two color theories. It is considered to be the true theory as color does not exist without light. Practical application of the light theory can be found in the upper grades in classes which pertain to stagecraft and lighting (see also JELLS and PAPERS).

To illustrate the light theory, one would use two prisms (see also PRISMS). By catching the sun's rays with the first prism, light would be divided into a spectrum of color ranging from red to violet, or infrared to ultraviolet (see also ULTRAVIOLET). During a rainbow, the sun's light filtering through the rain, which acts as a prism, will produce the same effect. If a second prism were arranged, in an inverted manner, to catch the spectrum of light, the resulting light from the second prism would be white light.

In the light theory, it is the refraction of white light which produces colors. Separation of the rays of light through absorption, reflection, and refraction will produce individual hues. Hence, in the light theory, white light is the mixture of all colors or a reflection of all light, while black is the absence of all color or the total absorption of all light.

Pigment theory: Inasmuch as the pigment theory is related to paint, this is the theory which is used most often in a practical manner in the schools. The pigment theory concerns itself with pigment or paint and consists of 12 colors arranged on a color wheel. These colors consist of the primaries, the secondaries, and the intermediates. The primary colors are yellow, red, and blue. It is from these three colors that all other colors on the color wheel can be produced. The secondary colors are green, violet, and orange. The intermediate colors are yellow-green, blue-green, blue-violet, red-violet, red-orange, and yellow-orange.

Color wheel: The color wheel (Fig. C-13) is a functional tool toward the understanding and utilization of color in the pigment theory. Note that the primary colors lie between the intermediates, and the intermediates lie between a secondary and a primary.

Mixing Colors: Beginning with the primary colors of yellow, blue, and red, one can arrive at a formula for the mixing of the secondary colors as well as the intermediates.

Secondary colors: Mix one primary with another primary.

$$Y + B = G \qquad B + R = V \qquad R + Y = O$$

Intermediate colors: Mix one primary with one secondary.

$$Y + G = YG \qquad G + B = BG \qquad B + V = BV$$
$$V + R = RV \qquad R + O = RO \qquad O + Y = YO$$

There are 3 primary colors, 3 secondary colors, and 6 intermediate colors.

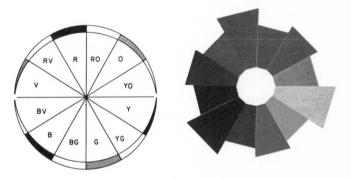

Fig. C-13

Tertiary Colors: The tertiary colors (three) are often erroneously called the intermediates. They are not the same and are not generally found on a conventional type of pigment color wheel. The tertiary colors are citrine, olive, and russet; they are formed through a mixture of the secondary colors in the following manner:

$$O + G = \text{citrine} \qquad G + V = \text{olive}$$
$$V + O = \text{russet}$$

Color Harmonies: Known color harmonies, sometimes called color schemes, are useful only insofar as knowledge about established color combinations is concerned. Students should not be confined to their memorization nor restricted to their use. Too often adults are afraid of color for they have heard all of the tales about what is acceptable and what is not. They live with feelings of timidity for there are so many contradictions. They have heard on one hand that red and orange are not acceptable together;

yet they inspect a flower and find that nature has contradicted man. We have come a long way in our acceptance of color combinations since the Fauves or Wild Beasts (see also FAUVES) put on their canvases color combinations that were previously thought of as being taboo. Witness in fabric designs the pinks and reds, the blues and greens, the reds and oranges, and the oranges and magentas! Known color harmonies, as they are described in color theory, are as follows:

Analogous colors: Those colors which are adjacent to each other on the color wheel and are usually in groupings of three, such as yellow-orange, orange, and red-orange; or blue, blue-green, and green. Analogous colors are sometimes called related colors.

Complementary colors: Those colors which are directly opposite each other on the color wheel. Examples of complements would be blue and orange, red and green, or yellow-orange and blue-violet. Complements when used side by side will produce the greatest visual contrast in the use of colors. This knowledge is often applied by sign painters. When complements are mixed together in equal proportions of paint, they will produce gray. When they are mixed together in unequal proportions, they will neutralize each other and produce an interesting rich color.

Split complements: Any three colors on the color wheel which have the following placement: one color plus the two colors which are adjacent to, or on either side of, its complement. For example, start with the color blue. The complement of blue is orange. The two colors which are adjacent, or on either side of orange, are yellow-orange and red-orange. The split complement would then contain the colors of blue, yellow-orange, and red-orange. The process may be reversed by starting with orange and selecting those two colors which lie adjacent to blue. Split complements can be worked out for any color on the color wheel.

Double Split Complement: Any four colors which have the following placement on the color wheel: four colors which lie adjacent to the two chosen complements. For example, let us again start with the color blue. The complement for blue is orange. The two colors which lie adjacent to orange are yellow-orange and red-orange. The two colors which lie on either side of blue are blue-green and

blue violet. This double split complement would then contain the colors of yellow-orange, red-orange, blue-green, and blue-violet. Double split complements can be worked out for any complement on the color wheel.

Monochromatic: Any one color which has been modified or changed in value through the addition of black or white and which produces a range of tints and shades of one color. The term monochromatic is taken from the word "mono" meaning one, and "chroma" meaning color.

Triad: Any three colors on the color wheel which have equal placement in terms of an equilateral triangle. For example, yellow, red, and blue; orange, green, and violet; or blue-violet red-orange, and yellow-green. The combination of three colors into a color harmony or scheme is sometimes referred to as being a triadic color combination.

Color Harmonies for Room Environment: The preceding material relating to color harmonies can, of course, be applied in classrooms for establishing color combinations for room environment. It is important to remember that not all colors in a given harmony should be used equally. One might be predominant, another subordinate, and the other or others might be used as accent colors. The limitations of the known color harmonies, in terms of numbers of colors used, will enhance the feeling of unity within the room.

In terms of color selection, one should be acutely aware of the kind of lighting the room affords. Does it have direct sun or shade? What is the size of the room? Is it large or small? If the room is large, use warm colors predominantly, with accents of cool colors. Warm colors advance and tend to make a room appear smaller. If the room is small, use cool colors predominantly, with accents of warm colors, for cool colors recede and tend to make a room appear larger. If the room is dark, utilize color harmonies of tints with accents of bold color. Cover bulletin boards with white burlap or white corrugated paper (see also BULLETIN BOARD, BURLAP, and PAPERS).

Once the color harmony has been established within the room, unity can be further achieved by repeating and picking up the same colors in different parts of the room. Mounting and matting of pictures within the room will enhance the feeling of unity if there is a relatedness of color in their use (see also MOUNTING and MATTING).

NOTE: There are from 100,000 to 300,000 different hues, tints, shades, and tones which the human eye is said to be able to distinguish.

COLORED TISSUE

See COLLAGE, PAINT SUBSTITUTES, PAPERS, and TISSUE (COLORED).

COLORS

See ACETATE COLORS and TEXTILE COLORS.

COLORS (STANDARD)

For purposes of ordering colored papers, construction, tonal (poster), or others, standard colors are as follows: red, orange, yellow, green, blue, and violet [see also PAPERS and SUPPLIES (CLASSROOM)].

COLUMN

Vertical pillar, often fluted, which consists of base, shaft, and capital (see also CAPITAL, CLASSICAL ORDERS, CORNICE, ENTABLATURE, and LINTELS).

COMPLEMENTARY

See COLOR.

COMPLEMENTS

See COLOR.

COMPOSITION

Term which is used interchangeably with design; the organization of the elements (see also DESIGN ELEMENTS). When a distinction is made between the two in terms of semantics, composition is one which involves the use of aerial or linear perspective (see also PERSPECTIVE).

CONCRETE

Oftentimes the terms concrete and cement are used interchangeably; this is a common error. They can be distinguished in the following manner:

Cement: Grayish white powder which can be mixed with water to achieve a stonelike mass.

Concrete: Cement is one of the ingredients of concrete but not the only one. A satisfactory formula for the mixing of concrete is as follows: Use ½ bag of cement to 20 shovelfuls of sand. Add water for the proper consistency. Textural effects can be achieved by adding gravel, rocks, or pebbles. Cracking can be avoided in concrete work by sprinkling the surface with water as soon as it has hardened. Regular sprinkling of water should be continued for one week or more until the concrete is seasoned (see also CARVING MATERIALS).

NOTE: Concrete is also available in premixed quantities.

CONE

See CERAMICS and CUBISM.

CONFIGURATION

Relates to design or composition; an analysis of how parts are distributed on a picture plane (see also DESIGN ELEMENTS).

CONSTRUCTIVISM

Type of sculpture which is an outgrowth of Tatlinism as developed by Vladimir Tatlin in Russia in 1916. Tatlin believed that no material was unworthy of utilization in three-dimensional form; he combined wire, wood, nails, and metals in sculpture. A sculpture created with wood scraps and Duco cement is shown in Fig. C-14.

Eventually the movement spread throughout Europe and came to America. Moholy-Nagy and Naum Gabo were its adherents. Subsequently, the movement of Tatlinism changed to Constructivism. Experiences in sculpture along the lines of Constructivism can be afforded to students of all ages. Scrap wood from lumber yards, nails, wire, and woodworking tools, plus a variety of scrap materials, will provide the necessary motivation (see also SCRAP MATERIALS and WOODWORKING).

CONTACT PAPER

See PAPERS.

C

Fig. C-14

CONTÉ

Type of drawing and sketching crayon which is available in rectangular 3″ sticks; available in hard, medium, and soft; sold by the stick or in boxes of 12. Most generally, Conté crayon is seen in black, but it is also available in sanguine, bister brown, and white (see also DRAWING).

CONTOUR

Limit or edge of a shape. When two shapes or forms share the same contour, it is called the common contour (see also DRAWING).

CONTRAST

Manipulation of elements of design in the use of texture, line, mass and space, or color in order to achieve opposition and interest (see also ACCENT, CHIAROSCURO, and DESIGN ELEMENTS).

CONVENTIONAL

See ACADEMIC.

COOKIE TINS

Used in marbling (see DECORATIVE PAPERS).

COOL COLORS

See COLOR.

COPPER ENAMELING

Materials Needed: Copper squares or circles, carborundum stone, penny coin, emery cloth, spatula, file, masking, gum solution (also called gum tragacanth), flux, enamels, threads, lumps, findings, adhesive (epoxy resin), asbestos pad, enameling fork, loading fork, and an enameling kiln.

Copper squares and circles: May be ordered from supply houses which handle copper-enameling materials and supplies. Shapes include circles, squares, and rectangles, as well as copper articles such as earrings, ash trays, and bracelets. The 1″ copper square is the recommended size for a student's first experience in the copper-enameling process in the intermediate and upper grades. As a student grows in his ability to handle materials, other shapes and copper articles may be given to him as an extension of his experience in working with the process.

Carborundum stone: Used as an abrasive for smoothing rough edges from copper; use is optional.

Coin: A penny coin will act as a prop or resting place for copper pieces when gum solution is painted on copper surfaces, when flux or enamel is dusted on surfaces, or when threads and lumps are placed on the surfaces of copper pieces. It is necessary to prop up the copper piece so that it may be picked up with the spatula and then placed on the enameling rack.

Spatula: Serves as an instrument to pick up the copper piece from the coin prop, as the use of fingers is avoided in this process.

File: Used to remove burnt edges from the copper piece after it has come from the kiln.

Masking: Copper protector which comes in paste form and protects pieces from fire scale. Used properly on the back of each piece of copper before firing, the masking will come off easily when the piece cools.

Gum solution: Adhesive solution for flux and enamel applications; copper piece should be thoroughly cleaned before applying gum solution.

Flux: An initial base coat of powder-like material applied to the copper piece to insure depth of color; use is optional.

Enamel: Powdered glass material which, when heated to a high temperature in an enameling kiln, will fuse and form a smooth, glossy surface on the copper. It is available in all colors including black, gray, and white, and in either opaque or transparent enamels (see also OPAQUE). Enamels are sold in 2-ounce, ½-pound, and 1-pound containers. They are applied on copper with a shaker over a coating of gum solution. Shaker tops can be purchased which will fit over the 2-ounce containers of enamels.

Threads: Linear threads of color which may be added for decorative detail; threads are picked up and placed on copper pieces with tweezers.

Lumps: Lumps of color which may be added for decorative detail or effects and will melt into spots of color.

Findings: Technical name for backs of earrings, cufflinks, tie clips, pin clasps, etc. These may be adhered to the backs of copper pieces with an all-purpose resin glue or epoxy resin (see also ADHESIVES).

Epoxy resin: See ADHESIVES.

Asbestos pad: Used for cooling of copper pieces after they come from the kiln.

Enameling rack: For firing one large copper object or several small objects at one time, such as earrings or small pendants; makes insertion and removal of copper pieces from the kiln much easier.

Enameling fork: For use with enameling rack; forks are 19″ long and have wooden handles. They are placed underneath the enameling rack to lift it into and out of the kiln. Copper pieces are placed on the enameling rack with a spatula.

Kiln: Copper-enameling kilns range in price from about $10.00 to $60.00. The studio kiln is an excellent size for small groups of students. It will fire small pieces as well as larger ones such as ash trays, bowls, and bracelets. The studio kiln heats to 1550° F, and the pivot lid provides easy access to copper pieces; it is equipped with a firing slot for viewing copper pieces when they are in the kiln. The kiln should be preheated before copper pieces are inserted. Heating a kiln for about 50 minutes before it is used will insure adequate heat for firing. Copper-enameling kilns should be given a coat of kiln wash along the bottom of the kiln about once a month if the kiln is used regularly (see also KILN WASH).

Procedure: File off the rough edges of the copper piece, using carborundum stone if available. Clean the copper piece thoroughly with emery cloth, or as a substitute, use a mixture of detergent and water. Cleaning is most important in this process. Fingers should stay off the copper pieces at all times because finger markings are oily and will prevent the flux, as well as the enamel, from spreading evenly. Hold the copper piece on the sides when cleaning.

Apply masking to the back of the copper piece with a small brush, and allow the masking to dry thoroughly. Masking will dry more readily if the copper piece is placed on top of the kiln. In fact, in any of the drying steps in the copper-enameling processes, drying can be accelerated in this manner. When the masking has dried, prop up the copper piece on the edge of a coin. In this position the masking will be on the bottom. Apply gum solution to the surface of the copper piece with a brush, shake powdered flux on the gum solution, and allow it to dry.

Slide the copper piece onto a spatula and then place the piece on the enameling rack. Place the loading fork underneath the enameling rack on which the copper piece rests, then place the enameling rack into the preheated kiln. When the surface of the copper piece appears to be smooth and shiny, remove the enameling rack and copper piece from the kiln with the loading fork. Lift the copper piece with a spatula, and place it on the asbestos pad for cooling. After the copper piece has cooled, remove the masking with a knife. Finish cleaning off the masking with emery cloth.

Once again, apply masking to the back of the copper piece, holding it between the fingers along the edge of the copper, and allow the masking to dry as before. Prop up the copper piece on a coin as described previously. Apply a coat of gum solution with a brush to the surface of the copper. Shake on the selected color of enamel, and if desired, place threads or lumps over the enameled surface for additional decorative effects. Allow to dry. Lift the copper piece from the edge of the coin with a spatula, put it on an enameling rack, and put the rack into the kiln with a loading fork.

C

Again, allow it to stay in the kiln until the surface appears smooth and shiny. This will take from 1 to 1½ minutes, depending upon the heat of the kiln and the type of enamel used. Remove from the kiln with a loading fork. Use a spatula to remove the copper piece from the enameling rack and place it on the asbestos pad for cooling.

When it is cool, again remove the masking with a knife, and finish with an emery cloth. If findings are to be attached to the copper piece, the findings should be cleaned with emery cloth and attached with epoxy resin or one of the white resin glues.

This technique represents but one of many in the copper-enameling processes; further experiences will promote experimentation and research. See Fig. C-15.

Fig. C-15

NOTE: There is an alternate method of attaching findings with solder. It is a rather tricky process for students, requiring a bit of dexterity and skill. The epoxy resin is recommended along with the white resin glue as it is a sure, quick, and easy method which involves less in the way of frustration.

COPTIC ART

Decorative and flat early Egyptian Christian art form in graphics. Predominantly in evidence from fourth to seventh centuries [see also CHRISTIAN ART (EARLY), EGYPTIAN ART, and GRAPHIC ARTS].

CORK TILE

May be used as a stencil board on which to pin fabric in textile designing using textile colors (see also PRINT-MAKING and TEXTILE DESIGN).

CORNICE

Uppermost part of a classic entablature; a support for the roof in architecture (see also CAPITAL, COLUMN, and ENTABLATURE).

CORRUGATED PAPER

Corrugated cardboard may be purchased in rolls; it is available in a wide range of colors including brown, black, and white (see also PAPERS). It is used extensively to establish additional bulletin-board areas in a classroom setting (see also BULLETIN BOARD and COLOR). It is also used for collages, marbling, and display work (see also COLLAGE and DECORATIVE PAPERS).

COTTON AND FLOSS

See YARNS AND STRINGS.

COTTON CHENILLE

See YARNS AND STRINGS.

COTTON ROVING

Large type of cotton yarn which is available in a wide range of colors; may be purchased by the spool or by the yard (see also YARNS AND STRINGS). It is a versatile material which is used to define areas on bulletin boards and display cases. It may be held in place with straight pins or staples (see also BULLETIN BOARDS). It may be pinned around a painting to create a frame (see also MOUNTING AND MATTING). It is also used to define lines in caricature drawings, for weft thread in weaving, and for detail work in stitchery (see also CARICATURE, STITCHERY, and WEAVING).

COTTON-ROVING MOBILES

Cotton-roving mobiles are not true mobiles in a literal sense. They are stiff cotton-roving forms which are sustained in shape and form through a starch saturation method. These forms may be hung from the ceiling with thread, hence the word mobile.

Students may "draw" with the roving after it has been saturated in liquid starch. They should do this drawing on large pieces of waxed paper. When the basic outline is completed, smaller bits of roving or wool yarn may be added for detail. These additional pieces of detail should touch the basic form in some manner, being pressed firmly to it, to insure sticking when the mobile has dried. When the form is completed, allow it to dry on the waxed paper. Drying will take from 2 to 3 days at room temperature. When the form is completely dry, it may be lifted from the waxed paper and it will retain its shape.

This technique of drawing with yarn for a mobile effect is particularly effective in carrying out a theme during the holidays (see also HOLIDAYS AND SPECIAL EVENTS). Forms may be hung from the ceilings at different heights to provide an interesting adaptation of the mobile idea. These forms will turn, bob, and sway when caught in the breeze (see also MOBILES).

COTTON WARP

See YARNS AND STRINGS.

COUNTERCHANGE

Alternate use of light against dark and dark against light on a common ground which has been divided in a predominantly horizontal, vertical, or diagonal manner. The device of counterchange is particularly effective in poster making, as shown in Fig. C-16 (see also POSTERS).

Fig. C-16

CRACKLED PAPER

See DECORATIVE PAPERS.

CRAFT PAPER

See PAPERS.

CRAFTS

Refers commonly to those art forms which have a utilitarian as well as an aesthetic value; these would include pottery, jewelry, and weaving. Often these crafts are called the minor arts as opposed to the fine arts which primarily have an aesthetic rather than a utilitarian value (see also FINE ARTS). However, as time goes on, contemporary philosophy makes less of a distinction between the two areas—the Bauhaus approach (see also BAUHAUS).

CRAYON

This convenient medium is one with which children have had experience long before they arrive at school. Generally, students use only the point of the crayon and possibly this is fostered by the idea of "filling in the spaces" of coloring books. Teachers have long accepted the idea that there is little creativity attendant to the coloring book. In times past, children found substitutes for the coloring book in some of the illustrations contained in reading and arithmetic workbooks. Recently, some workbook manufacturers have cooperated with teachers by including only colored illustrations in their workbooks, thus discouraging children from adding crayon details to them.

The best of crayon drawings are made from crayon discards, those broken pieces of crayon which have been rejected by the children. Some teachers never issue complete unbroken boxes of crayons to their children. They save the old crayons and break up the new ones. Then when it comes time to do some different kinds of crayon techniques, children need not suffer the trauma of breaking their own well-cared-for crayons or of peeling down the paper coverings. Keep the broken crayons in cigar boxes.

Demonstrate what can be done with crayons when they are used on their side; vary the pressure, and observe the gradation of color. Combine lines; put thin lines over broad crayon areas and heavy broad strokes over light crayon areas. Try combining crayon with other media such as crayon with black drawing ink, crayon with colored ink, crayon with tempera, or crayon with colored chalk (see also MIXED MEDIA). Vary the texture of the paper for different kinds of crayon experiences. Try using crayon on typing paper, brown kraft paper, butcher paper, paper toweling, or alphatone (see also PAPERS).

Try crayon rubbings over some highly textured surfaces, using crayon on the side and a lightweight newsprint (see also RUBBINGS). Cut some of these rubbings out of the newsprint and try pasting them to a piece of white drawing paper or a heavy board for a collage (see also COLLAGE). Crayons can be used creatively in the decorative papers; observe crayon laminations, crayon resist, and crayon etching (see also DECORATIVE PAPERS). Crayons are used to enhance glaze decoration in the resist technique in ceramic work (see also CERAMICS). They are also used as a coloring agent in candlemaking (see also CANDLEMAKING). Students may "paint" with crayons (see also CRAYON PAINTING, CRAYON TURP, and PAYONS).

Kindergarten-primary teachers sometimes melt broken crayons and put the melted colored wax into individual half-pint milk cartons. When the colored wax has cooled, the carton is torn away and individual blocks of colored crayons are made available for smaller children to grasp and draw colored murals. These are particularly favored for mural work as the blocks of crayon cover a good deal more of ground area with fewer strokes than the conventional type of crayon. Primary children should use the large, nonroll type of crayons which are available in boxes of 8 and 12. Intermediate and upper-grade students should use the smaller, more conventional type of crayon which is available in boxes of 8, 16, and 24 sticks. In addition, there are nontoxic, washable crayons available in boxes of 8 and 12 sticks [see also SUPPLIES (CLASSROOM)]. There are other types of crayons such as the broad line crayons which are flat and rectangular in shape. These crayons are effective in the rendering of design, lettering, and general poster work in the intermediate and upper grades (see also POSTERS).

CRAYON BATIK

Refers to crayon resist both in batik textile design and in decorative papers (see also BATIK and DECORATIVE PAPERS).

CRAYON ENGRAVING

See DECORATIVE PAPERS.

CRAYON FABRIC DESIGN

See TEXTILE DESIGN.

CRAYON LAMINATIONS

See DECORATIVE PAPERS.

CRAYON MARBLING

See DECORATIVE PAPERS.

CRAYON PAINTING

Involves the melting of crayons and then painting with the melted colored-wax medium. See Fig. C-17 for a

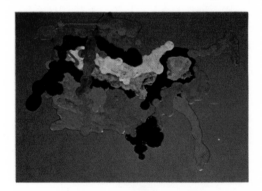

Fig. C-17

melted-crayon design. Crayons may be melted as follows:

1. Melt crayons in muffin tins using a sunlamp for heat.

2. Melt crayons in individual small cans, such as mushroom cans, in a kettle of water over an electric plate.

Students may paint with easel brushes directly on

heavy paper of cardboard ground (see also PAPERS). Wax crayon may be removed from brushes with turpentine (see also SOLVENTS).

CRAYON RESIST

See DECORATIVE PAPERS.

CRAYON TAPA CLOTH

See DECORATIVE PAPERS.

CRAYON TURP

Brush over a crayon drawing with a brush which has been dipped in turpentine. The effect when finished is somewhat like oil [see also CHALK (OILS) and SKETCHO].

CRAYON WATERCOLORS

See PAYONS.

CREPE PAPER

See CREPE-PAPER CRAFT, PAPERS, and VALENTINE BOXES.

CREPE-PAPER CRAFT

NOTE: Source books for teachers: *Fun with Crafts* and *Paper Arts and Crafts* (Dennison Books).

CREWEL NEEDLES

See NEEDLES and STITCHERY.

CRYSTOLON STONE

See ABRASIVES.

CUBISM

Early twentieth-century art movement which followed Postimpressionism (see also POSTIMPRESSIONISM). Lead by Paul Cézanne who believed that everything in nature could be treated in terms of geometric forms such as the cylinder, the sphere, and the cone; adherents included Juán Gris, Pablo Picasso, and Georges Braque.

Analytical Cubism: The earlier type of cubism which attempted to analyze nature into geometric relatedness.

EXAMPLE: "Gardanne," by Paul Cézanne.

Synthetic Cubism: Latter type of cubism which reorganized the geometric forms into cubistic designs.

EXAMPLE: "The Guitarist," by Georges Braque.

CURLED PAPER

See PAPER SCULPTURE.

CURSIVE WRITING

See CALLIGRAPHY and WRITING.

CURTAIN STRETCHERS

See STITCHERY.

CUTTING

When cutting paper, particularly around corners or small curves, greater detail can be achieved if the paper, not the scissors, is turned to change directions. The scissors always travels ahead in the same direction; it is the paper that is turned (see also PAPER SCULPTURE, SCISSORS, and SHEARS).

CYPRESS WOOD

See WOODS.

D

DADA

Art movement which developed under the leadership of Tristan Tzara in Zurich and lasted from 1916 to 1922. The Dadaists were considered to be nihilistic in their approach to subject matter. They held in contempt all that reflected adherence to established and accepted social traditions. Their art forms were biting, satirical, brash, and harsh. Like the Tatlinists and the Constructivists, they considered no material as useless or unworthy of experimentation (see also CONSTRUCTIVISM and SCRAP MATERIALS). Since the development of the Dada movement followed Word War I, it was considered to be a reaction to the aftermath of that war. The Dadaists were supposed to have said, "Nothing makes sense, so it makes sense to paint nonsense." The name Dada is significant in that it too is senseless. Dada in its literal translation means "hobby horse" and was selected at random from a French dictionary.

EXAMPLE: "Fur-Lined Teacup," by Meret Oppenheim.

DEC-ALL COLORS

Heat-setting color which will form a permanent bond with glass, ceramic ware, and metal. Decorated articles are placed in a kitchen oven and the temperature is allowed to rise gradually to 300° F. Dec-all colors are intense and smooth flowing on a brush; they will resist fading as well as deterioration on contact with acids and caustics. Dec-all colors include red, orange, yellow, green, blue, white, and black (see also CHINA PAINTING).

DECALS

Type of commercial design which is prepared on a gum-coated paper; available in designs, letters, and numbers in colors and in gold. Decals are placed in water for about 30 seconds and then affixed to surfaces face down; then the paper backing slides off, leaving the design face up on surfaces such as wood, metal, or glass (see also DECOUPAGE).

DECORATIVE ARTS

Relates to the decoration of any surface such as paper or wood (see also DECORATIVE PAPERS and DECOUPAGE).

DECORATIVE PAPERS

There are many applications of, and uses for, decorative papers including program covers, booklet covers, gift wrapping paper, box coverings, wastepaper basket coverings, as well as wallpaper for primary play houses (see also BOOKLET MAKING). Some of the known decorative paper techniques are as follows:

Chalk + Starch + Press:

Materials needed: Colored chalks, liquid starch, blunt-ended instrument such as the handle of a stencil brush, heavy, white construction paper, and an easel brush.

Procedure: Cover the entire paper with varied hues of heavily applied colored chalk. Brush liquid starch over the entire surface of the paper. Fold the paper in half. With the blunt end of a stencil-brush handle, press down and "draw" a design on one side of the paper which has been folded in half. Open up the paper. The result will be an interesting, symmetrical, linear drawing which is achieved through the pressure of the blunt instrument. In addition, there will be an interesting, textural quality to the paper which is achieved when the starch mixes with the colored chalk and is subsequently pulled away when the paper is opened. An example of this is shown in Fig. D-1.

Crackled Paper:

Materials needed: Lightweight white paper, tempera paint, and brushes.

Procedure: Soak a few sheets of paper in water for several minutes. Take one sheet of paper from the water and crumple it hard in the hands. Smooth out the paper and crumple it again. Repeated crumpling of the paper will break down the fibers of the paper's surface and allow the paint to seep through when it is applied with a brush.

Fig. D-1

Then smooth out the paper on a desk or table. Paint over the surface of the paper with a light tint (see also COLOR). While the paper is still damp, turn it over and paint the surface of the paper with a color of a deeper hue. When the paint has dried, hold the paper under running water so that the excess paint on both sides will be washed off. When the excess paint has been washed off, the crackle effect will be achieved. The darker color will seep through the cracks in the paper to the side painted with the lighter hue (see Fig. D-2). Crackled paper may be pressed with an iron to achieve a smoother surface.

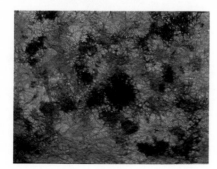

Fig. D-2

NOTE: For a different effect allow the color to drip and splash on the paper.

Crayon Engraving (Crayon Etching or Crayon Sgraffito):

Materials needed: White drawing paper, crayons, liquid soap, black tempera paint or black drawing ink, and a scratching tool.

Procedure: Cover entire surface of the paper with areas of colored crayon. Use many different colors and apply heavily. Cover the entire crayoned surface with black crayon. Using a scratching tool of some sort, a pointed scissors will do, scratch a design on the surface. See Fig. D-3.

Fig. D-3

An alternate method to using the black crayon would be to brush black tempera paint or black drawing ink on the surface. Add a few drops of liquid soap in order to insure that the paint will adhere to the waxed crayon surface. Liquid detergent will work as well as liquid soap. Wait until the tempera or black drawing ink has dried before attempting to scratch through the surface with a pointed instrument.

Crayon Lamination:

Materials needed: Old crayons, waxed paper, and an iron.

Procedure: Cut two pieces of waxed paper into identical sizes and lay one on top of a brown piece of kraft paper. The kraft paper is not part of the process but acts only as a protective covering on the table. Over the waxed paper, shave bits of colored crayon. Place the second piece of waxed paper over the first. Then place another piece of brown kraft paper over the waxed paper and iron with a medium-warm iron. When this step is finished, the heat from the iron will have melted the wax on the paper causing the two sheets of waxed paper to be bonded together. In addition, the heat from the iron will have melted the crayon shavings. These paper laminations should be adhered to window panes through which light may filter.

NOTE: In addition to using shaved crayons, try using some gold or silver thread as shown in Fig. D-4. Try

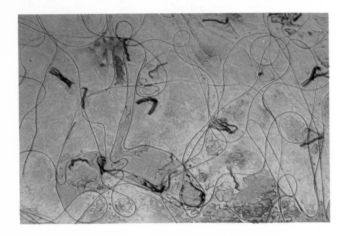

Fig. D-4

pressing maple leaves or flowers and putting these between sheets of waxed paper (see also PRESSING FLOWERS AND LEAVES). Try using overlays of colored tissue paper (Fig. D-5) and confetti (Fig. D-6) between sheets of waxed paper [see also COLLAGE, PAPERS, and TISSUE (COLORED)].

Fig. D-5

Crayon Resist:

Materials needed: Crayons, watery mixture of tempera paint, brushes, and white construction paper.

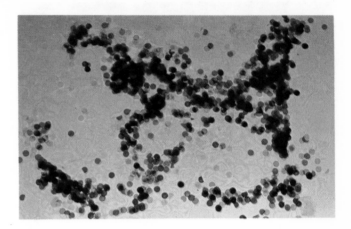

Fig. D-6

Procedure: Render a crayon drawing on the white construction paper. Paint over the crayon drawing with a light mixture of tempera paint. Crayoned areas will resist the paint and show through. Try crayon resist on paper toweling. Try white crayon on white paper with a colored wash for a touch of magic. See Fig. D-7.

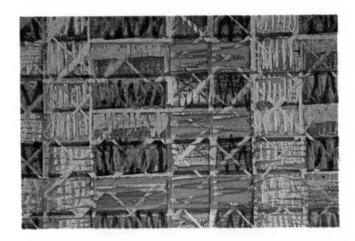

Fig. D-7

Crayon Tapa "Cloth": This paper technique for creating tapa, or Polynesian cloth, employs an economy of materials and yet achieves a rather striking effect which is not unlike the true tapa cloth. See Fig. D-8.

Fig. D-8

Materials needed: Brown paper bags and crayons.

Procedure: Soak the paper bags in water for about 2 or 3 minutes. Take the bags out of the water and open them at their seams so that they become long, brown strips of paper. Crumple the bags hard in the fist. Open up the bag and crumple it again. Repeat several times. Lay the brown paper flat on a table and smooth out with the hands. Allow to dry thoroughly. When dry, a design may be rendered on the paper bag in tapa fashion, utilizing some of the true tapa cloth colors such as black, brown, and white. Add another color of orange or red if desired.

Finger Painting (Direct Process):

Materials needed: Finger paint paper (shelf paper may be substituted), dry powder paint, liquid starch, and sponges.

Procedure: Cover working area with newspapers. Wet both sides of the finger paint paper with water by either dipping it into a pan or sponging it on both sides. The working surface is the glossy surface. Be sure this side is up when working. Put about 4 teaspoons of liquid starch on the center of the paper. Sprinkle some dry tempera powder paint on top. Mix the two together with the hands and cover the entire area of the paper, including the corners. Use fingers, fists, forearms, or palms in painting and rendering the picture or design. When finished, lift the painting by the corners and put it on a drying table which has been covered with newspapers. See Fig. D-9.

NOTE: Finger paintings tend to curl when they have dried. They may be ironed flat or weights may be put on the completed pictures.

Fig. D-9

Finger Painting (Indirect Process):

Materials needed: Large pieces of masonite (or a table top of formica), starch, powdered paint, and finger paint paper (or shelf paper).

Procedure: Draw the size of the paper to be used on the masonite working surface. This may be done with crayon or the lines may be defined with masking tape. Inside the boundaries, put about 4 teaspoons of liquid starch and sprinkle colored, powdered tempera on top. Mix with the hands directly on the masonite or formica surface and spread to all areas evenly. Draw, paint, or render design on the working surface. Lay the paper directly on top of the designed area, glossy side down, and run the hand lightly over the back of the paper to register the print. Lift the paper up and the design on the working surface will be transferred onto the paper. See Fig. D-10.

NOTE: Linoleum may be substituted for masonite or formica. Prepared, "home-brew" finger paint or commercially prepared finger paint may be substituted for the starch and tempera.

Fig. D-10

Fig. D-11

Finger Painting with Prepared "Home-Brew" Finger Paint: Commercial finger paint is sold by school supply houses. This is available in the solid jelly or in the powder form. Each requires the mixture of water on the paper. Some teachers prefer to mix their own finger paints. In this way, they have more control over colors, particularly in the shades, tints, and tones (see also COLOR). All that is necessary is to prepare a base which is cooked at home and add color in the form of powdered tempera or food coloring.

The prepared base is as follows: Beat with an electric or hand mixer 1 cup of flour, 1 teaspoon of salt, and 1½ cups of cold water. Add 1 cup of hot water and boil until clear. The mixture may be again beaten until the consistency is smooth. Allow to cool and store in mason jars. Add color when ready to use.

Glazed Paper: Apply a coat of shellac to a crayon or finger paint design (see Fig. D-11) for a high-gloss, glazed finish (see also SHELLAC).

Marbling (Chalk):
Materials needed: Colored chalks, knife, large enamel pan, and white drawing paper.
Procedure: Fill pan half full of cold water. Shave colored chalk dust onto the surface of the water. Lay a piece of 9″ x 12″ paper on the surface of the water. Lift up the paper. Apply fixative to the marbled paper when dry (Fig. D-12) (see also FIXATIVES and KRYLON).

Marbling (Crayon):
Materials needed: Crayons, turpentine, four small bowls or jars, enamel pan, a grater, and white drawing paper.
Procedure: Shave colored crayons and put each color into a separate jar. Add a small amount of turpentine to the crayon shavings. Allow mixtures to set for approximately 40 or 50 minutes or until the crayon shavings are completely dissolved. Fill enamel pan half full of warm water. Put a little of each color onto the surface of the water. Swirl the color to achieve the desired marbled

Fig. D-12

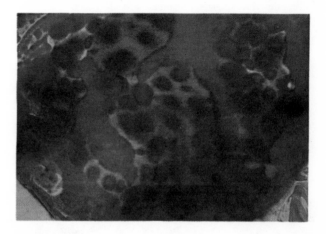

effect. Place a 9″ x 12″ sheet of paper on the surface of the water. Do not submerge the paper; float it. Then lift the paper, and the crayon marbling on the water's surface will have transferred to the paper. See Fig. D-13.

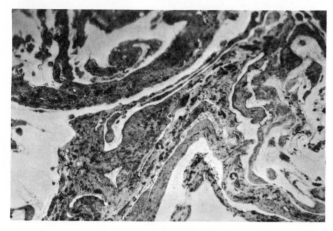

Fig. D-13

NOTE: For extra-large marbling using long strips of paper, use the bathtub.

Marbling (Felt Ink):

Materials needed: Felt-pen refill inks in several colors, enamel pan, and white drawing paper.

Procedure: Fill enamel pan about half full of water. Using different colors of ink, apply a little to the surface of the water. Swirl the ink with a pencil to achieve desired marbled effect. Lay paper on water and lift it up. See Fig. D-14.

NOTE: Colored drawing inks will not work; use only felt-pen refill inks (see also INKS).

Marbling (India Ink):

Materials needed: Black India ink or black drawing ink, enamel pan, and white drawing paper.

Procedure: Fill enamel pan about half full of water. Drop a little of the black drawing ink onto the surface of the water. Swirl the ink gently to achieve a marbled effect. Lay paper on the surface of the water and then pick it up for the desired "smoke-like" marbled paper. See Fig. D-15. Colored drawing inks will not work in this process.

NOTE: In all of the marbling techniques, a cookie tin or a roasting pan can substitute for the enamel pan which would have an approximate size of 14″ by 20″, or larger.

Fig. D-14

Marbling (Oil Paint):

Materials needed: Enamel paints (tubes of oil paints or oil printer's ink will substitute), enamel pan, turpentine, and white drawing paper.

Procedure: Using about three or four different colors of oil paints which have been thinned with turpentine, drop a little of the colors on top of the surface of the water.

Fig. D-15

D

Water will be contained in enamel pan (half full) as in other enameling processes. Swirl the paints on the surface of the water with the end of a pencil, if necessary, to achieve desired marbled effect. Lay a piece of paper on the surface of the water and pick up the marbled pattern. See Fig. D-16.

Fig. D-17

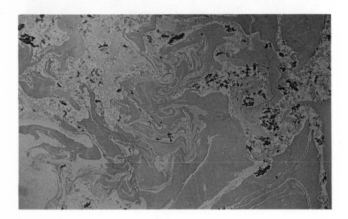

Fig. D-16

Rubber Cement Resist:

Materials needed: Rubber cement, light watery mixture of tempera paints, and white drawing or colored construction paper.

Procedure: Paint directly on the paper with rubber cement. Rubber cement may be dropped or trailed on the paper for interesting effects. Allow the rubber cement to dry thoroughly. Paint over the surface of the paper with a tempera wash. Use one color or many. When the paint is dry, rub off the rubber cement with the fingers. Where the rubber cement had been applied, the color of the paper will show through.

This process may be repeated again and again, blocking out areas of color with the rubber cement and applying other colors of tempera over the surface (see Fig. D-17). When this is done, the process is called paper batik because it resembles the textile batik process (see also BATIK).

Starch Paper: This process is much the same as the direct method of finger painting. However, instead of using the fingers, fists, and forearms to paint, cardboard combs are used. See Fig. D-18. These combs are made out of

Fig. D-18

chipboard and are passed over the surface of the paper which contains a starch-tempera mixture. Patterns are achieved through the manipulation of cardboard combs and the variations of the teeth. Examples of chipboard combs are illustrated in Fig. D-19.

Fig. D-19

58

D

DECOUPAGE

The art of decorating surfaces with assorted papers and glue. These may include colored tissue, gift wrapping, magazine pictures, newspaper photos, seed-catalog pictures, advertisements, and others. The art of decoupage is applied effectively in covering wastepaper baskets, lampshades, boxes, walls, and shelves. A coat of clear plastic protects decorated surfaces (see also DECALS, DECORATIVE ART, KRYLON, and SCRAP MATERIALS).

DESIGN

An organization of elements such as line, texture, mass and space, value, and color (Fig. D-20) (see also DESIGN

Fig. D-20

ELEMENTS). The degree to which these elements are used, in whole or in part, or varied in their use is a personalistic, selective process on the part of the artist. The degree to which these elements of design hold together and exhibit cohesiveness contributes to our understanding of unity in design and the degree to which the elements are varied contributes to our understanding of variety within unity in design. If the design of utilitarian objects is both functional and aesthetically pleasing, then the design will be successful both in concept and in resolution. Design is applied to all areas of the arts, including the decorative arts, the applied arts, the so-called minor arts, and the fine arts. Design is a truly creative act of expressiveness; it is original in concept, successful both in terms of execution and resolution, and aesthetically satisfying in terms of response (see also DESIGN ELEMENTS).

DESIGN ELEMENTS

Elements in design commonly refer to color, line, mass and space, texture, and value.

Color: Can refer to either the pigment theory or the light theory; more properly called hue (see also COLOR).

Line: Can be free flowing, as characterized in the graphic arts, or measured, as characterized in architecture or the applied arts.

Mass and Space: Space is given meaning with points of reference. Mass is called positive space, while the space that surrounds mass is called negative space.

Value: Light and shade; the lights, mediums, and darks of a rendered design or composition.

Texture: Of two types: visual, which can be seen but not felt; and tactile, which can be both seen and felt.

Related to the elements of art are the so-called principles of art which include terms such as rhythm, emphasis, balance, and proportion. Rhythm implies repetition or progression, emphasis relates to prominence, balance relates to equilibrium of vision, and proportion refers to size relationships.

DE STIJL

See NEOPLASTICISM.

DIE

For cutting a material, as in the use of a die press for mass-produced, machine-made articles (see also PLASTICS).

DIMENSION

Art forms are either two-dimensional or three-dimensional in character. Two-dimensional art forms relate to height and width, with *depth as an illusion,* as in perspective; they include flat work such as drawing, painting, printmaking, portraiture, or poster work (see also GRAPHIC ARTS). Three-dimensional art forms relate to height, width, and *depth as an actuality.* Such art forms would include modeling, carving, and all forms of sculpture (see also PLASTIC ARTS).

59

D

DIORAMA

For classroom experiences, a diorama refers to a scene which is both two-dimensional and three-dimensional in character and is rendered in a U-shaped box. See Fig. D-21. The diorama is effective as a correlated activity within

Fig. D-21

the curriculum in such areas as social studies, health, recreational reading, and science (see also PEEP SHOWS). Cardboard soup boxes may be used as well as smaller hat boxes. The top of the box must be cut away, as well as one side of the length of the box. When the basic working shape and area are established, the box will have three sides and a bottom.

It is on the sides and the bottom that the painting is done. For example, if one were to depict a wheat field, the sides and the back of the box might have distant hills painted on them. The bottom of the box would contain foreground detail which would be rendered in three-dimensional form to effectively carry out the theme (see also DIMENSION). Such objects as bundles of harvested wheat, as well as people in the fields who might be actively harvesting the wheat, might be placed there. The kinds of materials one might use in rendering the three-dimensional forms are limitless, for these might be carved, modeled, or cut from paper (see also CARVING MATERIALS, MODELING MATERIALS, and PAPER SCULPTURE).

DIPTYCH

Painting on two panels (see also TRIPTYCH).

DISPLAY

Visual arrangement such as bulletin boards, display cases, or exhibits (see also BULLETIN BOARD).

DISTORTION

Deviation from a photo effect such as in abstraction and caricatures (see also ABSTRACT and CARICATURE).

DOLLS (KACHINA)

Wood-sculptured dolls which are characteristic of American Indian art forms; chiefly of the Hopi, Zuni, and Pueblo tribes. Dolls are highly decorative with masklike faces, bright color, and feathers; they are approximately 10″ to 17″ tall. Kachina dolls represent an excellent kind of related carving experience for students who are studying comparative Indian cultures. Dolls can be carved from balsa wood, painted with tempera, and decorated with feathers (see also BALSA WOOD).

DOMINANT

Relates to emphasis in any of the elements of design; when one thing is dominant, the other is subordinate (see also DESIGN ELEMENTS).

DORIC

See CLASSICAL ORDERS.

DOUBLE SPLIT COMPLEMENT

See COLOR.

DOWELING

Round lengths of wood which may be obtained from lumber supply houses in varied diameters ranging in sizes from ¼″ to 3″ [see also SUPPLIES (VENDORS) and WOODS]. Smaller doweling is excellent for mobiles (see also MOBILES). Medium size doweling of ½″ to ¾″ is used in the making of stands for puppet heads (see also PAPIER-MÂCHÉ and PUPPETS). The medium size dowel is used in woodworking experiences in the lower grades; they are used as axles for wheels in construction. The large size dowel is used for a rolling pin in ceramic work relating to the slab method (see also CERAMICS).

DRAWING

Closed-Eye Drawing: Allow a student to select one object from memory such as a tree, an airplane, or a flower. Ask him to draw this object three times on his paper with his eyes closed. As a result of this experience, there will be many compositions with exceedingly interesting abstractions of forms. See Fig. D-22. A student may select the

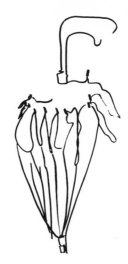

Fig. D-23

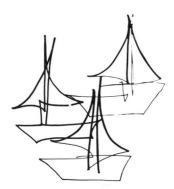

Fig. D-22

most interesting and meaningful lines and outline these with pen and ink. An extension of this experience would allow the student to further develop his compositions with color and texture.

Contour Drawing: Essentially, this drawing experience develops an awareness of the beauty of line as it defines the outer limits of a shape, or its contour. See Fig. D-23. The student may look at a subject such as a figure or a still-life arrangement. He then places his drawing instrument on the paper and continues looking at the subject, *not the paper,* while he draws. If the student wishes to stop, he may begin again by placing his pencil on the desired spot, but he must once again look only at the subject as he resumes his contour drawing.

Figure Drawing: Students tend to become inhibited about drawing the human figure once they have left the primary grades. As their awareness develops and they become addicted to realism, they become excessively self-critical of their efforts. At this point, they need some instructional guidelines, for the human figure is not easy to render. See Fig. D-24. Instead of giving such students any of the smaller drawing tools such as pencils, crayons, or char-

Fig. D-24

D

coal, allow them a margin for error by having them paint with sponges. The sponges can be charged with paint and the figure form can be stamped out without the worry of bothersome details. For a second, follow-up experience, use brush and black drawing ink or tempera paint. As a third experience, use colored chalk, encouraging the students to use the chalk on its side.

Related classroom experiences: Using students as models, try some 10-minute poses, some 5-minute poses, and follow these with quick, 2-minute, fast sketches. Reinforce these experiences by analyzing the human figure. Talk about it. How do the shoulders relate to the neck? Where do the arms bend with reference to the placement of the waist? When the arms are down, where do the fingertips end as they relate to the thigh? What is the angle of the pelvis when the weight is on the left foot? What is its angle when the weight is on the right foot? How many heads tall is the human figure? Is the ratio the same for children as it is for adults? Refer to the following chart for guidance:

Age (years)	Heads Tall
to 4	4 to 5
5 to 7	5½ to 6
10 to 16	6½ to 7
Adult	7½ to 9

Encourage students to be aware of how the limbs move when one walks, runs, squats, or kneels.

Finally, avoid making figure drawing a one-shot experience. Be mindful of the continuing need for experience in drawing the human figure, and provide correlated art experiences both in outdoor sketching and in murals. For a change of pace, introduce some of the modeling and carving media (see also CARVING MATERIALS and MODELING MATERIALS).

Head Drawing: In the primary grades as well as in the intermediates, students tend to draw the head shape as a circle and the features of the head are ill-placed. A simple blackboard demonstration relating to the following would help to clarify the shape of the head and the general placement of the features:

Head: Oval- or egg-shaped.

Eyes: Almond-shaped, with placement halfway down the head from the tip of the head to the tip of the chin. Allow the length of one eye to determine the approximate distance between one eye and the other.

Nose: Nostril line is placed halfway between the eyes and the chin.

Mouth: Mouth line is placed halfway between the nostrils and the chin.

Ears: Ear line placement begins with the top of the ear at the same approximate height as the eye line.

Neck: Treat this as a support of the head, coming from the jawline and forming the beginning lines of the shoulders.

Related classroom experiences: Use students as models. Begin with the full face, then the profile, and finally the three-quarter view. Additional experiences include the self-portrait, silhouettes, and caricatures (see also CARICATURES and SILHOUETTES).

NOTE: Some children are extremely self-conscious about being asked to pose as models for both head-drawing and figure-drawing experiences. Be sensitive to this and avoid arbitrarily choosing a child as a model. Allow the students to volunteer.

Outdoor Sketching: Here is an experience in drawing where the whole class can be taken outdoors with drawing boards, paper, and drawing tools such as charcoal, pencils, crayon, or colored chalk (see also CHALKS, CHARCOAL, CRAYON, and PENCILS). Encourage the students to block in areas in terms of mass and space and value. Sketches may be further developed later in the classrooms where details and textures may be added. See Fig. D-25.

Fig. D-25

Scribble Drawings: The student is encouraged to scribble aimlessly on paper and later try to find within the drawing some form, animals or human, which is pleasing or provocative in terms of development. If the student cannot find anything recognizable, he might select a portion of his scribble drawing as a nonobjective composition. He may then erase the extraneous lines and develop the area he finds pleasing. See Fig. D-26.

Fig. D-26

In all drawing experiences there are limitless materials for exploration and experimentation. Among these are drawing pencils, brushes, steel brushes, colored chalks, charcoal, pens, Conté crayons, crayons, and graphite sticks. It is always interesting to try the unconventional, such as dipping bamboo sticks in ink and drawing with them, or using pipe cleaners as drawing tools with ink.

DRAWING BOARDS

For indoor and outdoor drawing, use plywood, masonite, or thick chipboard as drawing boards. For adhering paper to boards while working, use thumbtacks for plywood, clothespins for masonite, and pins for chipboard (see also DRAWING).

DRAWING ERASERS

See ERASERS.

DRAWING INK

See INKS.

DRAWING INK PENS

See PENS.

DRAWING (MECHANICAL)

Drawing with the aid of mechanical tools or instruments, not freehand drawing. See Fig. D-27.

Fig. D-27

DRAWING PAPER

See PAPERS.

DRAWING PENCILS

See PENCILS.

DRAWING PENS

See PENS.

DRAWING (SCRATCHBOARD)

Drawing is done with a scratching tool or knife on special white-coated scratchboard. The white scratchboard is coated with black drawing ink and allowed to dry. The scratching tool is then used to render line drawings and reveals the white board underneath (see also KNIVES and PAPERS).

DRIFTWOOD

Trim off extraneous twigs, bark, and wood in order to develop an interesting basic form. Sand the driftwood with fine sandpaper and finish with fine steel wool. Apply several layers of household paste wax for final finishing (see also MANZANITA and WAX).

DRILLS

See WOODWORKING.

DRYING

For the drying of paintings, prints, tie-dyes, batiks, or other forms of two-dimensional artwork, string a wire across the room parallel to the back wall. Lay wet artwork across the wire or hang with clothespins. The wire can also serve as an excellent working area for balancing a mobile (see also MOBILES).

DRYING WEEDS

Collect decorative weeds from the fields, such as yellow yarrow, silver dollars, rye, wheat, brown tobacco, and thistle. Tie the long stalks together while they are still green and hang them upside down from a clothesline in the basement or garage. Cover them with waxed paper or plastic sheets to protect them from dust. Allow them to hang in this manner until they dry thoroughly and turn brown, then spray them with plastic spray (see also KRYLON). Use them for decorative arrangements in vases or bowls or for seasonal displays (see also HOLIDAYS AND SPECIAL EVENTS). They may be sprayed silver, gold, or any of the colors which are available in pressurized spray cans of paint (see also PRESERVING FLOWERS, PRESSING FLOWERS AND LEAVES, and SPRAYS).

DRY-MOUNT

Method of mounting photographs, drawings, prints, and other types of two-dimensional materials without the use of adhesives. A combination of heat and pressure, using dry-mount tissue, mounts with one easy action.

Materials needed: Dry-mount tissue, dry-mount press, and cardboard.

Procedure: Plug in the dry-mount press and set the thermostatic control at approximately 225° F; when the green light goes off, the press is ready for operation. Insert a piece of dry-mount tissue between the cardboard and the picture which is to be mounted. The cardboard and the picture should be exactly the same size as the tissue. If the tissue is too large, it may be trimmed off around the edges. Place a piece of white paper over the picture for protection. Place these in the press, face up, for 10 flashes of the red light. When finished, the picture will have adhered permanently to the cardboard.

NOTE: The ordinary household iron will substitute for the dry-mount press. Set the iron on medium heat and apply pressure to adhere the picture to the adhesive tissue and to adhere the adhesive tissue to the mounting board (see also DRY-MOUNT PRESS and DRY-MOUNT TISSUE).

DRY-MOUNT PRESS

The dry-mount press is automatic with a thermostatic control for timing and pressure. It is available in sizes relating to the platen: 8″ x 10″, 14″ x 17″, 15½″ x 18½″, and 18½″ x 23½″ (see also DRY-MOUNT and DRY-MOUNT TISSUE).

DRY-MOUNT TISSUE

Dry-mount tissue can be used with either the dry-mount press or with an ordinary kitchen iron. The dry-mount tissue comes in envelopes of 12 or in boxes of 12 dozen. The following dry-mount tissue sizes are available: 5″ x 7″, 8″ x 10″, 11″ x 14″, 14″ x 17″, 16″ x 20″, and in rolls of 16″ x 100′ and 32 ″ x 100′ (see also DRY-MOUNT and DRY-MOUNT PRESS).

DRY POINT

See INTAGLIO and PRINTMAKING (PROFESSIONAL).

DUCO CEMENT

See ADHESIVES.

DYES

Fabric Dyes: For general craft projects relating to fabric dyeing, use Putnam, Tintex, Rit, Ciba, and others. Read directions on containers relative to procedures for the specific dyes used (see also BATIK and TIE-DYE). Dyes may be set with mordants (see also MORDANTS). For information about home dyeing with natural dyes, write to: Superintendent of Documents, U.S. Government Printing Office, Washington, D.C.

NOTE: A liquid ink-dye is available in 4-ounce containers, including all colors and clear. It is manufactured under the name of Inko-dye and is available from Silk Screen Process Supplies Manufacturing Company, 1199 East 12th Street, Oakland, California. This Inko-dye has proved effective in the batik process utilizing the *brushing*, rather than the dipping, dye method of application (see also BATIK).

Leather Dyes: Used specifically for dyeing leather products in leather craft. Dyes are available in 3½-ounce, 4-ounce, 8-ounce, pint, and quart containers and are offered in a variety of colors, shades, tints, and tones (see also LEATHER).

Resin Dyes: These dyes are used for crafts relating to plastics, specifically clear-casting polyester (see also PLASTICS). Resin dyes are available from plastic supply houses in a limited range of colors, in 1-ounce containers, and in both transparent and opaque (see also OPAQUE and PLASTICS).

EARTHENWARE

Heavy type of pottery, heavier than china (see also CERAMICS).

EASEL BRUSHES

If the long handles of easel brushes get in the way of classroom traffic and of children who are painting at the easel, try sawing off about 3″ or 4″ from the wooden handle (see also BRUSHES).

EASEL PAPER

Painting experiences at the easel will be enhanced with a variety of easel papers in terms of size, shape, color, and texture. For a change of pace, hang easel paper vertically instead of horizontally. Change the color of the easel paper from day to day (see also PAPERS). Utilize different shapes for easel experiences such as ovals, circles, and free forms (see also FREE FORMS). For a variation of visual texture, hang newspaper at the easels, particularly the classified section. Try also the green section and the yellow section, as well as the comic section, for additional visually-textured papers (see also DESIGN ELEMENTS). Try kraft paper and butcher paper cut to easel size.

EASELS

School supply houses feature the double easel (Fig. E-1) with panels of 26″ x 20″ and with 50″ adjustable

Fig. E-1

heights. For kindergarten-primary classrooms there should be a minimum of two double easels in each classroom; for intermediate grades, one per classroom [see also SUPPLIES (CLASSROOM)].

E

EASEL SUBSTITUTES

Large pieces of chipboard which have been covered with oilcloth may substitute for easels in the kindergarten-primary grades. Paper may be fastened to them with clothespins. Another method of fashioning a substitute for an easel is to turn a primary chair upside down, with the back resting on the floor. The legs of the chair will serve as a back rest for the easel board. Other substitute easels may be fashioned from pieces of masonite or plywood. Stand these easels up on chalk trays for painting or drawing. Fasten paper on masonite with clothespins, on plywood with tacks, and on chipboard with either pins or clothespins (see also DRAWING BOARDS).

EASTERN ART

Eastern art, alternately called Oriental art, includes: Chaldean-Sumerian, Babylonian, Egyptian, Chinese, Assyrian, Hittite, Phoenician, Jewish, Persian, Indian, Japanese, and Byzantine [see also HISTORY (ART), and WESTERN ART].

EGG-KEEP

See SODIUM SILICATE.

EGG TREE

See MANZANITA.

EGYPTIAN ART

One of the arts of antiquity, 6000 to 50 B.C., a period of art history when monumental contributions were made including the pyramids and sculptured forms of gods and pharaohs which were carved in granite. Egyptian art initially showed great realism and eventually gave way to a form of flat stylization which remained for thousands of years (see also ANTIQUITY, BABYLONIA, and PAPYRUS). In the period of early Christianity, Egyptian painting took the form of flat, decorative, and/or Coptic rendering [see also COPTIC and CHRISTIAN ART (EARLY)].

ELEMENTS

See DESIGN ELEMENTS.

EMBOSSING

Lines which are rendered in relief on paper and can be seen as well as felt (see also DESIGN ELEMENTS and RELIEF).

EMBROIDERY FLOSS

See STITCHERY.

EMBROIDERY NEEDLES

See NEEDLES and STITCHERY.

EMERY CLOTH

See ABRASIVES.

EMPHASIS

See DESIGN ELEMENTS.

ENAMEL

See COPPER ENAMELING and PAINTS.

ENAMELING (COPPER)

See COPPER ENAMELING.

ENCAUSTIC

Ancient method of painting with colored wax which in turn was melted and burned into surfaces with hot irons (see also CRAYON PAINTING). Encaustic painting was considered a lost art when Leonardo da Vinci attempted to revive it in the sixteenth century. Currently the encaustic method is enjoying popularity with contemporary artists.

ENGOBE

See CERAMICS.

ENGRAVING

See INTAGLIO and PRINTMAKING (PROFESSIONAL).

ENLARGING

Enlarging a small drawing for a wall mural or a mosaic may be done in the following manner: Begin first by establishing a ground which will be proportionate in size to the smaller drawing (see also GROUND). Place the smaller drawing in the lower left-hand corner of a long strip of paper. Butcher paper or kraft paper is often used for enlargements (see also PAPERS). If the smaller drawing is horizontally placed on the paper, place the long strip of paper in a horizontal manner. If the smaller drawing is vertically placed on the paper, place the long strip of paper in a vertical manner. See Fig. E-2.

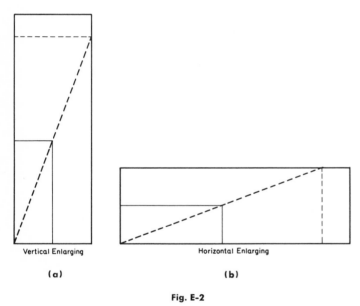

Vertical Enlarging   Horizontal Enlarging

(a)   (b)

Fig. E-2

Extend a diagonal line from the lower left-hand corner of the smaller drawing through its upper right-hand corner. Continue extending this line beyond the drawing until it reaches the upper edge of the long strip of paper. From the point where the diagonal line meets the edge of the long strip of paper, a line is dropped down which is perpendicular to the lower edge of the long strip. The paper which is contained on the right-hand side of the perpendicular line is to be discarded and thrown away. It is the paper on the left-hand side of the perpendicular

line which will be proportionate in size to the smaller drawing.

The transfer of the smaller drawing to the larger proportionate strip of paper may be done in sections or through freehand rendering. Thomas Benton was one artist who utilized the sectioning method in the enlargement of his drawings for large wall paintings or murals. Sectioning is accomplished by drawing a vertical line down the middle of the smaller drawing. A second horizontal line is drawn across the middle of the smaller drawing. Additional vertical and horizontal lines, spaced evenly, will section the smaller drawing into equal divisions of 16 or 64 areas. Similar line divisions are then established on the larger strip of paper, taking care to establish as many equal divisions on the larger strip of paper as are contained on the smaller paper. When one compares the detail of a section contained on the smaller drawing with the same section on the larger strip of paper, it is fairly easy to see where lines and placement go in terms of transfer (see also TRACING AND TRANSFER).

ENTABLATURE

Classic architectural section which extends beyond and above the columns consisting of a horizontal beam, frieze, and cornice. Figure E-3 shows the entablature

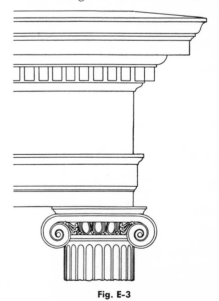

Fig. E-3

E

above the columns of the Parthenon (see also CLASSICAL ORDERS, COLUMNS, CORNICE, and FRIEZE).

EPOXY RESIN

See ADHESIVES.

ERASERS

Gum Eraser: Extremely soft eraser which does not mar or scratch the surface on which it is used; used for pencil drawings and taking up rubber cement; available in sizes: 1" x 1" x 1", 2" x 1" x 1" (see also DRAWING, DECORATIVE PAPERS, and PRINTMAKING).

Kneaded Eraser: Soft eraser which can be molded into a point or cut into any given shape; used for pastel, charcoal, and pencil drawings; available in large and small sizes (see also DRAWING).

Pencil Eraser: Soft rubber erasers are good practical tools for sketching and drawing experiences and will last longer than the gum erasers; available in large and small sizes and in soft and medium textures (see also DRAWING). These erasers are also handy tools for removing block-out solution from the edges of designs in the silk-screening process (see also SILK SCREENING).

ERASING KNIVES

See KNIVES.

ETCHING

See INTAGLIO and PRINTMAKING (PROFESSIONAL).

ETCHING CREAM

See ETCHING (GLASS).

ETCHING (GLASS)

Method of cutting a stencil and securing it to a glass surface with tape. Etching cream is then applied over the exposed glass surface through the stencil design and allowed to remain there for approximately 3 minutes. The stencil is then removed and the etching cream is washed off, creating a permanent, frosted, etched design on glassware as shown in Fig. E-4.

Fig. E-4

ETCHING PAPER

See PAPERS.

ETRUSCAN ART

One of the arts of antiquity which existed in central Italy, in Tuscany, 1800 B.C. to 200 B.C. Etruscan art forms included wall and tomb paintings, sculpture, terracotta plaques, pottery, and metalware. They were known particularly for their clay sarcophagi with figures of the deceased on stone coffin lids. Influenced by the Greeks, the Etruscans were considered to be the early link between Greek and Roman art forms. The Etruscans were the first Europeans to build irrigation channels, arched bridges, and vaulted gates [see also ANTIQUITY, HISTORY (ART), ROMAN ART, and SARCOPHAGUS].

EXCELSIOR

Common type of packing material which is somewhat like coarse straw in appearance. When it is dipped into a mixture of plaster of paris, it provides interesting free-form sculpture (see also PLASTER OF PARIS and SCULPTURE). Dip the excelsior into water and allow the excess water to drip off. Dip the excelsior into a mixture of plaster of paris. Arrange the excelsior over a form and allow it to dry; it will maintain the shape that was created through the use of supports and props.

EXCISED

Opposite of incised (see also INCISED). The design is drawn on the surface of clay, rock, wood, or other material and the background is carved away, leaving the pattern in low relief (see also RELIEF).

EXPRESSIONISM

Graphic and plastic art forms which rely upon emotional expression rather than the actual appearance of things. In this regard, expressionism may be considered a permanent characteristic of all art (see also GRAPHIC ARTS and PLASTIC ARTS). Children are considered natural expressionistic painters for it has been said of them, "They paint what they know, not what they see" (see also ABSTRACT-EXPRESSIONISM).

EXAMPLES: "Guernica," by Pablo Picasso and "The Intrigue," by James Ensor.

EXTENDERS

Extenders allow paints to go further without disturbing their intensity of color (see also COLOR). They are available for both tempera powdered paint and textile colors (see also PAINTS, SILK SCREENING, and TEXTILE COLORS).

EYELET PUNCH

Useful tool for securing eyelets to spines of books in booklet making (see also BOOKLET MAKING, EYELETS, and PUNCHES).

EYELETS

Small, round, 5⁄32″ metal eyelets which are used to finish holes which have been punched in spines of books in the booklet-making process (see also BOOKLET MAKING). They are adhered in place with an eyelet punch and provide the openings that allow twine and other fastening materials to hold the booklets together (see also PUNCHES).

EYE LEVEL

See PERSPECTIVE.

FABRIC DESIGN

See BATIK, TEXTILE DESIGN, and TIE-DYE.

FADELESS PAPER

See PAPERS.

FAUVES

See FAUVISM.

FAUVISM

Representative of a group of early twentieth-century French painters under the leadership of Henri Matisse. "Les Fauves," or the "Wild Beasts" as they were contemptuously called, were so named because of their unconventional use of brilliant color. The movement of Fauvism was considered significant in that it represented a breakthrough in what was academically considered to be "the correct use of color" (see also COLOR). Included in "Les Fauves" were Albert Marquet, André Derain, Maurice de Vlaminck, and Georges Rouault (see also COLOR).

EXAMPLE: "Red Trees," by Maurice de Vlaminck.

FELT

Used for appliqué in the stitchery process (see also APPLIQUÉ and STITCHERY). Felt is used in the making of felt prints in the printmaking process by gluing felt designs to squares of chipboard, inking surfaces, and printing (see also PRINTMAKING). It is used as a material in the creation of a collage, and for the decorative details in papier-mâché processes (see also COLLAGE, PAPIER-MÂCHÉ, and SCRAP MATERIALS). It is also used as a ground for

F

stitchery and murals (see also MURALS). It is available in colors, including black and white, at department stores in widths of 36".

FELT BOARD

Teaching tool which is used in the classroom, particularly in the kindergarten and primary area, for number work and story telling. Small pictures are stuck onto the felt board as the number lesson or story is being developed. Pictures will stick to the felt board by gluing small bits of sandpaper to the backs. Felt boards are made by gluing large pieces of felt to sheets of masonite, plywood, or chipboard (see also MAGNET BOARD).

FELT-PEN

See PENS.

FELT-PEN INK

See INKS.

FELT-PEN INK MARBLING

See DECORATIVE PAPERS.

FERRULE

See BRUSH and BRUSHES (CARE AND CLEANING).

FIGURATIVE

Relates to figures, objects, or images in a painting; opposite of nonfigurative, as in nonobjective painting (see also NONOBJECTIVE ART).

FIGURE

See DRAWING.

FIGURE FIELD

Also called figure ground; an interrelatedness of the figure with the surrounding elements in a graphic composition (see also DESIGN ELEMENTS and DRAWING).

FIGURINE

Small modeled figure using any of the plastic modeling or carving materials (see also CARVING MATERIALS, CERAMICS, CLAY, and MODELING MATERIALS).

FILM LINE CUTTER

See SILK SCREENING.

FILMS AND FILMSTRIPS (ART)

The following represents a partial list of sources for films, slides, and filmstrips:

American Library Colored Slide Co., 222 West 23rd Street, New York, New York

Bailey Films, Inc., 6509 DeLongpre Avenue, Hollywood 28, California

Charles Besler Company, 219 18th Street, East Orange, New Jersey

Brandon Films, Inc., 200 West 57th Street, New York 19, New York

Contemporary Films, Inc., 267 West 25th Street, New York 1, New York

Coronet Films, Coronet Building, Chicago 1, Illinois

Encyclopedia Britannica Films, 7250 MacArthur Boulevard, Oakland, California

Film Images, 18 East 60th Street, New York 22, New York

Girl Scouts of the USA, 830 Third Avenue, New York 22, New York

Indiana University, AV Center, Bloomington, Indiana

International Film Bureau, 57 East Jackson Boulevard, Chicago 4, Illinois

International Film Foundation, 1 East 42nd Street, New York 17, New York

National Film Board of Canada, 630 5th Avenue, New York 20, New York

Neubacher-Vetter Film Productions, 1750 Westwood Boulevard, Los Angeles, California

Picture Film Corporation, 487 Park Avenue, New York 22, New York

Prothmann, Dr. Konrad, 2378 Soper Avenue, Baldwin, Long Island, New York

Rembrandt Film Bureau, 267 West 25th Street, New York 1, New York

San Francisco Museum of Art, Civic Center, San Francisco, California

Society for Visual Education, 1345 Deversey Parkway, Chicago 41, Illinois

United World Films, Inc., 1445 Park Avenue, New York 29, New York

University of California, Film Rental Library, Berkeley, California

FINDINGS

Technical name for backs of earrings, cuff links, tie clasps, pins, etc. (see also COPPER ENAMELING and PLASTICS).

FINE ARTS

Categorically related to those art forms in either the graphic or plastic arts which adhere to pure aestheticism; no relation to utilitarianism or functionalism (see also MINOR ARTS).

FINGER PAINT

See DECORATIVE PAPERS and PAINTS.

FINGER PAINTING (DIRECT)

See DECORATIVE PAPERS.

FINGER PAINTING (INDIRECT)

See DECORATIVE PAPERS.

FINGER PAINT PAPER

See PAPERS.

FINISHING WOODS AND FURNITURE

See LACQUER, LINSEED OIL, SHELLAC, and VARNISH.

FIRING

See CERAMICS.

FISH PRINTS

See PRINTMAKING.

FIXATIF

Alternate term for fixative (see also FIXATIVE).

FIXATIVE

Liquid substance which is blown through an atomizer to prevent smearing of drawings, such as charcoal, pencil, pastel, colored chalk, and crayon drawings (see also ATOMIZERS). Fixative is available in small 8-ounce bottles (see also FIXATIVE SUBSTITUTES).

Atomizers are purchased separately and are placed into the small bottles. Krylon fixative is available in pressurized cans and alleviates the need for separate atomizers. Krylon also has a plastic spray in the pressurized can which gives a hard, more permanent finish (see also KRYLON).

FIXATIVE SUBSTITUTES

Dilute liquid starch with water and spray mixture onto drawings with a household spray can, or use one of the pressurized cans of liquid starch. Dilute canned milk with water and spray onto drawings with a household spray can. Use pressurized cans of hair lacquer, without oil base.

FLO-MASTER PEN

See PENS.

FLOUR AND SALT

See MODELING MATERIALS.

FLOWERS (PRESSED)

See PRESSING FLOWERS AND LEAVES.

FLUORESCENT PAPER

See PAPERS.

FLUTED

Refers to vertical grooves carved into pillars (see also COLUMN).

F

FOAM GLASS

An insulating material which is available at building supply houses in blocks of 4″ x 12″ x 15″. This material is easily carved with files, knives, spoons, and rasps. It can be finished with sandpaper. Foam glass is black and offers wide latitudes for experimentation in sculpture and carving (see also CARVING MATERIALS and SCULPTURE).

FOCAL POINT

That point at which other elements in design seem to converge (see also DESIGN ELEMENTS). Parallel lines appear to converge in perspective to gain the illusion of distance as shown in Fig. F-1 (see also PERSPECTIVE).

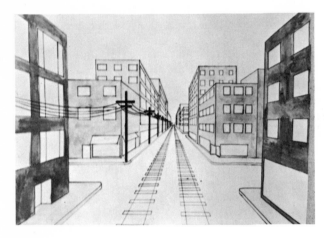

Fig. F-1

FOIL

Aluminum Foil: May be purchased in grocery stores in 12″ and 18″ rolls. Aluminum foil may be pushed or bent into shape to form an armature support for one of the modeling materials such as asbestos, sawdust, or pulp papier-mâché (see also ARMATURES, MODELING MATERIALS, and PAPIER-MÂCHÉ). It may be used as a texture for a collage or may be pressed over a wood or clay mask to provide a light three-dimensional mask (see also COLLAGE and PAPIER-MÂCHÉ). It may be used as a ground for drawing, decorative papers, and printmaking (see also ACETATE COLORS, ACETATE INKS, DECORATIVE PAPERS, GROUND, and PRINTMAKING).

Colored Foil: May be purchased from art supply houses in brilliant colors including red, blue, green, and gold. It is available by single sheets, by the dozen, or in a 12″ x 3′ size.

FOIL PAPER

See PAPERS.

FOLDED PAPER

See PAPER SCULPTURE.

FORESHORTENING

The illusionary shortening of objects, fingers, or forms as viewed from an angle (Fig. F-2).

EXAMPLE: "Dead Christ," by Andrea Mantegna.

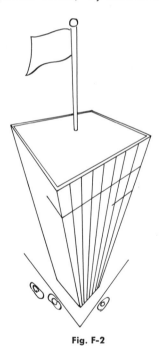

Fig. F-2

FORM

Refers to mass and shape; also refers to the organization of all of the elements in design or composition (see also COMPOSITION, DESIGN, and DESIGN ELEMENTS).

FOUND OBJECTS

Literally objects which have been found and, as such, may be considered as art forms unto themselves, for example, driftwood, lids, broken goblets, seashells, etc. Sometimes the found object is arranged with other things and is called *found art composed* or *art of the assemblage* (see also ASSEMBLAGE).

FREE FORM

Form which is not geometric in shape, for example, kidney-shaped. Figure F-3 shows a free-form design. Jean

Fig. F-3

Arp experimented with the free-form shape in painting and in sculpture.

FREEHAND DRAWING

Drawing which is done without the aid of mechanical instruments or tools, as opposed to mechanical drawing [see also DRAWING and DRAWING (MECHANICAL)].

FRESCO

Usually a wall painting which has been rendered on a wet ground of fresh lime and gypsum or wet "plaster" (see also GROUND, GYPSUM, LIME, and MURALS).

FRIEZE

Pictorial representation of a theme; usually contained within a classical entablature between the architrave, or horizontal beam, and the cornice. Most often the frieze is rendered in relief (see also CLASSIC, ENTABLATURE, and RELIEF).

FRUIT

See PAPIER-MÂCHÉ and PRINTMAKING.

FURNITURE FINISHING

See LACQUER, LINSEED OIL, SHELLAC, and VARNISH.

FURNITURE STAINS

See SALT.

FUTURISM

Followed Cubism, and originated in Italy in the early twentieth century. Futurism opposed the static qualities of painting and brought about a dynamic quality of movement characterized by repetition of many lines and superimposed shapes.

EXAMPLE: "Nude Descending a Staircase," by Marcel Duchamp.

GELATINE PAPER

See COLOR, JELLS, and PAPERS.

GENRE

Common and familiar scenes from life which are portrayed by artists.

EXAMPLE: "Boy with a Top," by Jean Chardin.

G

GESSO

White liquid mixture which is of the consistency of cream; basically a mixture of plaster of paris, glue, water, oil, and varnish. It is used as a coating on rigid panels such as wood and canvas for painting (see also CANVAS, GROUND, PLASTER OF PARIS, and VARNISH). It is available in either liquid or powder form at hardware or art supply houses. Gesso is used as a painting medium in some contemporary paintings. It can also be applied heavily on a rigid box, for example, and linear designs can be rendered with an incising tool.

GENUINE MAHOGANY

See WOODS.

GEOMETRIC

Angular or inorganic forms such as triangles, squares, rectangles, and hexagons (see Fig. G-1), as opposed to free

Fig. G-1

forms (see also FREE FORM). Geometric forms can be used effectively in rubbings and provide an interesting correla-

tion of geometry with design (see also RUBBINGS). Piet Mondrian and Wassily Kandinsky used geometric forms extensively in their paintings (see also NEOPLASTICISM).

EXAMPLES: "Broadway Boogie-Woogie," by Piet Mondrian; and "Emphasized Corners," by Wassily Kandinsky.

GLAZE

See CERAMICS.

GLAZED PAPERS

See DECORATIVE PAPERS.

GLAZE FIRING

See CERAMICS.

GLITTER

Powder-like, colored metallic material which is used for decorative purposes in candlemaking, poster making, etc. It is applied on surfaces by spreading resin glue and shaking the glitter on it. The excess glitter which does not stick to the glue can be shaken from the surface and put back into its container for further use. Glitter is available in 1-ounce or 2-ounce packages in the following colors: red, green, blue, yellow, pink, gold, copper, and black (see also ADHESIVES, CANDLEMAKING, and POSTERS).

GLOBES (LIGHT)

May be used in fashioning puppet heads or maracas with the papier-mâché process (see also PAPIER-MÂCHÉ).

GLOBES (WORLD)

See PAPIER-MÂCHÉ.

GLUE

See ADHESIVES.

GLYCERINE

Colorless, syrup-like liquid which is obtained at drug stores. It may be used in the preparation of water-soluble printing inks (see also PRINTING INK SUBSTITUTES). Glycerine is used in basketry to add to water in the soaking of reed (see also BASKETRY). It is used to retard drying on homemade, ink stamping pads in the printmaking processes (see also PRINTMAKING). It is also used with ceramic clay in the preparation of a nondrying substitute for plastic clay [see also CLAY (PLASTIC) SUBSTITUTE].

GOLD LEAF

Extremely fine sheets of pure gold which are light and fragile. Craftsmen pick up the leaves with combs which have been run through the hair. Gold leaf is used extensively in bookbinding, lettering, and in the finishing of frames; it is sometimes laminated between glass to form gold tesserae (see also BOOKLET MAKING, LETTERING, MOSAICS, and TESSERAE).

GOLD PAPER

See PAPERS.

GOODENOUGH TEST

An intelligence test for children based upon the instruction to draw a picture of a man with a pencil. The scale for measurement is based upon 51 possible points which relate specifically to detail of drawings and method of representation.

NOTE: The following is a source book for teachers: Florence L. Goodenough, Ph.D., *Measurement of Intelligence by Drawing* (New York and Chicago: World Book Company).

GOTHIC

Style of art and architecture which was prominent in Europe from the middle of the twelfth century until the end of the fifteenth century [see also HISTORY (ART)]. Characteristic of Gothic architecture were the cross-ribbed vaultings, the flying buttresses, the stained-glass windows, and the pointed arches in cathedrals.

EXAMPLES (architecture): Chartres Cathedral, Amiens Cathedral, Cologne Cathedral, and St. George's Chapel, Windsor.

GOUACHE

See PAINTING and PAINTS.

GRAPHIC

Relating to line (see also GRAPHIC ARTS).

GRAPHIC ARTS

Two-dimensional art forms which include drawing (Fig. G-2), painting, photography, and printmaking proc-

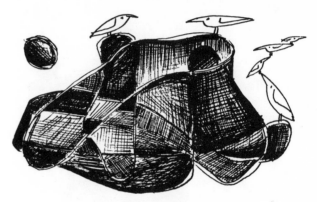

Fig. G-2

esses. The graphic arts would be opposed to the plastic arts, which are three-dimensional in character (see also DIMENSION and PLASTIC ARTS).

GRAPHITE PAPER

See PAPERS.

GRAPHITE STICKS

Graphite sticks are chiefly used in drawing; soft, black, and with a metallic luster, they are rectangular in shape (see also DRAWING).

GREASE STAINS

See SALT.

G

GREEK ART

One of the arts of antiquity, 900 to 100 B.C.; the Greeks were considered masters of sculpture and architecture [see also ACROPOLIS, ANTIQUITY, BALANCE, HELLAS, and HISTORY (ART)].

EXAMPLES (architecture): The Parthenon (Fig. G-3)

Fig. G-3

and the Erechtheum (Fig. G-4), both on the Acropolis in Athens. The photograph of the Erechtheum shows the

Fig. G-4

caryatids or statues of women used as supports for the entablature.

EXAMPLE (sculpture): The "Winged Victory" of Samothrace.

GROG

Mixed with modeling and carving materials to achieve additional body and texture (see also CARVING MATERIALS and MODELING MATERIALS). For example, sand can be considered as a grog when it is mixed with clay (see also CERAMICS). Zonolite and vermiculite are used as grogs in aggregate carvings (see also VERMICULITE and ZONOLITE).

GROUND

Any surface on which an artist draws, paints, or renders a design, whether that surface be a piece of paper, a canvas, or a wall (see also CANVAS and PAPERS). Secondary meaning relates to intaglio processes in printmaking in which ground refers to a protective film called etching ground. This ground resists the action of acids on metal plates and is primarily used in the etching and aquatint processes (see also INTAGLIO).

GROUT

See MOSAICS.

GROUT COLOR

See MOSAICS.

GROUT SEALER

See MOSAICS.

GUM ERASER

See DRAWING, ERASERS, and PRINTMAKING.

GUM (RED) WOOD

See WOODS.

GUM TRAGACANTH

See ADHESIVES and COPPER ENAMELING.

GUN STAPLER

See STAPLE GUN.

GYPSUM

Alternate name for plaster of paris (see also PLASTER OF PARIS).

HALF ROUND

See RELIEF.

HALFTONES

Those tones which are halfway between light and dark (see also SHADING SHEETS).

HAMMERS

See WOODWORKING.

HAMMOCK MOLD

See CERAMICS.

HAND DRILL

See WOODWORKING.

HAND PRINTS

There is nothing creative about allowing a child to make a print of his hand; yet fathers and mothers love them as gifts.

Hand Print in Clay: Form a round disk of ceramic clay about 1″ thick. Allow the child to make an imprint of his hand in the clay. Allow the clay to dry at room temperature; then glaze and fire in the kiln (see also CERAMICS).

Hand Print in Plaster: Pour a mixture of plaster of paris into a pie tin (see also PLASTER OF PARIS). It is not neces-

sary to fill the entire pan with plaster; a free form is most interesting. Place the child's hand into the plaster, instructing him to hold his hand lightly and not to press it down to the bottom of the pan. Allow the plaster to harden around the hand. This will take approximately 1½ minutes. The child may then take his hand out of the plaster and his hand print will remain.

NOTE: If you desire to hang the plaster plaque, insert a drinking straw through the top of the plaster form before it hardens.

Hand Print with Tempera: Paint the child's palm with one of the nontoxic tempera paints. Print the hand on paper.

Spray Hand Print: Place child's hand on a dark shade of colored construction paper and spray over the hand with a light watery mixture of tempera paint. Use a household spray can or dip a scrub brush in a tempera mixture and rub over a piece of screen. Apply the spray about 15″ from the hand. A thin spray is more effective than a thick, blotted one. See Fig. H-1 for an example of spray hand prints.

Fig. H-1

H

HAND PROTECTING CREAM

Available under commercial trade name of Pro-tek. An application of Pro-tek to the hands before starting to work in paint or dye will protect the hands from staining. When the job is finished, wash the protecting cream off the hands, and they will be free from stains.

HARD EDGE

Clean-cut definitive edge in painting, not blended. For example, paintings of Piet Mondrian (see also DE STIJL, NEOPLASTICISM, and SOFT EDGE).

HARD MAPLE

See WOODS.

HARMONY

Relates to unity of design; also to unity of color (see also COLOR and DESIGN ELEMENTS).

HEAD DRAWING

See DRAWING.

HELLAS

Ancient name for Greece which included all of the areas occupied by the Greeks in the era of historical antiquity beginning about 900 B.C. These areas included Greek cities in Asia Minor, Sicily, and parts of the Mediterranean coast [see also ANTIQUITY, ETRUSCAN ART, GREEK ART, HELLENISTIC PERIOD, and HISTORY (ART)].

HELLENISTIC PERIOD

Relates to Hellas or Greece; also relates to Hellenism, the culture of the early Greeks following the time of Alexander the Great, 333 to 63 B.C. [see also ANTIQUITY, ETRUSCAN ART, GREEK ART, HELLAS, and HISTORY (ART)].

HERRINGBONE TWILL

Weaving pattern; repetition of a V-shaped motif (see also WEAVING).

HIGGINS VEGETABLE GLUE

See ADHESIVES.

HIGHLIGHT

Specific point or area on the surface of a form, such as a vase or face, which reflects the highest degree of light.

HIGH RELIEF

See RELIEF.

HIGH RENAISSANCE

See RENAISSANCE.

HINGES

See SILK SCREENING and WOODWORKING.

HISTORY (ART)

Prehistoric and Primitive; 20,000 B.C. :
Paleolithic (Old Stone Age): Cave paintings in Spain and France.
Mesolithic (Transitional Age).
Neolithic (New Stone Age): Stonehenge, England.

Arts of Antiquity; 6000 B.C. :
Chaldean-Sumerian and Babylonian (Eastern); 6000 B.C.: Relief carvings, small mosaics, and metal sculpture.
Egyptian (Eastern); 6000 B.C.: Pyramids, stone and metal sculpture, glass blowing, murals, pottery, and jewelry.
Aegean-Cretan or Minoan (Pre-Hellenic Western); 4500 B.C.: High development of all art forms, particularly pottery.
Indian (Eastern); 4000 B.C.: Frescoes, textiles, and architecture.
Chinese (Eastern); 3000 B.C.: Calligraphy, painting, bronze castings, and pottery.
Hittite (Eastern); 2500 B.C.: Detailed stone relief; use of brick, stone, and wood columns in architecture.
Etruscan (Western); 1800 B.C.: Wall and tomb paintings, sarcophagi, stone carvings, terra-cotta plaques, pottery, and metalware.
Phoenician (Eastern); 1700 B.C.: Textiles, glassware, seals, and pottery.

Assyrian (Eastern); 1500 B.C.: Relief carvings, textiles, and textile decorations.

Greek-Hellenic (Western); 900 B.C.: Sculpture, architecture, relief work, pottery, and painting.

Persian (Eastern); 539 B.C.: Pottery, repoussé, relief sculpture, ornamental calligraphy, miniature paintings, and textiles.

Mayan (Western) 325 B.C.: Pyramids, relief carvings, sculpture, and pottery.

Roman (Western); 300 B.C.: Sculpture, painting, and architecture.

Arts from Early Christianity; A.D. 100:

Early Christian (Western); A.D. 100: Catacombs and frescoes.

Byzantine (Western); A.D. 400: Mosaics, manuscripts, illuminations, sculpture, and architecture.

Japanese (Eastern); A.D. 600: Calligraphy, painting, and sculpture.

Romanesque (Western); A.D. 800: Painting and architecture.

Inca (Western); A.D. 1200: Stone dwellings, pottery, metalwork, and textiles.

Gothic (Western); A.D. 1300: Painting and architecture.

Aztec (Western); A.D. 1325: Stone sculpture and pottery.

Renaissance (Western); A.D. 1400: Painting, sculpture, and architecture.

Baroque (Western); A.D. 1600: Architecture, sculpture, and painting.

Rococo (Western); A.D. 1700: Architecture, sculpture, and painting.

Classicism or Neoclassicism (Western); 1750: Painting.

Romanticism (Western); 1800: Painting.

Arts of the Modern Era:

Impressionism (Western); 1860: Painting.

Postimpressionism (Western); 1880: Painting.

Abstract and Abstract-Expressionistic (Western); 1900: Painting and sculpture.

HITTITE ART

Ancient art of a now extinct people who lived in a land called Khatti (now Anatolia, Turkey) in 2500 B.C.

Influenced by the Babylonians, they used building materials of stone and brick, as well as columns of wood. The gates and walls of their monumental structures were carved in relief [see also HISTORY (ART)].

HOLIDAYS AND SPECIAL EVENTS

In terms of planning for the school year for poster making, festivals, and commemorative celebrations, the following list is offered as a teacher's reference:

January:
    March of Dimes Month
    New Year's Day (1)
    New Mexico Statehood (6)
    Battle of New Orleans (8)
    Benjamin Franklin's Birthday (17)
    Robert E. Lee's Birthday (19)
    Stonewall Jackson's Birthday (21)

February:
    American Heart Month
    Boy Scout Week
    National Brotherhood Week
    Groundhog Day (2)
    Daniel Boone's Birthday (11)
    Abraham Lincoln's Birthday (12)
    Georgia Day (12)
    Arizona Admission Day (14)
    St. Valentine's Day (14)
    Florida Ceded to United States (22)
    Washington's Birthday (22)

March:
    American Red Cross Month
    Camp Fire Girls Week
    National Wildlife Week
    Save Your Vision Week
    Texas Independence Day (2)
    Pennsylvania Day (4)
    Andrew Jackson's Birthday (15)
    St. Patrick's Day (17)
    Spring begins (21)
    Maryland Day (25)
    Kuhio Day, Hawaii (26)
    Seward Day, Alaska (30)
    National Shut-in Day (30)

H

April:
 Cancer Crusade Month
 National Boys Club Week
 National Garden Week
 National YMCA Week
 Pan American Week
 American National Conservation Day
 April Fools' Day (1)
 Thomas Jefferson's Birthday (13)
 Oklahoma Day (22)
 Confederate Memorial Day (26)

May:
 Cerebral Palsy Month
 National Hearing Month
 Be Kind to Animals Week
 World Trade Week
 May Day (1)
 Mother's Day (12)
 Armed Forces Day (19)
 Maritime Day (22)
 Memorial Day (30)

June:
 Graduation Month
 National Swim for Health Week
 Kentucky Statehood (1)
 Jefferson Davis's Birthday (3)
 Kamehameha Day, Hawaii (11)
 Flag Day (14)
 Magna Carta Anniversary (15)
 Father's Day (16)
 West Virginia Day (20)
 Summer begins (21)

July:
 National Farm Safety Week
 Independence Day (4)
 Pioneer Day, Utah (24)

August:
 Colorado Day (1)

September:
 National Dog Week
 Labor Day
 California Admission Day (9)

Defender's Day, Maryland (12)
 Cherokee Strip Day (16)
 Constitution Day (17)
 Autumn begins (23)
 American Indian Day (26)

October:
 National Fire Prevention Week
 National Thrift Week
 United Nations Day
 Missouri Day (1)
 Alaska Day (18)
 Halloween (31)
 Nevada Admission Day (31)

November:
 American Art Week
 American Children's Book Week
 American Education Week
 Election Day
 Veterans Day (11)
 Thanksgiving

December:
 Forefathers Day (21)
 Winter begins (22)
 Christmas Eve (24)
 Christmas (25)
 New Year's Eve (31)

HORIZON LINE

 See PERSPECTIVE.

HUE

 See COLOR.

ICE-CREAM STICKS

See SCRAP MATERIALS and STICKS.

ICON

Small painting of sacred image; relates to Byzantine and Greek churches (see also BYZANTINE).

ICONOGRAPHY

Study of symbolism in art forms (see also CATACOMBS, SYMBOLIC, and SYMBOLISM).

ILLUMINATIONS

Small illustrations or extravagantly embellished letters which accompanied the text of hand-rendered manuscripts of the early Christian and Byzantine schools of book painting. Sometimes these were decorated with gold leaf (see also BYZANTINE, CHRISTIAN ART, GOLD LEAF, MANUSCRIPTS, and PARCHMENT).

ILLUSTRATION BOARD

See PAPERS.

IMPASTO

Paint which is applied in a thick manner to canvas or other grounds (see also GROUND, PAINTING, and PAINTS).

IMPRESSIONISM

Art movement which began in the latter half of the nineteenth century and lasted from 1860 to 1890. Leader of the impressionistic painters was Claude Monet, whose painting "Impression Sunrise" gave the movement and its adherents the name. Considered to be the beginning of modern painting, the movement was concerned with the colors of the spectrum, light, and the rather ethereal and formless impressions related to the utilization and interpretation of these two elements. Among the impressionistic painters were Claude Monet, Pierre Renoir, Alfred Sisley, Camille Pissarro, and Hilaire Degas. Later movements which developed and found direction from the Impressionists were Neoimpressionism and Postimpressionism [see also HISTORY (ART), NEOIMPRESSIONISM, and POSTIMPRESSIONISM].

INCA ART

See HISTORY (ART).

INCISED

Opposite of excised (see also EXCISED). Method of incising or cutting a line into a surface such as wood, metal, or stone (see also CARVING MATERIALS). Relating to the intaglio processes, incised lines would conform to the techniques used in engraving and dry-point etching (see also INTAGLIO). Incised lines are also seen in wood engravings (see also WOODCUTS and WOOD ENGRAVINGS). The term incise is also used in classroom printmaking processes, including the potato print, linoleum block print, gum eraser print, and others (see also INTAGLIO, PRINTMAKING, and RELIEF).

INDIA-INK MARBLING

See DECORATIVE PAPERS.

INDIA INKS

Black drawing inks (see also INKS).

INDIAN ART (EAST)

The Golden Age of Indian art, an Oriental art, was in the seventh century, although civilization was evident in 4000 B.C. Early Indian art forms show the influence of the Persians and the Greeks. Indian art is characteristically

I

decorative and symbolic with more emphasis on architectural decoration than on painting, although there were some frescoes. An example of late Indian Moslem style with graceful minarets, arches, and domes is seen in the Taj Mahal at Agra [see also HISTORY (ART)].

INKS

Are two basic types: liquid ink, which is used with pens and brushes in line drawing and lettering, and solid tube ink, which is used in printmaking processes on paper or textiles. See Fig. I-1 for an illustration of an ink print.

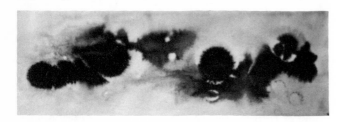

Fig. I-1

Acetate Inks: Water-soluble, liquid ink which is used with drawing pens or brushes; used for drawing on slick surfaces of plastic such as acetate sheeting, cellophane, or metal foils (see also ACETATE SHEETING, MAPMAKING, MOVIES (FILM), and PLASTICS). In 1-ounce and 8-ounce containers, acetate inks are available in either transparent or opaque and in a wide range of colors, including black and white (see also OPAQUE and TRANSPARENT).

Drawing Inks: Water-soluble, liquid ink which is used with drawing pens or brushes on papers and other suitable grounds; available in ¾-ounce, half-pint, 1-pint, and quart containers in a wide range of colors, including black and white (see also DRAWING and DECORATIVE PAPERS).

Felt-Pen Inks: Used for the refilling of felt pens; available in half-pint containers in a variety of colors, including black and brown (see also DECORATIVE PAPERS).

Ink Sticks: Oriental ink sticks represent black drawing ink in its solid form. The ink stick may be ground and water added to it to obtain the desired consistency, or a wet brush may be simply rubbed over the ink stick for a black ink medium. Ink sticks are suitable for line drawings and washes (see also DRAWING and PAINTING).

Spatter Ink: To be used with commercial spatter gun for spatter prints, available in 8-ounce containers in a wide variety of colors, including black and white (see also HAND PRINTS, PRINTING INK SUBSTITUTES, and PRINTMAKING).

Printing Inks: Available in water-base inks for paper work or oil-base inks for textiles. Both are supplied in tubes of 1″ x 4″ and in a wide variety of colors, as well as black and white (see also PRINTING INK SUBSTITUTES and PRINTMAKING).

Stamp Pad Ink: Used to revitalize old and dried stamp pads. Containers (1¼ ounce) come with stiff brush for application. Available in liquid form in black and colors (see also PRINTMAKING).

NOTE: Water-base printing inks are much simpler to use in the classroom than oil-base inks. Unless there is a need for permanency of color as in textile work, one would benefit by working only with water-base inks in terms of simplicity of use and easy cleanup (see also SOLVENTS and TEXTILE COLORS). The one advantage of oil-base over water-base printing inks is that oil colors tend to produce more intense colors on paper grounds (see also COLOR, GROUND, and PRINTING INK SUBSTITUTES). Printing inks are also available for the intaglio processes (etching, etc.), the planographic process (lithograph), the stencil process (serigraphic or silk screen), and the block printing process (woodcuts and linoleum) [see also PRINTMAKING (PROFESSIONAL) and SILK SCREENING].

INK SUBSTITUTES (PRINTING)

See PRINTING INK SUBSTITUTES.

INTAGLIO

Professional printmaking category which includes processes of aquatint, dry-point engraving, engraving, etching, and mezzotint and the products of which are called *prints* (see also PRINTS). The word intaglio is Italian and means "to cut in."

Engraving: Method of cutting into a metal plate with an engraving tool called a burin. The burin-engraved line creates a residue of metal along the incised area called the burr (see also INCISED and RELIEF). Since the primary aim of engraving is to achieve distinction of line, the burr is removed, the plate is inked, and the print is taken on an etching press. This process dates back to 1446.

Dry-Point Engraving: Method of creating an incised line directly on a metal plate with a sharp instrument such as a steel tool. The incised line creates a burr, as in engraving; in opposition to engraving, the burr is not removed but is allowed to remain on the plate. When the plate is inked, the burr will create a soft linear effect. The print is taken on an etching press. Rembrandt often combined dry-point engraving with etching (see also ARTISTS).

Etching: Method of "etching-in" or "biting-in" a line with acid on a metal plate, a process which dates back to 1513. Areas that will remain free from acid action are covered or protected with an etching ground (see also GROUND). The plate is inked and the print is taken on an etching press.

Aquatint: An etching process which primarily emphasizes tone; often combines tone and line as well as color. Tonal effects are achieved through treatment of the etching ground which becomes porous instead of being completely acid proof as in the etching process. The plate is inked and the print is taken on an etching press. Goya is known for his aquatints (see also ARTISTS).

Mezzotint: Method whereby a printing plate is treated to achieve rich, tonal qualities. This process was invented in the seventeenth century. A rocking tool is used to create a uniform distribution of burr over the entire plate. Distribution of value, or dark, medium, and light areas, is achieved on the plate with the use of a "scraper." The scraper removes the burr from the desired areas, and detail of form is achieved through skillful manipulation of value [see also DESIGN ELEMENTS and PRINTMAKING (PROFESSIONAL)].

INTEGRATION

With reference to classroom experiences, the term integration implies that a creative art process was linked with experience in the area of curriculum. With reference to art, integration relates to configuration and unity of design (see also DESIGN ELEMENTS).

INTENSITY

See COLOR.

INTERIOR DECORATION

See INTERIOR DESIGN.

INTERIOR DESIGN

Design as applied to the interiors of homes, offices, and public or private buildings; frequently called interior decoration.

INTERMEDIATE COLORS

See COLOR.

IRON AGE

The Iron Age followed the Ages of Stone and Bronze (see also BRONZE AGE and STONE AGE).

JAPANESE ART

Early Japanese art was based upon the Chinese concepts which came to them in the sixth century with Buddhism. Influenced later by the Greeks and Indians, their sculpture was carved in wood and ivory. Japanese art is noted for its porcelain, lacquer, enamels, damask fabrics, origami, and tie-dye [see also HISTORY (ART), ORIGAMI, and TIE-DYE].

JAPANESE FOLK ART

Called Mingei; relates to Japanese pottery, baskets, woodenware and textiles which are created today just as they were centuries ago.

J

JAPANESE ORIGAMI

See ORIGAMI.

JAPANESE RICE PAPER

See PAPERS.

JAPANESE SCROLLS

See KAKEMONO and MAKIMONO.

JAPANESE SHOJI PAPER

Laminated, transparent paper which is usually patterned with pressed butterflies and leaves. Figure J-1 illus-

Fig. J-1

trates how pressed leaves can be laminated between two sheets of waxed paper. A warm iron is used to apply pressure and heat, thus adhering the laminated sheets of paper with the melted wax (see also DECORATIVE PAPERS, LAMINATED, LAMINATED PAPER, and PRESSING FLOWERS AND LEAVES).

JAPANESE WATERCOLORS

Paper wafers of pigment which are put into water to produce a watercolor medium for painting (see also PAINTING and PAINTS).

JAPANNING

Process by which articles of wood, leather, and metal are given heavy, high-gloss finishes of lacquer type paint; subjected to heat for durability. Japanned furniture and coaches were popular in the eighteenth century.

JELLO WRAPPING

See PAPERS.

JELLS

Gelatine-colored paper which is used for lighting effects in stagecraft (see also COLOR and PAPERS). It is a versatile material in that it will stick to itself as well as other materials when moistened. It is commonly used to provide color to panels of stabiles and other forms of sculpture. It is particularly effective when light filters through a stabile with jell insets. The somewhat distorted shadow that is cast upon the wall or floor provides, in effect, another stabile form (see also SCULPTURE and STABILES).

JEWELRY MAKING

Pendants: Wrap a piece of soft wire around a piece of shattered marble. As you wrap the wire, fashion a hook. Loop a leather lacing through the wire hook for a pendant (see also MARBLES).

Drop some mixed plaster of paris onto a sheet of waxed paper. Allow the plaster to drop into interesting shapes. When dry, bore a hole through the top. String a length of leather lacing through the hole (see also PLASTER OF PARIS).

Another type of pendant may be made from ceramic clay, utilizing the slab technique. Cut the shape desired. Cut out a hole for stringing. Glaze and fire. Add leather lacing for necklace (see also CERAMICS).

Tie Clasps and Earrings: Fashion these from ceramic clay; glaze and fire. Glue to jewelry findings. (Findings are the backs of earrings, tie clasps, cuff links, etc.) Use basic jewelry findings for sea-shells, buttons, beads, etc. Don't overlook the possibility for jewelry design from copper enameling (see also COPPER ENAMELING).

Beads: See BEAD MAKING.

JEWISH ART

One of the early Eastern arts of antiquity, 1000 B.C. to A.D. 70. Early Jewish art was influenced by Aegean, Assyrian, and Phoenician cultures [see also AEGEAN ART, ANTIQUITY, ASSYRIAN ART, EASTERN ART and HISTORY (ART)].

JUTE

See YARNS AND STRINGS.

KAKEMONO

Japanese scroll painting which is hung vertically (see also MAKIMONO, QUADRA, and TONDO).

KEROSENE

See SILK SCREENING and SOLVENTS.

KEY

See COLOR.

KILN

See CERAMICS, COPPER ENAMELING, and KILN WASH.

KILN CEMENT

Semimoist cement preparation for the purpose of mending loose fire bricks in ceramic and copper-enameling kilns (see also CERAMICS and COPPER ENAMELING).

KILN WASH

Kiln wash protects the kiln from glaze droppings; available in powdered form and should be mixed with water to the consistency of thick cream. Apply with a brush.

Ceramic Kilns: Apply kiln wash to the floor and sides of kiln before each glaze firing to prevent glaze from sticking to the floor. A school-type ceramic kiln is shown in Fig. K-1 (see also CERAMICS).

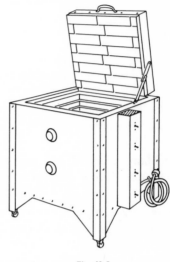

Fig. K-1

Copper-Enameling Kilns: Apply kiln wash to the bottom of the kiln only to protect from colored enamels. If the kiln is used regularly, an application will be needed about once a month. Figure K-2 shows two sizes of copper-enameling kilns (see also COPPER ENAMELING).

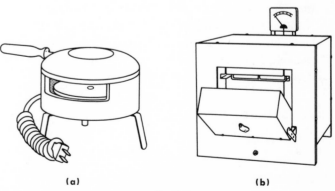

(a)　　　　　　(b)

Fig. K-2

K

KLING-KOTE LIQUID CLOTH

See ADHESIVES.

KNEADED ERASER

See ERASERS.

KNIVES

The following knives are available and will assist a teacher in an art program:

Leather Knife: Use standard square-point knives with approximate blade measurements of 5/8" x 3¾" (see also LEATHER).

Mat Knife: Many types of mat knives are available, including X-Acto Mat Knife, No. 6 (see also MOUNTING AND MATTING).

Painting Knife: Made of steel, with a wooden handle; available individually or in sets of 12 (see also PAINTING).

Palette Knife: Made with a steel blade and a wooden handle; has a 3" dull blade (see also PAINTING).

Putty Knife: Available with stiff or semistiff blades; blades are 2" long and 1¼" wide (see also WOODWORKING).

Scratch Knife: No. 330, Esterbrook scratch-knife blade will fit a pen holder, used for scratchboard drawing [see also DRAWING (SCRATCHBOARD)].

Scratch Knife for Erasing: No. 331, Esterbrook scratch-knife blade will fit a pen holder; can be used for erasing and cutting on grounds (see also GROUNDS and PAINTING).

Stencil Knife: Different types of stencil knives are available, including X-Acto Stencil Knife, No. 4; available with detachable blade and handle; used for cutting stencils (see also PRINTMAKING and STENCILS).

KRAFT GUMMED TAPE

See TAPES.

KRAFT PAPER

See PAPERS.

KRYLON

Krylon Fixative: Used as a "fixing" agent for crayon, colored-chalk, pastel, pencil, and charcoal drawings (see also FIXATIVES). The application of Krylon fixative will prevent smearing the surfaces of drawings; it is available in 12-ounce pressurized spray cans for classroom use (see also CHARCOAL, COLORED CHALK, CRAYON, DRAWING, PASTELS, and PENCILS).

Krylon Plastic Spray: Clear, acrylic, plastic protective covering for any of the graphic arts or crafts. It can be used on metals, glass, and leather, as well as on paper grounds. It will not discolor and will seal out dirt and water; it is available in 12-ounce pressurized cans.

LACQUER

Lacquers are available in clear form as well as in colors. Clear lacquer is used in paper-collage techniques as an adhesive; it is also used to give a high-gloss covering to furniture (see also ADHESIVES, COLLAGE, and WOODWORKING). To cover a given piece of wood furniture with lacquer, first clean the piece thoroughly and sand it, if necessary. The first coat of lacquer should be thinned down with lacquer thinner to allow for penetration into the wood (see also SOLVENTS). Succeeding coats of lacquer should be applied and allowed to dry thoroughly, rubbing lightly with steel wool over the surface between each coat. Start with a coarse steel wool, and on each successive coat, use a finer-gauge steel wool abrasive. The number of coats of lacquer will depend entirely upon individual preference. Some lacquered furniture has as many as nine or ten coats. When finished, give the piece a final coating of paste wax (see also LACQUER WARE and WAX).

LACQUER SUBSTITUTE

See SODIUM SILICATE.

LACQUER WARE

Art form of China and Japan which sometimes involves elaborate insets and inlays of mother-of-pearl, gold, silver, and ivory; sometimes called lacquer work (see also JAPAN-NING, LACQUER, and MARQUETRY).

LAMINATED

Refers to layers, as in wood, paper, or plastics. Layers are glued and pressed together to form one welded piece. Plywood is an example of laminated wood. Paper lamination is illustrated by the technique of crayon lamination with waxed paper in the decorative-paper processes. Figure L-1 shows onion skins laminated betwen two sheets of

Fig. L-1

waxed paper with the aid of a warm iron (see also DECO-RATIVE PAPERS, JAPANESE SHOJI PAPER, and LAMINATED PAPER).

LAMINATED PAPER

Laminated paper is an exciting process which offers limitless possibilities for sculpture (Fig. L-2) and design. (See also SCULPTURE.) The process involves the building

Fig. L-2

up of paper layers with an adhesive, using newsprint or newspaper as the paper base. The first sheet of newsprint is laid flat upon the table and wheat paste is brushed over the entire surface with a 1½″ enamel or varnish brush (see also BRUSHES and WHEAT PASTE). A second sheet of paper of the exact size is then laid on the first sheet of newsprint. The process is repeated until there are four or five layers of paper pasted together. Paste should be omitted from the top of the final sheet of paper.

When the laminated paper is still wet, it may be picked up and bent into three-dimensional forms with the use of rolled or wadded paper props. Laminated paper may be wrapped around molds such as jars, hats, or baskets. It may even be wrapped around figures to make form-fitting capes or serapes. When laminated paper is dry, it achieves a hard finish much like sculptured wood. It may be sanded if desired, painted with tempera paint, and given a coat of shellac (see also ABRASIVES, PAINT, and SHELLAC).

LAMINATED RESIN

The art of laminating with resin is a fairly new process, but it has limitless possibilities for exploration and experimentation in the classroom. While the product may appear awesome, the process is very simple. A clear liquid laminating resin is mixed with a hardening agent. It is stirred and then poured either into a mold, such as a custard cup,

L

or onto a flat cord-outlined shape which has been defined and glued onto a sheet of acetate (see also ACETATE SHEETING). When the resin dries, it assumes the character of a clear glasslike material. Forms in molds can be tapped out, while poured resin shapes can be lifted off the acetate.

One often sees objects such as coins, buttons, and leaves, imbedded in laminating resin, particularly in the mold type for paper weights. In the poured type, one can envision possibilities for mobiles and stabiles, as well as hanging ornamental shapes for window décor (see also MOBILES, PLASTICS, STABILES, and STAINED GLASS).

Paperweight:

Materials needed: One pint of clear, liquid, laminating resin, hardening agent (liquid), paper medical cup with ounce measurements, custard cup mold, household spray wax, and decorative buttons.

Procedure: Spray the inside of the custard cup with household spray wax. Mix two ounces of laminating resin with twenty drops of hardening agent. (NOTE: Different commercial resins and hardening agents will vary in terms of mixing proportions.) Stir resin with hardening agent with a small wooden stick. Pour this mixture into the custard cup and allow it to set for approximately half an hour, or until the mixture appears to be setting. Place decorative buttons upside down on top of the resin mixture. Mix an additional two ounces of resin and hardener (20 drops), and pour over the top. Allow to dry for 24 hours. When dry, turn the custard cup mold upside down and tap out the resin paperweight.

Free-Form Ornamental Hangings:

Materials needed: One pint of clear, liquid laminating resin, hardening agent (liquid), paper medical cup with ounce measurements, gold or silver cording (cotton roving will substitute), white resin glue, acetate sheeting (12" x 18"), pieces of colored broken glass. NOTE: Broken colored glass can be obtained from stained glass window establishments or craft shops. In addition, one may break colored bottles inside heavy brown paper bags. Blue milk of magnesia bottles, brown medicine bottles, and green carbonated beverage bottles are but a few of the possibilities (see also ACETATE SHEETING, ADHESIVES, COTTON ROVING, and STAINED GLASS WINDOWS).

Procedure: Place the acetate sheet over a piece of chipboard or similar board. Glue gold or silver cording to the acetate in the shape desired. This may prove to be somewhat difficult, but if the shape is rendered and the glue is trailed along the inside of the shape, it will adhere to the acetate. To allow for hanging, form a loop with the cording at the top of the shape. Allow the glue to dry for approximately 25 minutes. When the cording has been securely glued to the acetate, and is dry, begin to place pieces of colored glass within the outlined shape. Place them fairly close together. Mix 2 ounces of laminating resin with 20 drops of hardening agent, stir and then pour over shape. It is not important that the resin cover the glass, but that it is poured between the pieces of glass. It is important that the resin touch the gold or silver cording. When the resin has been poured, lift up the chipboard and transfer the design to a drying area. This drying period will take 24 hours. When dry, peel the acetate from the shape. The glass will be imbedded in resin and will be outlined with gold or silver cording.

NOTE: In all instances when working with laminating resin, make sure that there is adequate ventilation. Avoid prolonged inhalation of fumes, and avoid contact with the skin. Read directions on containers relative to safety precautions.

LANDSCAPE

Refers to drawings or paintings of outdoor scenes, usually involving hills, trees, foliage, and sometimes figures. Claude Lorrain is considered to be the "father of landscape painting" for he was the first to use landscape as a subject unto itself, instead of as a backdrop for subject matter, see also BARBIZON SCHOOL and SEASCAPE).

LAPIDARY

The art of working with precious and semiprecious stones, as in cutting, polishing, and setting. Ornamental stones, excluding precious gems, include; alabaster, fluorspar, jade, jasper, labradorite, lapis lazuli, and malachite (see also ALABASTER).

LASCAUX

Cave in southwestern France which has Paleolithic paintings and drawings of bulls, galloping horses, oxen, bison, and deer. The caves were discovered in 1940; similar paintings and drawings exist in the caves of Altamira in Spain (see also ALTAMIRA).

LATHES

See CERAMICS, STICKS, and WOODWORKING.

LAYOUT

Used extensively in commercial advertising and relates to the preliminary working sketch of a planned design before it is rendered in its completed form.

LEATHER

Leather craft has enjoyed great popularity in the secondary schools. Elementary teachers find that schools seldom provide the materials necessary for a program in leather craft. However, it is easy to improvise tools and materials for such a program. Discarded leather trimmings may be purchased inexpensively at leather supply houses. Often these will be given to a teacher. Calfskin is considered to be the most desirable leather for tooling. Such leathers as alligator, lizard, and morocco are the only leathers that cannot be tooled. Heavy steel crochet needles and nutpicks may substitute for leather-tooling instruments. The leather process is quite simple once it is understood that leather can only be tooled, or incised with a design, when the leather is damp.

An excellent first experience in leather tooling is to incorporate a lesson on the monogram with the tooling of a bookmark. Scraps of leather provide ample rectangles for bookmarks. After the student has rendered his design on paper, he may transfer the design to the leather in the following manner: Dampen the leather with a sponge. Place the design over the leather and trace the design with a crochet needle as a drawing implement. The slight pressure of the needle together with the dampness of the leather will transfer the design onto the bookmark.

By applying greater pressure to the transferred design, the student may begin to tool his leather. Tooling requires a steady hand and even pressure; a well-tooled line is deep and shiny.

If the student wishes to apply color to his bookmark, he may use one of the commercial leather dyes or plain shoe polish. Leather dyes are available in a range of colors in 3½-ounce, 4-ounce, 8-ounce, pint, and quart containers (see also DYES). It is always better to apply several light coats of dye or polish rather than one heavy coat.

LEATHER DYES

See DYES.

LEATHER-HARD

See CERAMICS.

LEAVES (PRESSED)

See PRESSING FLOWERS AND LEAVES.

LEPAGES GLUE

See ADHESIVES and SOLVENTS.

LETTERING

There are a few basic rules to remember in the rendering of hand lettering. Once these rules have been assimilated and understood, lettering should not prove too difficult. Whether one is using a lettering pen, a lettering brush, a steel brush, or cutting letters from paper, the most important first basic rule is to make sure that the guidelines running horizontally are straight.

Secondly, it is important to have sufficient familiarity with upper-case and lower-case letters so that they are not confused and used inappropriately. For example, it is not uncommon to see a lower-case letter placed in the middle of a word that contains only upper-case or capital letters. Sometimes this is a technique employed by contemporary sign artists. However, it is never difficult to ascertain when such a technique is used for design quality as opposed to when it is used with unawareness and naïveté. It is also a good idea to check the letters against a letter chart for accuracy in rendering. The letters "S" and "N" are often reversed in hand lettering.

Finally, it is important to understand that letters within a given word generally are not all the same size, for example, look at the letter "I" as opposed to the letter "M". Never attempt to stretch a narrow letter out to make it appear the same width as the wider letters, for if you do, the word will appear to have spotted areas of white which will be distracting. The crossbars on an "I" are rather short; it will not help the unity of the word to stretch out the crossbars so that they will occupy the same width as the letter "M", for example. Conversely, never attempt to compress a wide letter into a small space because of poor planning and a desire to finish a word on the same line. It never works; the word will appear to have a compressed area of black in it which will also be distracting.

Possibly the most important rule to remember is this: *Letters, as they stand within words, do not occupy the same amount of horizontal spacing.* By way of illustration, you will observe in Fig. L-3 the word ITALY. Figure L-3*a* was

ITALY

(a)

ITALY

(b)

Fig. L-3

done with mechanical spacing, or spacing which was identical between each letter in the word. Observe how the letters "I" and "T" almost stand alone. The relationship between "A" and "L" is better, but the "Y" is too far removed from the rest of the word. Figure L-3*b* shows how the "I" and the "T" can be moved in closer. The "A" may cut into the "T" territory as the "Y" may cut into the area which was alloted to the "L." This technique in letter spacing is not only permissible, it is a necessity. Angle letters consume too much space and need to cut into the areas of the surrounding letters.

By attempting to equalize the negative space surrounding letters, one can more adequately rely upon *visual spacing* rather than on faulty *measured mechanical spacing.* Practice lettering with a drawing pen, marking pen, steel brush, or lettering brush. Use newspaper liners for practice paper. Liners are found in the classified sections of daily newspapers. Vertical columns of advertising may be turned horizontally to provide ready-made guidelines for lettering [see also ALPHABET, BRUSHES, BRUSHES (STEEL), and LETTERS (CUT-PAPER)].

LETTERING BRUSHES

See BRUSHES.

LETTERS (CUT-PAPER)

Cut-paper letters can be a chore or a joy, depending entirely upon one's point of view. Some teachers make master copies of individual letters out of tagboard and trace and cut letters each time a display caption is needed. Others have discovered that there is more latitude for speed in the "deck-of-cards" type of cutout letters. This type of lettering breaks a few rules; specifically, it takes the stand that all letters are the same width and height, in the cause of expediency, and it disregards the fact that the "W" as well as the "M" often take more space.

All letters in the "deck-of-cards" system of cutouts are the same width and height with the exception of the "I," which is narrower, and the "Q," which is a trifle longer. The rules for cutting are simple:

1. Cut several strips of colored paper. The width of the strips will depend upon how high one wishes his letters to be. If one wished to cut letters which would be 3″ high, the width of the paper strips would be 3″.

2. Begin to fold the paper in the manner indicated in Fig. L-4. The first fold would be determined by one's preference as to how wide each letter would be. There is no need to measure; using one's eye is faster.

3. Fold the paper back and forth in accordion fashion (Fig. L-5), maintaining the width of the original fold.

4. Using the folds as guidelines, cut at the folds so that you have a pack of identical squares or rectangles.

5. Using the letter guide illustrated in Fig. L-6, snip away corners and areas to form the cut-paper letters.

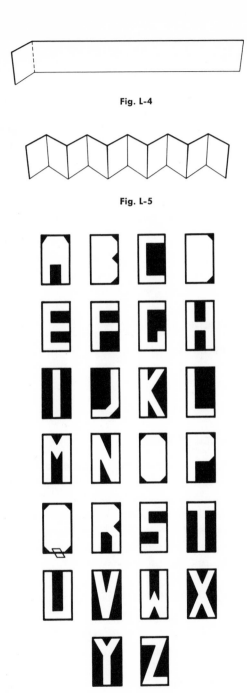

Fig. L-4

Fig. L-5

Fig. L-6

Initial experiences may necessitate the use of pencil guidelines in cutting the letters. But as one practices, the use of guidelines will become unnecessary. Notice that the width of the letter is never altered, nor is the height. Remaining within the confines of the cards, all letters will automatically be uniform in height and width, with two exceptions: The "I," by necessity, needs to be narrower and the "Q" will need an individually cut tail. The "Q" you will notice is an "O" with a tail pinned or pasted on. The important thing to remember is that the width of the stems, or legs of the letters, must be uniform. Once the width of the stems is determined, whether these be fat or slim, all letters must be consistent and conform.

Using this plan for cutting letters, one may cut low and wide letters as easily as one cuts tall and narrow ones. The determining factors are:

1. The width of the strips which determine the height of the letters.

2. The initial fold which will determine the width of the letters.

3. The size of the stems which will make for relatedness and unity within words.

4. The crossbars on letters such as the bar on the "A" and the bar on the "E" should be at the same height to promote and maintain unity and family relatedness.

Cutting Larger Letters: If there is a need for cutting letters for large display areas or halls, use the precut 9″ x 12″ or 12″ x 18″ colored construction paper as the base size for the "deck of cards." In this manner, the deck of cards is already cut and no folding or cutting of strips of paper is necessary.

Faster Letter Cutting: Faster letter cutting can be achieved by cutting many letters at the same time. Determine how many of the same letters are contained in a given caption or word, and tabulate these on a slip of paper. Cut the needed number at one time. For example, if you needed three "O" letters, put three cards together, one on top of another, and snip off the four corners. Some may be bothered by the fact that the letters are solid and that there are no holes in the "A" and in the "R," for example. If this bothers one excessively, the holes may be cut out with an X-Acto knife or a scissors. Students tend to read the letters

L

easily and are seldom bothered by the fact that they are solid [see also ALPHABET, LETTERING, and LETTERS (PLASTIC)].

LETTERS (PLASTIC)

These letters, shown in Fig. L-7, are designed for bulletin boards of cork and similar materials. Each letter has

Fig. L-7

a pin-back which allows them to be pinned into bulletin-board areas. They are permanent and may be easily cleaned with household abrasives (see also ABRASIVES). Letters are available in white, black, red, green, yellow, and blue in both upper-case and lower-case letters (see also ALPHABET). Letter sizes are: 1″, 1½″, 2″, and 3″ [see also BULLETIN BOARDS, LETTERING, and LETTERS (CUT-PAPER)].

LIGHT AND SHADE

See CHIAROSCURO and DESIGN ELEMENTS.

LIGHT THEORY

See COLOR.

LIMBA WOOD

See WOODS.

LIME

White, bulky powder of calcium oxide which is used in mortar, plaster, and whitewash (see also FRESCO and LIMESTONE).

LIMESTONE

White, sedimentary rock composed of calcium carbonate; source of lime (see also ADOBE, LIME, and PLANOGRAPHIC).

LINE

See DESIGN ELEMENTS.

LINEAR PERSPECTIVE

See PERSPECTIVE.

LINERS

See PAPERS.

LINOLEUM BLOCK CUTTERS

For cutting into linoleum in linoleum block printing. These tools are fashioned so that they fit into cutter handles. Cutter handles should be ordered when ordering cutters. Speedball linoleum cutters come in the following sizes and shapes: No. 1 liner; No. 2, V-shaped gouge; No. 3, large liner; No. 4, U-shaped gouge; No. 5, large gouge; and No. 6, knife (see also PRINTMAKING).

LINOLEUM BLOCK PRINTING PRESS

A metal press which prints blocks up to 8″ in width and will press prints from both mounted and unmounted linoleum (see also LINOLEUM BLOCKS and PRINTMAKING).

LINOLEUM BLOCK PRINTS

See PRINTMAKING and RELIEF.

LINOLEUM BLOCKS

Linoleum which is mounted on laminated wood and used in linoleum block printing (see also LAMINATED and PRINTMAKING). They are available in sizes: 3″ x 4″, 4″ x 5″, 4″ x 6″, 5″ x 7″, 6″ x 8″, 8″ x 10″, 9″ x 12″, and 12″ x 12″ (see also LINOLEUM BLOCK CUTTERS and LINOLEUM BLOCK PRINTING PRESS).

LINSEED OIL

Used as a binder in oil painting (see also BINDER, PAINT, and PAINTING). It is used in the process of making synthetic parchment paper (see also PARCHMENT PAPER). Linseed oil is also used in the finishing of wood.

Finishing Wood with Linseed Oil: Rub linseed oil into the wood with a soft cloth. Further applications may be put on the wood about once every four months until the desired effect is achieved. Apply a mild abrasive such as pumice to a soft cloth, and go over the entire surface of the finished wood with a gentle, swirling motion (see also ABRASIVES). Clean off the excess pumice powder with a clean soft cloth, and finish the wood with a coating of paste wax (see also WAX).

LINTEL

Architectural term which applies to a horizontal slab or bar which may be fashioned from wood, stone, or other material. It is placed over a door or window for the purpose of supporting weight from above (see also CAPITAL, CLASSIC, CLASSICAL ORDERS, COLUMN, ENTABLATURE, and FRIEZE).

LIQUID CLOTH

See ADHESIVES.

LITHOGRAPHIC CRAYONS

See PLANOGRAPHIC.

LITHOGRAPHS

See PLANOGRAPHIC.

LITHOGRAPHY

See PLANOGRAPHIC.

LITURGICAL ART

Refers to liturgy; art of the Church.

LOG (SHIPS)

See PARCHMENT PAPER.

LOOM

See WEAVING.

LOWER-CASE LETTERS

Small letters; letters which are not capitals (see also ALPHABET).

LUCITE

Clear plastic which can be sawed, carved, or cemented and is used in plastic art crafts (see also PLASTICS). Lucite may be cut into desired shapes with a coping saw (see also WOODWORKING). Rough edges may be rubbed down with pumice powder (see also ABRASIVES). Findings may be attached with lucite cement (see also ADHESIVES and FINDINGS). Lucite is available in sheets of ⅛″, ³⁄₁₆″, ¼″, and in blocks of 5″ x 8″.

LUCITE CEMENT

See ADHESIVES.

LUMINOSITY

Skillful use of paint to give feeling of dimension in transparency. This is often accomplished in painting by allowing the ground to show through in a transparent manner (see also GROUND and PAINTING).

M

MAGAZINES (ART)

The following represents a partial list of art periodicals:

American Artist, Watson-Guptill Publications, 24 West 40th Street, New York 18, New York.

Artforum, 723½ North La Cienga, Los Angeles, California; 839 Howard Street, San Francisco, California; 255 Seventh Avenue, New York, New York.

Art News, Art Foundation Press, 32 East 57th Street, New York, New York.

Arts, Art Digest, Inc., 116 East 59th Street, New York 22, New York.

Arts and Activities, Jones Publishing Company, Department 210, 8150 North Central Park Avenue, Skokie, Illinois.

Arts and Architecture, John D. Entenza, Publisher, 3305 Wilshire Boulevard, Los Angeles 5, California.

Craft Horizons, American Craftsmens Council, 29 West 53rd Street, New York 19, New York.

Creative Crafts, Fred de Liden, Oxford Press, 6015 Santa Monica Boulevard, Los Angeles 38, California.

Everyday Art, American Crayon Company, Sandusky, Ohio.

Print, 535 Fifth Avenue, New York 17, New York.

School Arts, The Davis Press, Worcester, Massachusetts.

MAGNESITE

Building material which provides a versatile medium for classroom art programs. Magnesite is used for sculpture (Fig. M-1), modeling, and as a base for mosaics (see also MODELING MATERIALS, MOSAICS, and SCULPTURE). Magnesite may be used with or without an armature (see also

ARMATURES). It becomes hard and durable at room temperature. Drying times are as follows: wet-dry, 2 to 4 hours; medium dry, 5 to 8 hours; and very dry, 12 to 16 hours. One of the interesting features of magnesite is that appendages and/or additions may be added to the sculptured or modeled form when it is already dry.

Materials needed: Magnesite, magnesium chloride (liquid), and waxed paper (see also BICYCLE PUMP).

Fig. M-1

Procedure: Mix the magnesium chloride solution with the powdered white magnesite to the consistency of dough. Mix it and knead it thoroughly. If the magnesite mixture tends to become sticky while working with it, dip the hands in a little magnesium-chloride liquid solution and this will alleviate the stickiness. Work on waxed paper and allow the form to dry on it. When it has dried, it may be carved with knives and rasps; or it may be modeled when wet, and finished with tools when it has dried.

Try using magnesite as a base for a mosaic tile. Roll out the magnesite with a rolling pin and cut the tile to the desired shape. Add some beads or other decorative mosaic-like details on the surface of the tile. Try filling the metal top of a cottage-cheese container with magnesite and add decorative mosaic-like details to the surface. The metal top will contain the tile and will provide a neat container for hanging. This is a particularly applicable mosaic experience for kindergarten-primary children (see also MOSAICS).

NOTE: When magnesite is used over an armature in sculpturing experiences, it tends to crack if it dries too readily. Drying can be retarded by placing a damp cloth over the form.

MAGNESIUM CHLORIDE

Brownish liquid which is available in gallon containers and is used in the preparation of magnesite in its plastic form for modeling and sculpture (see also MAGNESITE).

MAGNET BOARD

Type of auxillary teaching tool which is used in the same manner as a felt board (see also FELT BOARD). Consists of a sheet of metal which would act as a board and create a magnetic field with magnets. Small magnets of the approximate size of ¼″ x ¼″, are available at hardware stores and can be purchased individually or in lots of twenty or fifty. These small magnets are adhered to the backs of visual materials with masking tape. When these visual aids are placed flush against the metal board, magnetic contact will be made, and the pictures will remain securely in place. Magnet boards are excellent in story telling, arithmetic experiences, and other types of classroom activities.

MAHOGANY (GENUINE)

See WOODS.

MAKIMONO

Japanese scroll painting which is hung horizontally (see also KAKEMONO, QUADRA, and TONDO).

MANILA DRAWING PAPER

See PAPERS.

MANUSCRIPTS

Bound volumes of parchment which were hand-lettered and richly embellished with illuminations (see also ILLUMINATIONS and PARCHMENT). Manuscripts were a departure from scrolls which were used in periods of antiquity (see also ANTIQUITY).

MANUSCRIPT (WRITING)

See CALLIGRAPHY and WRITING.

MANZANITA

A well-formed branch of manzanita (Fig. M-2) will serve as the base for a Christmas tree decoration, an Easter

Fig. M-2

egg tree (Fig. M-3), or a Valentine tree (see also HOLIDAYS and SPECIAL EVENTS). The manzanita branch may be trimmed of· extraneous branches and sanded if necessary. It may then be anchored into a container with a mixture of plaster of paris (see also PLASTER OF PARIS).

Christmas Trees: Add small ornamental Christmas balls, tiny birds, stars, etc. (see also CHEESECLOTH).

Easter Egg Tree: Children can bring eggshells from home which may be effectively decorated with colored flo-ball pens (see also PENS). Easter eggshells may be decorated with sequins, bits of felt, colored paper, etc. An easy method of removing the egg from the shell is as follows: Crack a small opening in one end of the egg. Puncture the other end of the egg with a small pinhole. Blow the egg from the shell into a container using the pinhole end for blowing.

Fig. M-3

Valentine Tree: Tie tiny valentines on the manzanita branches with narrow red ribbon (see also VALENTINE BOXES).

MAPLE (HARD)

See WOODS.

MAPMAKING

Outline Maps: Outline maps are made with the aid of an opaque projector. The picture of the map is inserted into the projector and the map is thrown on a section of the wall which has been covered with a strip of butcher paper. The outline of the map can be traced on the paper from the projected image. See Fig. M-4 for an example of an outline map used in an elementary school social studies bulletin-board display.

Overlay Maps: This type of map makes it possible to show geographical locations of natural resources, industry, agriculture, and topography through a series of acetate-sheeting overlays placed over a basic, flat, outline map (see also ACETATE SHEETING). Symbolic keys may be used, such as factories to indicate industry, lettuce to indicate agriculture, and trains to indicate transportation. Symbolic key drawings may be rendered on paper and adhered to the acetate sheets with rubber cement, or they may be drawn directly on the acetate with special acetate colors or inks (see also ACETATE COLORS and ACETATE INKS).

Fig. M-4

The acetate key sheets may be placed one by one over the basic outline map, or they may be set up in book or chart form with the basic map outline underneath. As the sheets of acetate are flipped over, the series of map overlays clearly pinpoint regions of concentrated development, as well as regions of lack of concentrated development. Such maps also pinpoint a state's or country's characteristics and obviates the necessity of seeing a cluttered, overactive map which attempts to "tell all" in one glance. For an additional experience in globe making (see also PAPIER-MÂCHÉ).

Relief Maps: Outline maps serve as contour guides for relief maps. Once the outline is established on paper, the map can then be cut out and used as a guide for tracing on a piece of plywood. The relief map may be built up with one of the following modeling materials: pulp papier-mâché, salt and flour, asbestos, and wheat paste, or sawdust and wheat paste (see also MODELING MATERIALS and PAPIER-MÂCHÉ). The map may be given a smoother texture with the application of spackle over the surface of the modeling material when it has dried (see also SPACKLE).

MARACAS

See PAPIER-MÂCHÉ.

MARBLE PAPER

See PAPERS.

MARBLES

Marbles may be used as a form of tesserae in mosaics. They are particularly effective when they have been shattered (see also MOSAICS).

MARBLING

See DECORATIVE PAPERS.

MARQUETRY

The art of inlay of ivory, wood, stones, or metals into a wood ground; popularized in the seventeenth century (see also LACQUER WARE and PERSIAN ART). Wood inlay experiences are excellent for students on an upper-grade level. One needs only a supply of thin veneer woods with different color ranges and grains. Such woods are available in 36 different kinds, colors, and grains at the extreme thinness for cutting of ¼₈″.

NOTE: For additional information and a catalog relating to marquetry and supplies available, write to: Immerman and Sons, 1924 Euclid Avenue, Cleveland 15, Ohio.

MASKING TAPE

See TAPES.

MASKS

See PAPIER-MÂCHÉ.

MASONITE

See CANVAS SUBSTITUTES, DECORATIVE PAPERS, DRAWING BOARDS, and EASELS.

MASS AND SPACE

See DESIGN ELEMENTS.

MASTIC TILE ADHESIVE

See ADHESIVES.

MAT

See MOUNTING and MATTING.

MAT BOARD

See PAPERS.

MATTE

Surface without gloss; a dull finish (see also CERAMICS, PAPERS, and TAPES).

MATTING

See MOUNTING and MATTING.

MAYAN ART

See HISTORY (ART).

MECHANICAL DRAWING

See DRAWING (MECHANICAL).

MEDIA

Plural of medium, for example, "different kinds of media such as colored chalk, paint, and crayons" (see also MEDIUM and MIXED MEDIA).

MEDIEVAL ART

Also called the art of the Middle Ages; following the period of late antiquity and continuing until the Renaissance, encompassing both the Romanesque and Gothic periods [see also ANTIQUITY, CHRISTIAN ART, GOTHIC, HISTORY (ART), and ROMANESQUE]. Relating to religious themes with high stylization in rendering, medieval creative expression took the forms of reliefs in stone, wood, bone, and cast metals, including the paneled diptych and triptych; icons and small paintings, including the illuminations on manuscripts; glass painting; and architecture in the form of the basilica and round churches (see also BASILICA, DIPTYCH, ICONS, ILLUMINATIONS, MANUSCRIPTS, RELIEF, and TRIPTYCH).

MEDIUM

Term refers to the type of material which is used in the rendering of an art form; this might refer to a pencil as a medium for expression in the graphic arts or to clay as a medium for expression in the plastic arts (see also GRAPHIC ARTS, MEDIA, and MIXED MEDIA).

MESOLITHIC PERIOD

Transitional period between the Paleolithic period (Old Stone Age) and the Neolithic period (New Stone Age) [see also ALTAMIRA, HISTORY (ART), LASCAUX, NEOLITHIC PERIOD, and PALEOLITHIC PERIOD].

MEZZOTINT

See INTAGLIO.

MIDDLE AGES

See MEDIEVAL ART.

MIDDLE TONE

See HALFTONE.

MIMEOGRAPH STENCIL BACKS

See PAPERS.

MINGEI

See JAPANESE FOLK ART.

MINOAN ART

Alternate name for Pre-Hellenic or Aegean-Cretan Art [see also AEGEAN ART, HISTORY (ART), and PRE-HELLENIC ART].

MINOR ARTS

See CRAFTS.

MIRACLE TAPE

See TAPES.

MITER

Relates to treatment of corners in woodworking and paper work (see also BOOKLET MAKING). A mitered corner (Fig. M-5) would represent the result of two strips of paper or wood meeting to create an oblique line which would bisect the outside corner with two adjacent angles of 45°. To cut mitered corners, particularly in the construction of picture frames, a miter box is an indispensable yet inexpensive tool.

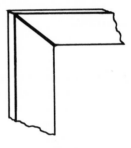

Fig. M-5

MIXED MEDIA

Combination of media, such as using colored chalk with black drawing ink, watercolor with crayon, or a combination of these with the collage technique (see also COLLAGE, MEDIA, and MEDIUM).

MOBILES

Moving, suspended form of sculpture (Fig. M-6) popularized by the noted American artist, Alexander Calder (see also SCULPTURE). Mobiles are based on the principle of creating a design which has both balance and motion. The mobile will change with the movement of the air; thus it is not a static form of sculpture.

Materials: Materials which can be used for the basic construction of mobiles are bamboo sticks, thin doweling, balsa wood, stove wire, or coat-hanger wire.

Procedure: String a wire across the room from which to hang the basic, horizontal wood or wire construction. Coat hangers can be used effectively for horizontal bars and can be cut with wire cutters (see also WIRE and WIRE CUTTERS). Since there is more movement with the bent form, the wire should be curved slightly. Use thin nylon

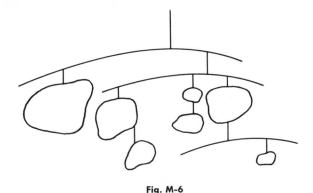

Fig. M-6

cord or nylon thread for hanging forms to the basic curved, or horizontal, line structure. Forms may be cut from paper, cardboard, tin cans, or thin wood. Color may be added with paint or overlays of colored tissue [see also PAINTS and TISSUE (COLORED)].

These cut forms must be placed on the horizontal wood or wire construction so that the desired balance and movement will evolve. This will necessitate starting the placement at the bottom and working up. When balance is achieved, glue each cord or thread from which the form or shape is suspended in place with Duco cement or resin glue (see also ADHESIVES).

MODELING MATERIALS

Asbestos:

Type 1: Add water to asbestos flakes until mixture holds its shape for modeling (see also ASBESTOS).

Type 2: Add mixture of wheat paste and water to asbestos until it holds its shape for modeling (see also WHEAT PASTE).

Type 3: Add mixture of glue and water to asbestos until it holds its shape. Use 3 parts water to 1 part glue (see also PRESERVATIVES).

Carving Materials: Some of the carving materials may be used for modeling while still in their wet stage (see also

CARVING MATERIALS). Experiment with the materials at your disposal; combine them. Try combining vermiculite and wheat paste for a golden type of modeling material; try combining sawdust and asbestos with wheat paste. Try adding some plaster of paris to asbestos or sawdust and add water instead of wheat paste (see also PLASTER OF PARIS).

Clay: See CERAMICS.

Clay (Nonfiring): See CLAY (NONFIRING).

Clay (Plastic): See CLAY (PLASTIC).

Magnesite: See MAGNESITE.

Pulp Papier-Mâché: See PAPIER-MÂCHÉ.

Salt and Flour:

Type 1: Mix dry 1 part salt and 1 part flour. Slowly add enough water to make a modeling material which will hold its shape.

Type 2: For a more highly-textured, salt-flour modeling material, mix dry 2 parts salt and 1 part flour. Slowly add enough water to the mixture until it holds its shape for modeling.

NOTE: The one limitation of the salt and flour mixture is that if it is used in a thick manner, it will mold and crack in the drying stage. When depth is needed, such as in the modeling of detail on relief maps, build up by layers, allowing each layer to dry before the next one is laid down. In some instances it is possible to hasten the drying stage by setting salt and flour objects in a warm oven.

Sawdust: Mix 4 parts sawdust to 1 part wheat paste (see also WHEAT PASTE). Slowly add water until the mixture holds its shape for modeling.

NOTE: When obtaining sawdust from lumber yards, specify *pine sawdust*. Redwood sawdust is undesirable for modeling projects because of the likelihood of slivers and subsequent infections. When sawdust mixtures have dried completely, they may be sanded or allowed to remain in their highly-textured natural state.

MODERN ART

Refers to contemporary art movements. The term was given impetus after the Armory Show in New York in 1913. The Modern Art movement began with the impressionistic painters in the last half of the nineteenth century and has continued until contemporary times [see also ARMORY SHOW, HISTORY (ART), and IMPRESSIONISM].

M

MOLDS

Used for duplication of forms; usually made of plaster. They can be made or purchased commercially (see also PAPIER-MÂCHÉ and UNDERCUTS).

MONOGRAMS

Designs which are achieved through the use of initials or letters (see also ALPHABET, LEATHER, and LETTERING).

MONTAGE

Essentially, the gluing of parts of representational pictures to create a new pictorial image; fanciful, creative activity with an emphasis on design. Pictures may be cut from magazines, catalogs, or may be actual photographs. When photographs are used, the resulting design is called a photo-montage. Parts of pictures or photos are glued down on a thick paper ground such as chipboard, illustration board, or oak tagboard (see also PAPERS).

MORDANTS

Dye-setting solution which is used in all craft experiences relating to fabric dyeing processes (see also BATIK and TIE-DYE). Some dyes contain mordants, but it will do no harm to take the added precaution of using mordants for all dyeing to insure permanency and fastness of color.

Cottons: Place cold water in an enamel pan. Add 10 percent Glauber's salt as compared to the total weight of the fabric which has been dyed. Place the fabric in the mordant solution for several hours or overnight. Hang cottons in the shade or inside to dry.

Silks and Woolens: As these fabrics contain animal and vegetable fibers, a different mordant solution is used. Place cold water into an enamel pan and add 10 percent acetic acid (28 percent solution of acetic acid) as compared to the total weight of the fabric being dyed. Allow the fabric to remain in the mordant solution for several hours or overnight. Again, hang the fabric in the shade or inside to dry.

NOTE: Remember *always* to add the acid to the water, *never* the reverse!

Heat setting method for fabrics: Wrap the fabric in aluminum foil in the following manner: Place fabric on top of foil and wrap fabric and foil into a roll. Secure the ends and place the foil package into a cold oven. Set the temperature at 250° F and allow the oven to remain at this temperature for 20 minutes; then, shut it off. Allow the foil-wrapped package to remain in the oven for an additional hour or until the oven has cooled.

MOSAICS

Materials Needed: Tile or tesserae, tile cutter, carborundum stone, white resin glue, grout, and baseboard.

Tile: Called tessera or tesserae (plural); consists of squares of enamel, glass, porcelain, stone, or plastic which are used in making mosaics. Commercially made tesserae can be purchased from craft supply houses or tile stores. However, tile scraps and imperfect large tiles may be cut with tile cutters and used as well. The actual size of commercially made tesserae varies. Ceramic tile is usually $\frac{13}{16}''$ square; Venetian glass tile, $\frac{3}{4}''$ square; porcelain tile, $\frac{3}{8}''$ square; and plastic tile, $\frac{11}{16}''$ square. Tiles come in varied hues, shades, tones, and tints which are transparent as well as opaque. There are some forms of tesserae which are patterned and textured. In addition, there are multipebble tiles which have irregular shapes.

NOTE: A new mosaic tile has been developed called Artile. It is available from Bergen Arts and Crafts, Box 689sa, Salem, Massachusetts. Artile is easily cut, can be broken with the hands, and is available in 26 brilliant colors. It has a soft clay body, but a hard glossy top glaze. This material would be particularly appropriate for smaller children in the elementary grades.

Tile Cutter: Students should use the 10-ounce tile cutters with 8″ handles. It is always recommended that they cut their tiles inside a paper or plastic bag, or cup a gloved hand over the tile. The reason for this precautionary measure is that shattering glass is apt to travel and render injury to skin and eyes.

Carborundum stone: This abrasive is used to smooth the rough edges on the tiles after cutting them. Carborundum stone should be used under running water so that the glass dust will be washed down the sink instead of floating about in the air.

Glue: White resin glue is suitable for small mosaics; for larger ones, such as wall mosaics, use mastic tile cement and a cement spreader (see also ADHESIVES).

Grout: Grout is used to fill the spaces between tiles, and it works to make a firmer bonding with the baseboard. Grout is mixed with water to the consistency of batter. The directions for mixing the grout are usually found on the container.

Baseboard: Use either plywood, fiberboard, wooden box tops, cement stepping stones, or walls.

Procedure: Render in color a design which will be used as a cartoon for the mosaic (see also CARTOON). The size of the design will be the exact size of the baseboard. Transfer the design to the baseboard with pencil (see also TRACING AND TRANSFER). Begin to arrange the tile on the baseboard without glue in an effort to duplicate with tile the color harmony which was created on paper. This will involve some tile cutting with the tile cutter.

When the tesserae have been arranged satisfactorily, begin to "butter" each tile separately (apply adhesive to tessera) with glue or mastic and place on the board. When the mosaic has been completed in terms of gluing down each separate tessera, allow the mosaic design to dry overnight.

Mix grout and spread it over the entire surface with the hands, taking precaution to see that it is spread evenly so that it will work itself between the tesserae. Allow the grout to set for approximately 20 minutes. Then wipe the surface clean of grout with a large, damp sponge. Do not allow the grout to stay on beyond the 20 minutes prescribed or it will be exceedingly difficult to remove. A film of grout will remain after the grout has been removed. This may be taken off with a mild abrasive the next day. Use a damp cloth with some household Ajax—or similar household cleansing agent.

Sometimes grout color is added to the grout to match tesserae or for purposes of contrast. Grout color is available in small, 1-ounce containers of red, green, yellow, and black. A grout sealer with a silicone base will protect the grout from grease and dirt and will also render it nonporous.

When you become more adept at the art of mosaic making, you may wish to try making your own tesserae out of clay. Roll out the ceramic clay in a slab method to a thickness of about ½". Cut the shapes of tesserae with a knife. Allow them to dry; glaze and fire (see also CERAMICS). Try making salt and flour tesserae (see also MODELING MATERIALS). Roll out the salt-flour mixture on a board and cut desired shapes with a knife. Salt-flour tesserae may be painted with tempera and sprayed with plastic, or food coloring may be added to the mixture (see also KRYLON).

Do not overlook the possibility of using other materials as tesserae; use pieces of colored glass, pebbles, and beads. Visit wrecking yards, automobile glass-repair shops, and stained-glass window manufacturers for assortments of broken glass which are generally yours for the asking. Bring a pair of gloves.

Multicolored glass marbles are excellent for tesserae, especially when they have been shattered and broken by the following method: Place marbles on a cookie tin and put them in a hot oven (or an electric frying pan) for a length of time. When the marbles are hot, take them off the cookie tin (use gloves) and drop them into a kettle of ice water. If all of the marbles do not shatter after placing them in ice water, put them on a hard surface, cover them with cardboard, and hit them with a hammer.

NOTE: When these marbles are used as tesserae, it is most effective to glue the smooth bottom surface to the mosaic ground, allowing the jagged edges to serve as a textured type of tesserae.

Color Harmonies for Mosaics: Mosaic tesserae are often clustered together in the following ways:

1. Cool colors grouped together, for example, blue, blue-green, and green.

2. Warm colors grouped together, for example, red, red-orange, and orange.

3. All cool colors grouped together with an occasional accent of a warm color, for example, blue, blue-green, and green with a spot of vermilion here and there.

4. All warm colors grouped together with an occasional accent of a cool color, for example, red, red-orange, and orange with a spot of blue-green here and there.

5. Monochromatic colors grouped together with different values, for example, light-green, medium green, and dark-green.

6. Unlike colors grouped together with like values, for example, dark-green, dark-blue, and dark-purple, or light-green, light-blue, and light purple (see also BROKEN COLOR and COLOR).

Other types of "nonpermanent" mosaics:

1. Use cutout or torn pieces of colored construction paper on a ground of chipboard.

2. Use magazine illustrations for cutting or tearing on a ground of chipboard.

3. Use eggshells which have been either painted with tempera or dyed with food coloring, and glue these to a chipboard ground.

4. Try seeds, bottle tops, buttons, and macaroni; try making your own tesserae from some of the modeling materials (see also MODELING MATERIALS).

MOTIF

Subject or theme which is treated in a creative manner.

MOUNTING AND MATTING

There are as many techniques for mounting and matting as there are teachers. It is always an interesting excursion to visit classrooms and to observe how teachers have developed ideas of their own in this area. While experimentation is encouraged, it should always be remembered that a mount or a mat plays a *subordinate* role to the subject being displayed. Once a mount or a mat overpowers a picture either by size, shape, color, or texture, it ceases to perform its subordinate function.

Matting: Using a mat knife and a steel-edged ruler, cut a window from a piece of matboard (see also KNIVES, PAPERS, and RULERS). Tagboard or heavy paper may be substituted for a heavy, textured matboard. The window area should be ½″ smaller all around than the actual size of the picture being displayed. In terms of actual measurement of the mat, the sides and top of the mat should be equal and the bottom slightly wider. When the window is cut with the mat knife, the picture should be fastened to the back of the mat with masking tape (see also TAPES). A well-cut mat (Fig. M-7) can be used over and over again, providing it has been stored flat.

Fig. M-7

Mounting: Generally speaking, the term mount refers to the pasting or pinning of a picture to an accented color and then to a neutral background paper. In a given picture, one can determine which accent color to use by noting the color which is least used in the picture. This color might be represented by a dash of red, a splash of orange, or perhaps a touch of blue.

Fig. M-8

The accent color should be duplicated with either construction or tonal paper and placed directly in back of the picture with an extending border of about ½″ or less all around. Place the picture and the accented paper on a neutral paper such as gray, buff, off-white, or plain tagboard. The margin on the neutral paper should be greater than the accented color, approximately 1½″ to 2″ around, as shown in Fig. M-8.

Another method of mounting is described in the dry-mount technique. This method utilizes stiff cardboard backing which is the same size as the picture. The cardboard backing and the picture are adhered together with a special dry-mount tissue (see also DRY-MOUNT).

NOTE: If a given picture has but two colors in its color scheme, use the complement of one of the colors for the accent (see also COLOR).

MOVIES (FILM)

An actual film-making project wherein students may utilize old, discarded 16-millimeter film from school audio-visual libraries in the creation of animated movies of their own design. The film coating of the old film may be removed with acetone (see also ACETONE). Thereafter, it is a simple matter of alloting each student a portion of the film for designing purposes. Use acetate colors, acetate inks, flo-ball pens, and black drawing inks and pens for drawing on the film (see also ACETATE COLORS and ACETATE INKS).

Students may choose to render their designs in the individual frames, or they may prefer to use the film sideways, utilizing wavy or jagged lines. Film designed sideways will, of course, appear vertical on the screen. Sgraffito effects may be achieved by scratching through the inks and colors with a scratching knife or similar tool (see also KNIVES). When the film is completed in terms of design, it may be wound around a take-up reel and viewed through a projector. Allow about 6 feet of clear film at the beginning for winding purposes.

Additional tips: Old pieces of film may be patched together with Scotch cellulose tape (see also TAPES). Clear, leader film may be used instead of old film. Leader film may be obtained from photographic supply houses and the cost is approximately $2.00 per 100′ of film. Motivation for this project might come with the showing of the two Norman McLaren films entitled, *Begone Dull Care* and *Fiddle Dee Dee,* which are both available from the National Film Board of Canada [see also FILMS AND FILMSTRIPS (ART)].

While the movie is being shown, a background of music from a recorder will enhance the production. Experimentation is needed in order to find a long-playing record that will suit the jerking, moving, and wavy motion of the rendered designs on film.

MOVIES (PAPER)

The pictures for these movies are drawn in "frames" of long strips of paper, either butcher or kraft; they are shown in constructions of cardboard or wooden boxes (Fig. M-9).

Fig. M-9

The pictures follow a planned sequence and either tell stories or illustrate important concepts relative to the curriculum. Such movies provide experiences in art as well as correlated experiences in writing and speaking, for children often caption the frames and offer narration for the movies as they are cranked in the boxes and shown.

Frames or constructions for these movies may be easily made from cardboard boxes. The top flaps of the cardboard box are removed. The frame for viewing is cut from a side of the box. The box is set on its bottom with long lengths of doweling inserted from side to side, one at the top and one at the bottom. The end of the paper strip (end of the movie) is taped to the bottom dowel, and the strip is then rolled up with the picture toward the outside. The other end of the paper strip (beginning of the movie) is taped to the top dowel, again with the picture toward the outside. Then, by turning the top dowel,

M

the movie is seen through the frame and is shown in sequence, passing from bottom to top.

MUFFIN TINS

Excellent for individual color selections in tempera painting or printmaking processes (see also PAINTING and PRINTMAKING).

MUNSELL COLOR THEORY

Relates to a color theory which involves five basic colors on the color wheel: red, yellow, green, blue, and purple (see also COLOR).

MURALS

Murals may be painted on walls or on panels which may be attached to walls. For classroom experiences, murals are rendered on panels of paper or plain fabric and are fastened to walls (see Fig. M-10) in display areas or within classroom settings (see also FRESCO and FRIEZE).

Fig. M-10

Approach: Students may individually design a cartoon which would represent the finished mural and select the most appropriate one for enlargement (see also ENLARGING). Another approach, which is particularly applicable in

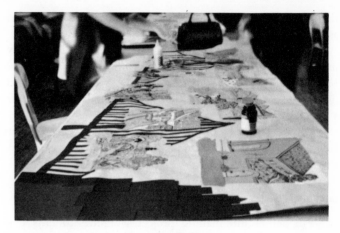

Fig. M-11

the kindergarten-primary grades, is to work directly on the paper ground. This is usually done after an initial session of group planning where general placement was discussed and understood, or when the design was blocked in with white or yellow chalk.

Media: Type of media is limitless, depending entirely upon the ground on which it is rendered. Some murals use only one medium, such as tempera, while others use mixed media (Fig. M-11) (see also GROUND, MEDIA, MEDIUM, and MIXED MEDIA). On a ground of paper, one may use colored chalk, colored inks, black ink, colored tempera, crayons, or mixed media. Cutout shapes and forms relate to paste-up murals, and these can be rendered in either two-dimensional flat or three-dimensional paper sculpture (see also DIMENSION and PAPER SCULPTURE). On grounds of burlap, use felt with an adhesive of white resin glue; on grounds of canvas, use a combination of felt or fabric and colored tempera paint or felt pens (see also ADHESIVES, BURLAP, PAINTS and PENS).

Planning the Mural: Since the mural is essentially a pictorial representation of a theme, many small, related pictures will be distributed throughout the panel, as well as larger ones. Some of these areas will, by necessity, be subordinate and others will be dominant. Color, size, shape, and placement will be some of the factors which will determine the areas of emphasis. It is well to try to pull some of these areas together by distributing some of the stronger colors throughout the mural rather than allowing them to become isolated in one section of the panel.

Another unifying technique is to rely heavily upon line as a means of achieving unity and relating one area to another. For example, in a mural relating to communication, telephone poles and telephone wires might act as a source for unification, through line, and pull the smaller, pictorial areas together with areas of more dominance and emphasis. Railroad tracks will act in the same manner in a mural relating to transportation; sidewalks, for communities; streets and trails, for neighborhoods; etc.

Size: The size of the mural generally depends upon the size of the space it will occupy. There are no restrictions as to size or shape of murals. They may be long vertical panels, long horizontal ones, or square.

Subject: The subject of a mural relates to a theme either factual or fanciful.

MYSTIC TAPE

See BOOKLET MAKING and TAPES.

NAILS

See WOODWORKING.

NATURALISM

See REALISM.

NEEDLE-NOSE PLIERS

See WIRE TOOLS.

NEEDLES

Crochet Needles: Used as substitute tools for tooling leather (see also LEATHER).

Embroidery Needles: Also called crewel needles; used as sewing needles for children in kindergarten-primary grades.

Raffia Needles: Available 20 to a package, No. 18 size. They are used for working with raffia in stitchery, or in the application of decorative detail relating to work with papier-mâché in either puppetry, animal, or mask-making (see also PAPIER-MÂCHÉ and PUPPETS).

Sewing Needles: Available 20 to a package; all steel, with assorted lengths (see also STITCHERY).

Tapestry Needles: Long, 6″ tapestry needles are used for weaving (see also WEAVING).

NEGATIVE SOLUTION

See SILK SCREENING.

NEGATIVE SOLUTION SOLVENT

See SILK SCREENING and SOLVENTS.

NEGATIVE SPACE

See DESIGN ELEMENTS and SILK SCREENING.

NEOCLASSICISM

See CLASSICISM.

NEOIMPRESSIONISM

Followed Impressionism; a technique of painting with tiny dots of pure color on a canvas; also called pointillism (see also BROKEN COLOR and IMPRESSIONISM).

EXAMPLE: "Sunday Afternoon on the Island of La Grande Jatte," by Georges Seurat.

NEOLITHIC PERIOD

Refers to the New Stone Age [see also HISTORY (ART) and PALEOLITHIC PERIOD].

EXAMPLE: Ruins of Stonehenge in England.

NEOPLASTICISM

Alternately called de Stijl; also related to Purism, Classical Abstraction, and Nonobjective Art (see also NON-

N

OBJECTIVE ART). Neoplasticism developed in Holland in 1917, led by artists Piet Mondrian and Theo van Doesburg. Artists in this group worked for simplicity of form using rectangular planes of pure color. Later, they were to influence the Bauhaus, and eventually their art forms were applied to exterior design in architecture (see also ARCHITECTURE and BAUHAUS).

EXAMPLE: "Composition (1936)," by Piet Mondrian.

NEWSPAPER

See PAPERS.

NEWSPAPER LINERS

See PAPERS.

NEWSPRINT

See PAPERS.

NIPPERS

See MOSAICS and WIRE TOOLS.

NONFIGURATIVE

See FIGURATIVE and NONOBJECTIVE ART.

NONOBJECTIVE ART

Nonobjective art need not rely upon material subject matter for either inspiration or subsequent modification. It can be a simple arrangement of geometric forms or lines as illustrated in some of the paintings of Wassily Kandinsky and Piet Mondrian, or it can be related to the work of the abstract-expressionistic painters such as Jackson Pollack. Nonobjective art need have no counterpart in nature (see also ABSTRACT-EXPRESSIONISM, DE STIJL, and NEOPLASTICISM).

NONREPRESENTATIONAL

See NONOBJECTIVE ART.

NONSPECTRAL COLORS

Relates to hues not found in the color spectrum or on a color wheel, for example, burnt umber, brown, etc., (see also COLOR).

NOTAN

Form of design in which negative space takes on the quality of positive space, as in an optical illusion. Figure N-1 shows a potato print notan (see also DESIGN ELEMENTS).

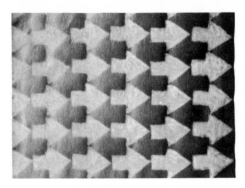

Fig. N-1

OAK (RED)

See WOODS.

OAK TAGBOARD

See PAPERS.

OAK (WHITE)

See WOODS.

OIL INKS

See INKS and SILK SCREENING.

OIL OF CLOVES

See PRESERVATIVES.

OIL OF PEPPERMINT

See PRESERVATIVES.

OIL OF WINTERGREEN

See PRESERVATIVES.

OIL PAINT

See PAINTING and PAINTS.

OILS

Commonly refers to tubes of oil paints which are used in oil painting; also refers to the medium of oil painting (Fig. O-1) (see also MEDIUM, PAINTING, and PAINTS).

Fig. O-1

ONION BAGS

See STITCHERY.

OPAQUE

Quality of not being transparent; relates to paint such as tempera, poster, gouche, and oil (see also PAINTING and PAINTS). It also relates to matte glazes and matte enamels (see also CERAMICS and COPPER ENAMELING), to cellulose tape with matte finish (see also TAPES), and to acetate sheeting which is nontransparent (see also ACETATE SHEETING).

ORIENTAL ART

See EASTERN ART.

ORIGAMI

Japanese art of paper folding using square, lightweight paper called origami paper (see also PAPERS). This folding will produce such forms as houses, birds, animals, balls, and hats. Forms hold their shape in three dimensions without the use of adhesives, and no cutting is involved.

NOTE: One of the available source books for teachers: Tokinobu and Hideko Mihara, *Origami* (San Francisco, Calif.: Oriental Culture Book Company).

ORNAMENTS

See LAMINATED RESIN, ORIGAMI, PAPER SCULPTURE, and PAPIER-MÂCHÉ.

OVERLAY MAPS

See MAPMAKING.

OZALID PAPER

See PAPERS.

OZALID PRINTS

See PRINTMAKING.

PAINT

All paint consists of three basic ingredients: the pigment, or color; the binder, or that material which holds the pigment together; and the vehicle, or that material which makes the pigment and binder flow as a painting medium (see also BINDER, PAINTING, PAINTS, PIGMENT, and VEHICLE).

PAINTER'S VARNISH

See VARNISH.

PAINTING

In order to identify types of painting media and their characteristics, the following will illustrate casein, finger paint, gouache, oil, poster paint, tempera, and watercolor:

Casein:

Characteristics:

1. Water soluble.
2. Tube paint.
3. Used in same manner as watercolors.
4. Colors can be fully diluted and will resemble watercolors; if used in a thicker manner (impasto), it will resemble gouache.
5. Colors dry fast with great intensity.
6. Colors dry waterproof. Corrections can be made on top of painting when it is dry, and it will not disturb the underpainting.

Casein paint is available in 1″ x 4″ tubes and can be purchased individually or in sets. It is considered a sophisticated medium and generally is not used in school programs, except occasionally on a secondary level. Watercolor brushes or soft, sable, oil brushes are used with casein. Heavy cardboard, canvasette, or heavy watercolor paper are used as grounds (see also BRUSHES, PAINT SUBSTITUTES, and PAPERS). Paintings can be given a coating of painter's varnish when dry (see also VARNISH).

Finger Paint: See DECORATIVE PAPERS.

Gouache:

Characteristics:

1. Water-soluble tube paints.
2. Used in same manner as watercolors.
3. Is opaque in quality.
4. When dry, colors are not as intense as casein.
5. Not waterproof.
6. Paintings can be given a coating of picture wax when dry (see also WAX).

Use watercolor brushes and a few stiff easel brushes for gouache painting. Use illustration board or heavy watercolor paper as a ground (see also BRUSHES and PAPER).

Oils:

Characteristics:

1. Not water soluble.
2. Opaque oil medium is in tube form.
3. Paint is thinned with a mixture of ½ artist's turpentine and ½ linseed oil.
4. Extremely slow drying medium.
5. Color is squeezed on a palette from tubes with cool colors on one side and warm colors on the other (see also COLOR).
6. Sometimes painting is done with a palette knife or a painting knife (see also KNIVES).
7. Painter's varnish is used to highlight areas, or used over the entire canvas. Use is optional (see also VARNISH).

Obtain as a starter set: zinc white or titanium white (large tubes for white only), ivory black, burnt umber, raw sienna, ultramarine blue, yellow ochre, cadmium light yellow, cadmium medium red, alizarin crimson, and viridian green. Also, obtain 8-ounce containers of turpentine and linseed oil, palette, palette knife, oil and turpentine cups for palette, and a supply of old rags. Small and large, soft, sable oil brushes will be needed, as well as one medium and one large bristle oil brush (see also BRUSHES). Use canvas, canvasette, or one of the canvas substitutes as a ground [see also CANVAS, CANVAS SUBSTITUTES, PAINT SUBSTITUTES, PAPERS, and SUPPLIES (CLASSROOM)].

Poster Paint:

Characteristics:

1. Water-soluble, concentrated bottle paints.

2. Used for illustration work, design, and posters.

3. Opaque paint.

4. It is not waterproof.

Poster paint is available in bottles of 2, 8, 16, and 32 ounces and also in gallons. Use watercolor or lettering brushes with poster paint (see also BRUSHES). Use illustration board, poster board, railroad board, or heavy paper as a ground for poster paints (see also PAPERS and POSTERS).

Tempera Paint:

Characteristics:

1. Water-soluble, powder-type paint which is available in shaker cans; and is used extensively in all school art programs.

2. Has opaque quality when mixed properly; mix 2 parts tempera powder paint with 1 part water.

3. More water can be added for a transparent mixture.

4. Preservatives may be added to insure freshness if paints are to be kept over a period of time (see also PRE-SERVATIVES).

Tempera paint is available in 1-pound cans in all colors, including "flesh." Extenders are used to make paints go further (see also EXTENDERS). Use easel brushes for tempera powder paint (see also BRUSHES). Use newsprint, white art paper, or manila paper as a ground; use kraft paper or butcher paper for mural work (see also MURALS and PAPERS). Try mixing tempera powder paint with liquid starch for an interesting painting medium. Starch may be diluted with water. A kindergarten tempera painting rendered on the back of oilcloth is shown in Fig. P-1.

Watercolor:

Characteristics:

1. Transparent, water-soluble medium in cake or tube form.

2. Slow drying; not waterproof.

3. White paint is not included in watercolor sets, but is achieved characteristically by allowing the paper or ground to show through (see also GROUND).

4. It is a "fresh," quickly rendered medium and should not be overworked or overpainted.

Fig. P-1

5. It has been said of watercolor painting that it takes four hours to plan and four minutes to paint. See Fig. P-2.

Fig. P-2

Watercolor paints are available in boxes, in sets of 4, 7, 8, and 16 colors, and as semimoist cakes of paint. They are also available in ½" x 2" tubes. Use watercolor or oriental brushes with watercolor paints. Use watercolor paper, newsprint, white art paper, or manila paper as a ground [see also BRUSHES, PAPERS, SUPPLIES (CLASSROOM), and WASH].

PAINTS

Paints may be classified as follows: water-base paints, oil-base paints, and household paints which are used for wood finishes. Water-base paints which are used extensively in art programs are: casein, finger paint, gouache, poster, tempera, and watercolor (see also ACETATE COLORS and PAINTING). Oil-base paints which are used in art programs are referred to as "oils" and are used specifically for oil canvas-type paintings. Household paints may be classified as enamels, acrylic, rubber-base, varnishes, shellacs, lacquers, and stains (see also LACQUER, SHELLAC, SOLVENTS, SPRAYS, and VARNISH).

NOTE: Water-base or oil-base paints should not be confused with water-base or oil-base inks which are used specifically for printing processes (see also INKS, PRINTING INK SUBSTITUTES, and TEXTILE COLORS).

PAINT SUBSTITUTES

Casein-Like Mixture: Mix powdered paint with canned milk.

Enamel-Like Mixture: Mix equal amounts of powdered tempera with spar varnish.

Gouache-Like Mixture: Use poster paint as a thicker medium.

Oil-Like Mixture: Mix tempera powder with white resin glue.

Poster-Like Mixture: Use tempera as a thicker medium.

Watercolor-Like Mixture: Use casein, poster paint, or tempera, each fully diluted. A type of "Japanese watercolor" mixture can be made by soaking some colored tissue paper in water and using the resulting colored water as a painting medium [see also JAPANESE WATERCOLORS, PAPERS, and TISSUE (COLORED)].

PAINT THINNERS

See SOLVENTS.

PALEOLITHIC PERIOD

Refers to Old Stone Age [see also ALTAMIRA, HISTORY (ART), LASCAUX, and NEOLITHIC PERIOD].

EXAMPLES: Cave paintings at Altamira, Spain, and at Lascaux, France.

PAPER CUTTER

Standard size of paper cutter (Fig. P-3) is 18″ x 18″ and is recommended as a basic size for both elementary and secondary schools. The ration of distribution is one paper cutter per four classrooms on an elementary level and one paper cutter per art classroom on a secondary level [see also SUPPLIES (CLASSROOM)].

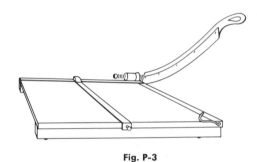

Fig. P-3

PAPERS

Standard sizes: 9″ x 12″, 12″ x 18″, 18″ x 24″, 24″ x 36″, and 36″ x 54″.

Standard colors: Red, orange, yellow, green, blue, and violet.

Ground: Any surface on which one draws or paints; relates to cardboards as well as papers in this categorical listing.

Quire of paper: 24 sheets.

Ream of paper: 20 quires or 500 sheets.

Ply: Refers to thickness of paper in laminated effect such as 1 ply, 2 ply or 3 ply; thickness increases proportionately with numbers (see also LAMINATED PAPER).

Rag content and weight: Refers to quality of paper; rag content denotes quality paper, as does a heavier weight.

Kinds of Papers and Cardboards:

Alphatone: Rough-textured, oatmeal-type paper; used for colored chalk, watercolor, crayon, and printmaking; available in standard sizes and in rolls of 36″ x 300′.

Blotting paper: Absorbent; used to pick up excess water in watercolor painting and as a ground in printmaking. Standard size is 18″ x 24″.

Bogus paper: Absorbent and gray; used for charcoal,

pen and ink, chalk, and printmaking; available in standard sizes.

Bristol board: Smooth-surfaced cardboard which can be used on both sides; available in various plys from 1 to 5 and in colors, including white. It is used extensively by professional artists for pen and ink drawings, pencil, crayon, and water-soluble paints. The standard size of Bristol board is 22½″ x 28⅛″.

Butcher paper: White, slick-surfaced, roll paper which is used for finger painting, crayon, sgraffito, and mural making; available in rolls of 1000′ with widths of 15″, 18″, 24″, 30″, and 36″.

Canvasette: Inexpensive replacement for canvas board; used for oil as well as casein painting; available in packages of ten sheets, in sizes 9″ x 12″, 12″ x 16″, and 16″ x 20″.

Carbon: For duplication or transfer of designs onto another surface or ground; available in sizes 8½″ x 11″ and 19″ x 26″ and in colors of blue, black, green, red, white, and yellow. Colored carbon is useful in transferring a design onto a fabric ground as in stitchery.

Cellophane: Thin, transparent, colored waterproof paper which is available in individual sheets of 20″ x 30″ or in rolls.

Charcoal paper: Used specifically for fine charcoal drawings; may be purchased by the sheet or quire in standard size of 19″ x 25″.

Chipboard: Heavy gray cardboard in varied thicknesses: No. 40 (thickest), No. 50, No. 60, and No. 70 (thinnest). It is used in booklet making and, in its thickest ply, for drawing boards and easels. It is available in a standard size of 26″ x 38″.

Colored tissue: See Tissue and Tissue (colored) in this listing.

Construction paper: Most common colored paper found in school art programs. It is a heavier paper than tonal or poster paper, and it is used for paper sculpture, mounting and matting, painting, crayon, charcoal, and printmaking. It is available in standard sizes and in a wide range of colors, tones, tints, and shades.

Contact paper: Paper with adhesive backing which makes immediate contact with wood, concrete, or plaster; available in patterns as well as solid colors; can be pur-

chased by the yard or roll, in widths of 18″ and 36″.

Corrugated paper: Wavy, corrugated, textured paper; available in a wide range of colors, including black, gray, and white. It is used for bulletin boards, stage sets, mounting and matting, collage techniques, and decorative papers. It can be purchased in rolls of 49″ x 25′.

Craft paper: See Kraft paper in this listing.

Crepe paper: Soft, textured paper which is available in all colors, including black, white, gray, gold, silver, and copper. It is used extensively in costume making, decorations, and crepe-paper crafts. It can be purchased in folds of 20″ x 7½′ and in streamer rolls of 2½″ x 35′.

Display-tex: See Corrugated paper in this listing.

Drawing paper (white): An all-purpose, slightly rough-textured paper which is most commonly used in general art programs in the schools. It is available at the utilitarian, economical weight of 60 pounds and at the finer heavier weight of 80 pounds. It is used for ink, watercolor, pencil, crayon, charcoal, decorative papers, and printmaking and is available in standard sizes.

Drawing paper (manila): An all-purpose, slightly rough-textured, cream-colored paper which is most commonly used in general art programs in the schools. It is available in standard sizes and is used for the same purposes as listed for white drawing paper.

Dry-mount tissue: For mounting work with the dry-mount press; available in envelopes of 12, in boxes of 144 sheets, in sizes: 5″ x 7″, 8″ x 10″, 11″ x 14″, 14″ x 17″, 16″ x 20″, and in rolls of 16″ x 100′ and 32″ x 100′.

Easel paper: See Newspaper liners, and Newsprint in this listing.

Etching paper: Fine type of paper made especially for etchings, lithographs, and block prints; available in sizes 20″ x 30″ and 22½″ x 30½″.

Fadeless paper: Colored paper in vibrant hues which resists fading.

Finger paint paper: Glazed on one side; available in packages of 12, 24, and 100 sheets in size 16″ x 24″.

Fluorescent paper: Glows in sunlight or at night under light; available in vibrant colors of blue, cerise, chartreuse, red, orange, yellow-orange, red-orange, and green. It may be purchased by the single sheet or in packages of 12 or 100, in sizes 9″ x 12″ and 12″ x 18″.

Foil paper: Foil, backed with paper; available in brilliant colors in individual sheets or in rolls of 26″ x 10′, 26″ x 25′, and 26″ x 100′.

Gelatine paper: Available in sheets of colored, transparent paper, in size 20″ x 26″; used extensively in stagecraft for lighting effects and, in some instances, as color inlays in sculpture work relating to the stabile (see also JELLS).

Gold and silver paper: Not a foil paper; dull gold and dull silver paper with plain paper or gummed backing; may be purchased by the single sheet or in packages of 12 or 100, in size 20″ x 26″.

Graphite paper: Thin paper coated with graphite which is used to transfer drawings onto another ground; available in size 17″ x 22″.

Illustration board: White, smooth-surfaced cardboard for pen and ink drawings, pencil, crayon, or water-soluble paints; used for illustration work in advertising. It is available in varied thicknesses or plys and in sizes from 20″ x 30″ to 30″ x 40″.

Japanese paper: See Rice paper in this listing.

Jello wrapping: Obtained from packages of Jello; used as a substitute material for stencil paper.

Kraft paper: Brown, roll paper which is used for murals, pastels, etc.; available in rolls of 1000′ and in widths of 15″, 18″, 24″, 30″, and 36″.

Liners: See Newspaper liners in this listing.

Manila paper: See Drawing paper (manila) in this listing.

Marble paper: Commercially made marbled paper which is available in rolls of 26″ x 45′ and 26″ x 10′; used as decorative lining sheets in booklet making.

Mat board: Available in traditional white or cream with egg-shell texture or in color, in varied ply, and in standard size of 30″ x 40″.

Mimeograph stencil backs: Used as a substitute material for stencil paper.

Newspaper: May be used to cover working areas during art activities, as a textured material for the collage, for the montage, and as a ground for easel painting and printmaking.

Newspaper liners: Want-ad sections of newspapers; used as a practice paper in rendering lettering. Turned sideways, the paper presents ready-made guidelines for letters. Liners are also used as a substitute for easel paper and as a textured paper for printmaking and the collage.

Newsprint (plain or natural): Used for all easel painting, including watercolor, pencil drawing, crayon, chalk, and charcoal, and for decorative papers and printmaking processes; available in standard sizes.

Newsprint (colored): Used for same purposes as listed for plain newsprint; available in colors of yellow, blue, pink, green, and orange and in standard sizes.

Oak tagboard: Strong, tough, manila-colored cardboard which folds without cracking; used for mounting, matting, charts, and stencils; available in standard size of 24″ x 36″.

Onion-skin paper: Used for tracing and transfer of designs; available in reams in size 8½″ x 11″.

Origami paper: Used for the art of Japanese paper folding known as origami; available in colors.

Ozalid paper: Used for ozalid copying machines and for classroom art experiences in the making of ozalid prints; available by the ream in size 8½″ x 11″.

Paper towels: School-supplied paper toweling as well as kitchen toweling is used as a ground for block printing, crayon resist, and the final finishing coats in the strip papier-mâché process.

Parchment: Available in genuine sheepskin or in synthetic parchment; used for scrolls and diplomas. Synthetic parchment is less expensive than the genuine, although they are quite similar in appearance. Synthetic parchment is available in semitransparent, semiopaque, and mottled finishes. It is sold by the single sheet or by the yard.

Poster board: Cardboard which is colored on one side only; used extensively for poster work and is available in varied thicknesses from $\frac{1}{16}$″ to ⅛″. Sizes range from 22″ x 28″ to 30″ x 40″.

Poster paper: Also known as tonal paper; available in the same colors as construction paper, but it is lighter in weight and easier for small children to cut. It is used in mounting and cut-paper work, as well as in printmaking and is available in standard sizes.

Pre-Sure-Stick paper: Opaque, white paper with an adhesive backing which will stick to any surface with pressure; used for labels and masking. It may be used for nameplates for social affairs and conventions, eliminating the need of pins.

Railroad board: Cardboard with a smooth surface and colored on both sides; used for poster work and matting; generally available in a 4-ply thickness, in size 22″ x 28″.

Rice paper: Imported, textured paper which is extremely lightweight; used for block printing and other printing processes. It is available by the single sheet, in packages of 12, 100, and in ream quantities in sizes 20″ x 30″ and 24″ x 36″.

Scratchboard: Plain white cardboard which can be coated with black ink for scratchboard drawing. Scratchboard is also available with a black coating which is ready for use. It is available in sizes 11″ x 14″ and 22″ x 28″.

Shelf paper: Available in rolls at variety or hardware stores, in either colored or white; used as a substitute for finger paint paper.

Showcard board: Extremely heavy, colored cardboard, heavier than poster board; generally available in 14-ply thickness, in standard size of 22″ x 28″.

Silhouette paper: Smooth-surfaced paper which is black on one side and white on the other; available in single sheets or in packages of 12 or 100, in size 20″ x 26″.

Stencil paper: Transparent, moisture-resistant paper; usually heavily waxed. Transparency allows for tracing and eliminates use of carbon for transfer of design. It is available in 12- and 20-sheet packages, in sizes 9″ x 12″, 12″ x 18″, and 18″ x 24″.

Tagboard: See Oak tagboard in this listing.

Tissue: Available at variety or department stores in folds of 8 sheets, in size 20″ x 30″; colors include white, green, pink, blue, yellow, and red. NOTE: This tissue is not to be confused with imported Belgian colored tissue which is referred to consistently in this book.

Tissue (colored): Brilliant and intense colors; in spectral hues, including tints, shades, and tones. Nonspectral colors are also included such as sienna, umber, black, and gray. Tissue is sold both by the quire and by the ream, in size 20″ x 30″.

Tonal paper: See Poster paper in this listing.

Tracing paper: See Onion-skin paper in this listing.

Tru-Tone paper: Colored paper in vibrant hues which resists fading.

Watercolor paper: Used exclusively for watercolor painting; may be purchased by the single sheet in lots of 12, 24, or 100, or in a ream. It is also available in tablet form. It has varied weights, from 72 pounds single to 140 pounds double, and a range of textures from smooth to very rough.

Waxed paper: Paper with a waxed surface which is available in grocery stores in rolls. It is used in general art programs particularly for laminated papers such as shoji.

Woodgrain paper: Simulated wood effects on paper; used as lining sheets in booklet making; available in varied woods and in rolls of 26″ x 30′ and 26″ x 45′.

NOTE: Sizes may vary with different papers and vendors.

PAPER SCULPTURE

The art of paper sculpture employs the following techniques, either alone or in combination, to achieve three-dimensional paper forms (Fig. P-4):

Fig. P-4

Curled Paper: Achieved by cutting a strip of paper and holding it between the thumb and the sharp, open edge of a scissors' blade. The paper is pulled toward the person doing the curling and light pressure is applied with the thumb.

Cut Paper: See CUTTING.

Folded Paper: Used in cutting symmetrical forms, either a single symmetrical form by folding once or multiple symmetrical forms by folding the paper in accordion fashion.

Scored Paper: Achieved by "scoring" or cutting the grain of the paper with an X-Acto knife. The paper is not cut all the way through. It is cut just enough so that when the paper is bent in the opposite direction from the scoring, it will provide a paper hinge and will achieve dimension to the flat paper plane (see also DIMENSION and KNIVES).

Torn Paper: See TORN PAPER.

The art of paper sculpture is an exciting process wherein flat, two-dimensional paper can achieve a third dimension of depth by cutting, curling, folding, tearing, and scoring. Paper-sculptured forms can be achieved with or without the use of adhesives and can be used effectively on bulletin boards, dioramas, charts, masks, murals, peep shows, and posters (see also DIORAMAS, MURALS, PEEP SHOWS, and POSTERS).

NOTE: Suggested source books for teachers include: Pauline Johnson, *Creating with Paper* (Seattle, Wash.: University of Washington Press, 1958); Marie Gilbert Martin, *Pasteless Construction with Paper* (New York: Pageant Press); and Edith C. Becker, *Scissors and Paper* (Scranton, Pa.: International Textbook Company, 1959).

PAPIER-MÂCHÉ

Basically there are two methods of working with papier-mâché: the pulp method and the strip method.

Pulp papier-mâché: Picked up by the hand and patted or molded into shape. The use of an armature support depends entirely upon the size of the article. Pulp papier-mâché can be used to cover models, molds, or armatures, or to build relief maps (see also ARMATURES, MAPMAKING, and MODELING MATERIALS). Coloring such as powdered tempera may be added to the pulp before modeling with it, or it may be applied to the surface of the form when the pulp papier-mâché is dry.

To make pulp papier-mâché, one would tear or shred approximately 30 sheets of newspaper. Soak the shredded newspaper in warm water for 48 hours. Squeeze out as much of the water as possible. Add a wheat-paste mixture to the pulp using 1 part wheat paste to 4 parts pulp (see also WHEAT PASTE). The pulp is now ready for use as a modeling material or for covering an armature. If the mixture is to be kept for any length of time, add a few drops of oil of cloves or some other type of preservative agent (see also PRESERVATIVES).

Additional pointers: Add a little plaster of paris to the pulp mixture to attain extra hardness. Use plaster in dry form. When using pulp papier-mâché for relief maps, add 1½ teaspoons of glue to the pulp mixture. This will increase the adhesive quality of the material and will allow it to stick to plywood more effectively (see also MAPMAKING).

Strip papier-mâché: Literally laid down over a form, strip by strip. The difference lies in the fact that when pulp papier-mâché is used, the pulp becomes the article being formed; while when the strip papier-mâché is used, the strip can either become the article being formed or can duplicate a form or mold and be lifted off. It is used primarily to duplicate modeled objects such as puppet heads made of plastic clay or masks made of earth clay. It can be used over commercial objects such as bowls for purposes of duplication. The strip method can also be used over crumpled newspaper armatures in order to build up the form in terms of detail and give it a final even-textured finish (see also ARMATURES).

The size of the article being reproduced with the strip method will determine the size of the strips to be used. Use large strips of paper for larger areas and smaller pieces for small, detailed areas. The strips are dipped into a mixture of wheat paste (see also WHEAT PASTE). Pull these strips of paper between the fingers to remove the excess paste. Apply the strips directly to the modeled form. Lay on the strips in all directions to insure strength. A slight overlapping is necessary.

At least five layers of strip papier-mâché should be applied to larger objects. Smaller objects may take as few as three layers. It is recommended that different kinds of paper be used so that one might easily determine where one layer ends and another begins.

First layer: Newspaper liner sheets
Second layer: Green sports-section sheets

Third layer: Comic section

Fourth layer: Paper toweling (for a fine-textured finish)

Fifth layer: Toilet tissue or Kleenex (for a finer-textured finish)

If extremely large articles are being made, use a layer of torn, brown paper bags or brown kraft paper for the third layer in place of the comic section to insure strength.

Additional pointers: If the strip papier-mâché is being used over crushed newspaper forms and will not be lifted from the form, use paste on the first layer and on all succeeding layers. On the other hand, if the strip papier-mâché is to be used over a form or mold, for purposes of duplication, *do not use paste on the first layer of paper applied.* Simply dip the strip paper in water and allow the water to provide the adhesive necessary for the first layer of paper which will cover the form. This will insure easy removal when the dry strip papier-mâché is either pulled from the form or cut away from it.

An alternate method to dipping the strip paper in water is to apply a thin coating of petroleum jelly to the object or form being duplicated. The strips of paper will adhere to the object or form with the help of the petroleum jelly. Succeeding layers, of course, will necessitate the use of wheat paste. Make certain that the strips follow the contour of the form. Do not allow a large piece of strip papier-mâché to take the place of several smaller strips. Large strips in small areas will fold over and create a bumpy surface.

It will be necessary in fine detail work, such as working around the areas of the nose and mouth in puppetry, to press the small strips down with a nail file, modeling tool, or similar kind of instrument. Allow the papier-mâché to dry thoroughly before attempting to take it from a mold, if a mold is used. Generally, papier-mâché will dry thoroughly in 24 hours if only one layer is involved; two or more layers will take at least 48 hours. It is not necessary to allow one layer to dry before another is added, although in finer papier-mâché work, it is highly desirable. It is better to tear the strips rather than to cut them. Cut-paper strips appear harsh when dry.

Paper toweling is always used for the final finishing coat. The texture is rich and interesting and provides a desirable surface for painting. However, as indicated earlier, a finer finish may be achieved by using either Kleenex or toilet tissue over the paper toweling. If a mask or a bowl is being reproduced with the strip method, the papier-mâché is easily removed from the mold when it is dry, provided, of course, that there are no undercuts (see also UNDERCUTS).

With modeled puppet heads or animals made of clay, the strip papier-mâché is cut from the form in two separate halves and is then patched together with another layer of papier-mâché. For puppets, animals, and other forms made from crushed newspaper, with or without an armature inside, the strip papier-mâché acts as a finishing layer, or layers, over the form. The crushed newspaper and/or armature, if one is used, is not removed.

Papier-Mâché Animals:

Type 1: Construct armature of wire. Pad with newspaper, tying it in place with string. Cover with strip papier-mâché. Paint with tempera, shellac, and add decorative details such as button eyes, raffia tails, etc. (see also ARMATURES, PAINT, SCRAP MATERIALS and SHELLAC).

Type 2: Form animal with crushed newspaper. Bend, crush, and press newspaper into shape and tie with string. Tie appendages to main form if necessary. Use masking or cellulose tape for additional strength. Cover animal with strips of papier-mâché. Paint with tempera, shellac, and add decorative details (see also PAINT, SCRAP MATERIALS, and SHELLAC).

Type 3: For smaller animals, model forms with either plastic or earth clay [see also CERAMICS and CLAY (PLASTIC)]. Plastic clay will not necessitate a period of waiting for it to dry, but earth clay will. When modeling, exaggerate the details and avoid the four-legged animals, that is, avoid modeling four separate legs. It is better to suggest the four legs through depressions between the front and back legs. This will not only create a better design but will insure greater strength for standing. Cover form with strips of papier-mâché. Make certain that the first layer does not contain paste, since the papier-mâché shell will be cut from this animal and the lack of paste on the first layer will insure easy removal.

After the papier-mâché is dry, begin to cut it away from the clay form, using an X-Acto knife (see also

KNIVES). Cut horizontally across the top back. Continue cutting in a line which goes between the ears on the head, down the middle of the face, under the neck, between the depressions on the legs, and under the stomach. Continue cutting until the animal is halved. Pull the two halves away from the clay form. Place the two halves together and patch the animal whole again with strips of papier-mâché along the cut edges only. Allow to dry, then add paint, shellac, and decorative details. See Fig. P-5 (see also PAINT, SCRAP MATERIALS, and SHELLAC).

Fig. P-5

Papier-Mâché Bowls: Use a commercial bowl of any sort as a mold, provided, of course, that it does not have any undercuts (see also UNDERCUTS). Cover the outside surface of the bowl with a thin coating of petroleum jelly. Apply the first layer of strip papier-mâché without using wheat paste. Build up five or six layers of strip papier-mâché over the bowl. When dry, remove from the bowl, paint with tempera, decorate, and varnish (see also VARNISH). For an additional experience, use papier-mâché over boxes fastened together to build a totem pole (see also TOTEM POLES).

Papier-Mâché Figures: May be constructed in the same manner as types 1, 2, and 3 of the animal forms described previously.

Papier-Mâché Fruit: Apply a thin layer of petroleum jelly on the surface of the fruit which will be used as molds for duplication. Use bananas, pears, apples, oranges, or plums. Add several layers of strip papier-mâché. When the papier-mâché is dry, cut the form in half with an X-Acto knife and pull away from the fruit mold, as previously described. Paint, shellac, and add decorative details such as colored pipe cleaners for stems, etc. *Try this with vegetables too!* (See also PAINT, SCRAP MATERIALS, SHELLAC).

Papier-Mâché Globes: Weather balloons make excellent forms for the construction of papier-mâché world globes. They can be obtained from surplus stores and sometimes from weather stations. Attach a metal hook to the ceiling and hang the weather balloon from it with a piece of wire. Apply layers of strip papier-mâché to the balloon after first giving it a coating of petroleum jelly.

In this process, the weather balloon may remain inside permanently or the world-globe shell may be cut away. In the first instance, the petroleum jelly will act as a lubricant to allow the balloon to drop from the shell when the air in it eventually escapes. Without this lubricant, the balloon would pull the globe inward, disturbing the symmetry of the form. In the second instance, if the shell form is to be cut from the balloon, the petroleum jelly will afford easier removal, as described previously. Additional geographical details may be added later with a light application of pulp papier-mâché. The globe may be finished with a covering of spackle when the papier-mâché is thoroughly dry (see also SPACKLE).

Papier-Mâché Maracas: Cover ordinary light bulbs with four or five layers of strip papier-mâché. When the layers are thoroughly dry, tap the light bulb form sharply on a hard surface. The light bulb will break inside the covering of papier-mâché and the broken bits of glass inside will make the "music" when the maracas are shaken. Should the maracas dent a little when they are hit over the hard surface, the dents can be pulled up with the aid of a large needle or similar instrument. Another coating of strip papier-mâché will repair the damage. Paint the maracas with bright colors, adding streamers of ribbon or raffia to the handles.

NOTE: In classroom projects involving the breaking of light bulbs, it would be well if the teacher assumed the responsibility of doing the breaking.

Papier-Mâché Masks:

Type 1: Fashion mask with earth clay on a flat board or piece of masonite; allow it to dry thoroughly. Apply five layers of strip papier-mâché to the mask. For reasons previously described, make certain that the first layer does not contain paste. Either dip the strips of paper in water or apply a thin layer of petroleum jelly to the mask. When the papier-mâché has dried, lift the mask from the clay mold. If your mask does not contain any undercuts, it will lift up easily (see also UNDERCUTS). Trim the edges with a pair of scissors, and finish them with masking tape (see also TAPES). Give the entire area of the outer edge a coating of strip papier-mâché as a final finishing. Allow to dry, then add paint, shellac, and decorative details (Fig. P-6) (see also PAINT, SCRAP MATERIALS, and SHELLAC).

Fig. P-6

Type 2: Fashion mask with plastic clay and proceed as directed in type 1. Plastic clay does not need to harden and papier-mâché may be added immediately [see also CLAY (PLASTIC)].

Type 3: Fashion mask with crushed newspaper in the following manner: Wrap crushed newspaper in a single sheet of newspaper and tape it closed with masking tape at the back (see also TAPES). Open up a folded sheet of newspaper so that it is a long rectangle in shape. Roll this into a long cylinder. Lay the cylinder on a table and flatten it with the hands into a long strip. Wrap this band or strip around the edge of the crushed newspaper form and tape the edges down around it, overlapping if necessary. This is the working base for a mask.

Build up the features by using crushed newspaper, styrofoam, or pieces of cardboard and tape them into place (see also STYROFOAM). Cover the entire mask with strip papier-mâché. When finished, paint with tempera and shellac, and add decorative details.

NOTE: If you wish this mask to "lift off," do not cover the back of it with strip papier-mâché. Simply build up the layers of strip papier-mâché to the front and sides of the mask form. When the papier-mâché is dry, you may carefully pull the "stuffings" out from the back of the mask.

Type 4: Using stuffed paper bags or blown up balloons and the same techniques as described in type 3, papier-mâché masks may be formed.

Papier-Mâché Ornaments: Roll small balls of pulp papier-mâché in the hands and stick paper clips into the top of the balls while the pulp is still wet. Allow these balls to dry, paint with tempera, shellac, and add glitter (see also GLITTER, PAINT, and SHELLAC).

Papier-Mâché Puppets:

Type 1: Fashion puppet with plastic clay around a wooden dowel stand. A wooden dowel stand consists of a 10" length of round, ½" doweling which has been nailed perpendicularly to a 6" square wooden base, as shown in Fig. P-7 (see also DOWELING). As the puppet head is

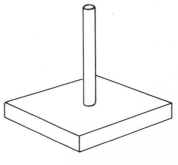

Fig. P-7

P

being fashioned on the dowel stand, keep in mind that the features should be exaggerated and that the neck will have to be formed around the dowel with clay. When finished with the modeling of the head, apply strips of papier-mâché to the clay head and neck. Remember not to add paste to the first layer!

Several layers of strip papier-mâché will be needed. Because the object is small, use small pieces of strip papier-mâché. When the papier-mâché has dried, cut the shell head off the clay head with an X-Acto knife (see also KNIVES). Start cutting from the top of the head with a cutting motion which runs from ear to ear. Cut to the ears on each side, down in back of the ears, and down the neck. Pull the two halves of the shell head off the puppet head form. Put the two halves together and patch with strips of papier-mâché. Paint with tempera and shellac, and add decorative details. Use raffia or yarn for hair and eyebrows (see also RAFFIA and YARNS AND STRINGS).

Puppet hands may be fashioned from plastic clay on the dowel stand once the puppet head has been removed. Strips of papier-mâché are applied to the hand form in the same manner. The shell hands are cut away from the plastic-clay hand molds in a vertical manner, and they are patched together again with strips of papier-mâché. Hands are painted, shellacked, and sewn to the puppet costume at the sleeves. The puppet head is sewn to the puppet costume at the neck.

Type 2: Put a light bulb into a wooden base, or set the light bulb into a base of plastic clay. Cover it with a thin layer of petroleum jelly. Apply several layers of strip papier-mâché to the light bulb. Build up the features with plastic clay. Cover this again with several layers of strip papier-mâché. The puppet is cut off the light bulb in the same manner as was described in type 1. It is then patched together, painted with tempera, shellacked, and decorative details are added.

NOTE: For additional ways of making puppets, excluding the use of the papier-mâché process (see also PUPPETS).

PAPIER-MÂCHÉ ANIMALS

See PAPIER-MÂCHÉ.

PAPIER-MÂCHÉ BOWLS

See PAPIER-MÂCHÉ.

PAPIER-MÂCHÉ FIGURES

See PAPIER-MÂCHÉ.

PAPIER-MÂCHÉ FRUIT AND VEGETABLES

See PAPIER-MÂCHÉ.

PAPIER-MÂCHÉ GLOBES

See PAPIER-MÂCHÉ.

PAPIER-MÂCHÉ MARACAS

See PAPIER-MÂCHÉ.

PAPIER-MÂCHÉ MASKS

See PAPIER-MÂCHÉ.

PAPIER-MÂCHÉ ORNAMENTS

See PAPIER-MÂCHÉ.

PAPIER-MÂCHÉ PUPPETS

See PAPIER-MÂCHÉ.

PAPIERS COLLÉS

French term meaning "pasted papers"; an alternate term for collage (see also COLLAGE).

PAPYRUS

Ancient Egyptian method of making paper. The stems of the rush plant were cut into long strips, and placed horizontally, then vertically, on a flat working surface. These strips were first moistened, then pressed, and allowed to dry. The final step in the process was rubbing the surface of the papyrus with an abrasive of some sort and polishing it to a hard surface for writing. Egyptians used reed pens for writing on papyrus (see also EGYPTIAN ART, PAPER, PARCHMENT, and PENS).

PARAFFIN WAX

See WAX.

PARCHMENT

Historically, man first wrote on papyrus, then on parchment. Early parchment was used in the Byzantine era in book making and in the rendering of illuminations (see also BYZANTINE and ILLUMINATIONS). Parchment was made from stretched animal skins which had been rubbed smooth with abrasives (see also PAPYRUS). When parchment pages were ripped or torn, they were sewn together again with needles and thread.

Parchment which is made of sheepskin is called genuine parchment. There are less expensive synthetic parchment papers also on the market (see also PAPERS). Students have used the synthetic parchment in schools when making ship logs in correlation with studies relating to early commerce. The parchment is dipped into lemon juice or coffee to give the appearance of age. These pages are then put into the oven for additional browning and aging. Sometimes the corners of the parchment pages are burned to enhance the "weathered" look. The booklets or ship logs are most effective when they are bound in wood (see also BOOKLET MAKING). Ship logs provide motivation for historical exploration and research and chronicle the history of the United States as related to discovery and commerce.

Making Parchment Paper: Use tagboard or butcher paper. Mix 4 parts linseed oil with 1 part turpentine. Brush the mixture onto one side of the paper. With a soft cloth or a piece of Kleenex, rub this mixture into the grain of the paper. Repeat this process on the other side of the paper. Two coats of the linseed-turpentine mixture are more effective than one. When finished, lay the parchment between two sheets of absorbent paper, such as newsprint, until all of the excess oil has been absorbed.

PARCHMENT PAPER

See PAPERS and PARCHMENT.

PASTE

See ADHESIVES.

PASTE BRUSHES

See BRUSHES.

PASTELS

Similar to colored chalks; however, pastels are of a finer quality. They are used primarily in landscapes, seascapes, and portraitures. They are available in single sticks or in sets of 12 to 300 sticks. Pastels are used in the same manner as colored chalks. They are rubbed with the fingers, paper stumps, and chamois skins. The chief disadvantages of pastels for school programs are that they break easily and are rather costly as a medium. There are, however, pastel holders which are made of aluminum, and these help to keep the sticks of soft pastels from breaking.

PASTE WAX

See WAX.

PATCHING PLASTER

See SPACKLE.

PATTERNS

Repetition of a design or a motif; also called allover patterns and repeat patterns; commonly used in the printmaking processes such as the potato print, rubber tube print, stencil print, and gadget print, among others. Figure P-8 shows standard types of repeat patterns: (a) full repeat, (b) full-drop repeat, and (c) an alternate full-drop repeat.

Encouraging students to experiment will develop an awareness relative to how the character of the same design can change through variations of placement. Further experimentation will extend understanding and promote more latitudes for freedom of placement in allover-pattern design. Slight irregularities of placement, inverting, overlapping, and mixing media are all part of the discovery process which relates to the extension of understanding and a more sophisticated performance level. See Fig. P-9 which illustrates an allover pattern utilizing mixed media (see also MIXED MEDIA).

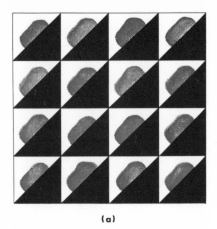

(a)

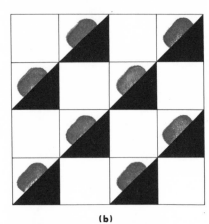

(b)

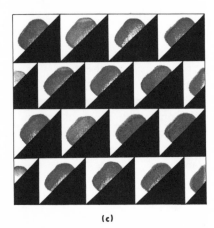

(c)

Fig. P-8

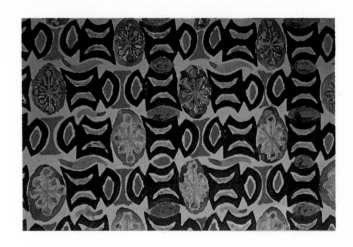

Fig. P-9

PAYONS

Payons are used like crayons but can be painted over with water to achieve a watercolor effect; it is a painting crayon. Sticks are 3½″ x ⁵⁄₁₆″ and are available in sets of 8 colors (see also CRAYONS, PAINT, and PAINTING).

PEEP SHOWS

Students may create pure designs or related social studies scenes within a shoebox for peep shows. A peephole is cut from one end of the box; and it is from this end that the viewing is done. A larger frame window is cut from the top of the box and covered with colored cellophane (see Fig. P-10). This larger frame window will emit the necessary light for the "show" (see also PAPERS). The scenes

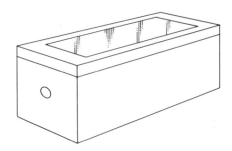

Fig. P-10

inside may be rendered with paint, crayon, chalk, or mixed media; and there can be a combination of two-dimensional as well as three-dimensional forms. Paper sculpture can be effectively used in peep shows, as can any of the modeling materials (see also DIMENSION, MIXED MEDIA, MODELING MATERIALS, and PAPER SCULPTURE, and for a related experience on a larger scale, see DIORAMAS).

PENCILS

Charcoal Pencils: Available with four degrees of hardness: hard, medium, soft, and extra soft (see also CHARCOAL).

Colored Pencils: Colored pencils may be brushed over with water and will produce watercolor effects, available in sets of 8, 12, and 24.

Drawing Pencils: These pencils have degrees of hardness and softness. A standard code which is stamped on some drawing pencils indicates whether or not a pencil is hard, medium, or soft:

Hard pencils: 4H, 5H, 6H, 7H, 8H, 9H (hardest)
Medium pencils: B, HB, F, H, 2H, 3H (hardest)
Soft pencils: 7B, 6B, 5B, 4B, 3B, 2B (hardest)

The pencil which is most commonly used for commercial illustration work is the pencil HB.

NOTE: Using a long point, which will break easily, is a good rule of thumb for the sketching artist. It will teach him to work lightly. Avoid the use of a pencil sharpener, for good pencil drawings, as it tends to produce a characterless line; use a sharp knife and rub the point on sandpaper or emery board (see also ABRASIVES and DRAWING).

PENS

Bamboo Pens or Reed Pens: Made from bamboo for use with black drawing ink; available in large, medium, and small sizes.

Cado Pens, Felt Pens, Flo-Master Pens, Magic Markers, etc.: Made to produce a continual flow of either black or colored ink from a felt nib point. These are excellent tools for chart work and drawing; they can be used on fabrics, papers, wood, glass, and metals. These pens can be purchased individually or in sets. Assortments of nibs or points are available, as well as assortments of refill inks (see also INKS).

Drawing Pens, India-Ink Pens, and Lettering Pens: Available in varied sizes and shapes within sizes; to be used with pen holders and black or colored drawing inks (see also INKS). Two brand names, Esterbrook and Speedball, are widely used in school art programs and are described here to show the range of pens available [see also PENS (CLEANER)].

Esterbrook Drawlet Lettering Pens: Available in round, square, and shading points in the following sizes:
Round points: 0 (smallest), 1, 2, 3, 4, 5 (largest)
Square points: 6 (smallest), 7, 8, 9 10 (largest)
Shading points: 11 (smallest), 12, 13, 14, 15, 16, 17, 18, 19 (largest)
These pens are available individually, by the dozen, or in sets of assortments.

Speedball Lettering Pens: Available in square, round, oblong, and oval tips in the following sizes:
Square tips, style A: A-5 (smallest), A-4, A-3, A-2, A-1, A-0 (largest)
Round tips, style B: B-6 (smallest), B-5, B-4, B-3, B-2, B-1, B-0 (largest)
Oblong tips, style C: C-6 (smallest), C-5, C-4, C-3, C-2, C-1, C-0 (largest)
Oval tips, style D: D-5 (smallest), D-4, D-3, D-2, D-1, D-0, D-00 (largest)
Use square tips for square Gothic and block letters; round tips for round Gothic or uniform lines; oblong tips for Roman, text, and shaded italics; and oval tips for Roman, text, and italics (see also ALPHABET and LETTERING). These pens are available individually, by the dozen, or in sets of assortments [see also BRUSHES (STEEL)].

PENS (CLEANER)

For removing dried waterproof drawing ink from nonabsorbent surfaces; available as Higgins Pen Cleaner in 2½-ounce containers. Articles can be immersed in this fluid from 30 minutes to 8 hours, depending on the condition of the pen or article. Rinse with water.

NOTE: All drawing pens, whether fountain or separate points, should be cleaned immediately after using them (see also PENS).

P

PERIODICALS

See MAGAZINES (ART).

PERSIAN ART

Early Persian art began in 539 B.C. and is considered one of the arts of antiquity. By the seventh century it was well established with art forms in pottery, figurines, and bronzes. After the conquest of Alexander the Great in 331 B.C., Persian art took on the flavor of the Greeks and Romans. It was also influenced by the conquest of Jenghiz Khan in A.D. 1215. By the fourteenth century the arts of book illuminations, tile marquetry, miniature paintings, and carpet designs developed [see also HISTORY (ART) and MARQUETRY].

PERSPECTIVE

There are two types of perspective: aerial, which is used by painters, and linear, which is used by draftsmen.

Aerial Perspective: In painting or other colored media, an illusion of space and distance is achieved through modification of color. Generally speaking, in the distance, dark colors become less intense or paler, and light colors become less intense and somewhat darker. For example, a black ship never appears jet black in the distance or on the horizon line of the ocean, it appears gray. A stark white ship never appears stark white in the distance or on the horizon line of the ocean, it appears gray. Therefore, to achieve the illusion of distance or perspective in aerial theory, the darks in the distance are not as dark as they would appear if they were in the foreground, nor are the lights in the distance as light as they would appear if they were in the foreground.

The foreground of the picture plane contains the darkest darks and the lightest lights. The middle plane of the picture, or that area between the background and the foreground, contains those colors which are not as pale or modified as the background colors or as intense and high-key as the foreground colors. Hence, through modification of color on the flat picture plane, one can achieve the illusion of space; this is called *aerial perspective*.

Linear Perspective: Relates to line; specifically, creating the illusion of distance and space through converging lines which, in actuality, are parallel. First, one establishes an eye-level line. This eye-level line is exactly what it implies: a line which is level with the eyes as one stands or sits and looks at a scene which would be duplicated on paper.

The eye-level line is not the same as the horizon line in placement, but runs parallel with it. One looks at a scene either above the horizon line, as on a hill looking down; on the horizon line, as at sea level, or looking straight across; or below the horizon line, as in a deep valley looking up. In any instance, the eye-level line is established on paper to correspond with the position of the viewer. It is on this line that a vanishing point, or points, are established. One would establish one vanishing point for one-point perspective and two, for two-point perspective.

One-point perspective: In Fig. P-11, you will note a cigar box as it is viewed head-on from *above* the eye-level line, *on* the eye-level line, and *below* the eye-level line.

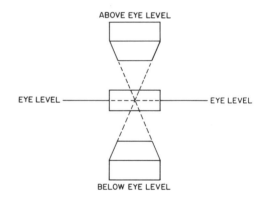

Fig. P-11

Two-point perspective: On the eye-level line, establish two vanishing points, as shown in Fig. P-12. Then establish the vertical line which is nearest to you, the viewer. In order to draw a cube, run lines from the top and bottom of the vertical line to vanishing point 1, and then to vanishing point 2. Next, draw a vertical line in the area of the converging lines leading to vanishing point 1 in order to delineate the side of the cigar box. Run a line from the top of the newly-established vertical line to vanishing point 2. Now draw a vertical line in the area of the converging lines leading to vanishing point 2 to delineate the other side of

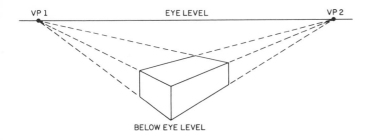

VP 1　　　　EYE LEVEL　　　　VP 2

BELOW EYE LEVEL

Fig. P-12

the cigar box. Run a line from the top of the established, second vertical line to vanishing point 1.

Figure P-12 shows a view of a cigar box as seen below one's line of vision. In other words, if one were standing up in a room and looking straight ahead, one's line of vision, or eye-level line, would be somewhere in the neighborhood of 5′ or 6′ high, established for pictorial purposes on the wall at which one would be looking. But, as one stood in this same position and looked down at a desk top on which there was placed a cigar box, the cigar box would be represented pictorially as below the eye-level line, and would appear as illustrated in Fig. P-12.

Try drawing a cigar box above the line of vision, as it would appear if one were sitting on the floor and looking up at a glass desk top. Once these simple rules for perspective are practiced and understood, it will become easier to convert a cigar box into a gabled house or a barn.

PHOTO MONTAGE

See MONTAGE.

PICTURE WAX

See WAX.

PIGMENT

Relates to color in paints; together with the binder and the vehicle, a medium for painting is produced (see also BINDER, PAINT, PAINTING, PAINTS, and VEHICLE).

PINCERS

See WOODWORKING.

P

PINE

See WOODS.

PIPE CLEANERS

Use pipe cleaners as an introductory lesson in wire sculpture (see also SCULPTURE, WIRE, and WIRE TOOLS). Use colored pipe cleaners to fashion figures, or armatures for figures, to be used in dioramas and peep shows (see also ARMATURES, DIORAMAS, and PEEP SHOWS). Use pipe cleaners as a drawing tool with black drawing ink. They achieve interesting linear effects when used on wet paper (see also BAMBOO STICKS, DRAWING INKS, and PAPERS). Pipe cleaners are available in white and assorted colors.

PLANE

Level, flat, two-dimensional surface on which one draws or paints; also called the picture plane. A secondary meaning refers to flat areas which are rendered in design and composition.

PLANOGRAPHIC

One of the processes of the graphic arts; specifically refers to lithography, also known as surface printing. This technique was discovered in 1798. In the lithographic process, plates are prepared directly on a flat stone. The artist draws on it with lithographic crayons which are high in grease composition. The stone is then moistened and a greasy type of ink is applied; where there is moisture, the grease ink will be repelled and where there is greasy crayon, the ink will adhere. The paper is then placed on the stone and run through a lithographic press. Figure P-13 shows a lithograph by Georges Braque.

The lithographic process uses plates of zinc and aluminum as well as limestone. In addition to the lithographic crayon, special lithgraphic inks and tusche are used. The planographic process is essentially a surface method of printmaking, as the print will reproduce what is rendered on the plate. It is opposed to the relief or intaglio processes, where lines are incised into the plate or bitten in with acids [see also INTAGLIO and PRINTMAKING (PROFESSIONAL)].

P

Fig. P-13

PLASTER OF PARIS

Plaster of paris is a derivative of gypsum; it is a white chalky material which is available in 25- and 100-pound sacks. A 100-pound sack of plaster of paris costs approximately $2.00.

Directions for mixing plaster of paris: Use 2 cups of plaster of paris to 1¼ cups of water. Pour water into a bowl and add plaster slowly. Use either a spoon or the hands to mix the plaster; avoid "beating" it. When the plaster begins to thicken to about the consistency of thick cream, pour it into a mold. If coloring is desired, mix dry tempera powder paint or poster color into the mixture. To waterproof plaster for outdoor displays, paint with resin which is available at hardware stores [see also CARVING MATERIALS, CASTING (SAND), CHEESECLOTH, EXCELSIOR, LAMINATED RESIN, and SCULPTURE].

PLASTIC ARTS

Relates to three-dimensional art forms as opposed to the graphic arts which are two-dimensional. Plastic arts would include all forms of sculpture as well as ceramics (see also CARVING MATERIALS, MODELING MATERIALS, PLASTIC ARTS, RELIEF, and SCULPTURE).

PLASTICS

Wide assortments of plastic materials are now available for school art programs; these include acrylite, castolite, vinylite, cellulose acetate, lucite, fiberglass, laminates, phenolite, plexiglass, polyester resins, styrofoam and vinoflex (see also ACETATE SHEETING LAMINATED, LAMINATED RESIN, LUCITE, and STYROFOAM). In addition, there are auxiliary tools and materials available to use with plastics, including jewelry findings, hot pack ovens and heaters, buffing motors and wheels, resin dyes, adhesives, and plastic die presses (see also ADHESIVES, DIE, DYES, and FINDINGS).

NOTE: All of the aforementioned plastics and auxiliary tools and materials are available from Cope Plastics, Highway 100, Godfrey, Illinois.

PLASTIC SPRAY

See KRYLON.

PLIERS

See WIRE TOOLS and WOODWORKING.

PLY

Refers to thickness of papers and boards as well as of wood, as in plywood; a lamination (see also LAMINATED). Thicknesses are referred to as being 1 ply, 2 ply, 3 ply, etc. The increasing numbers designate thicker paper or wood (see also PAPERS and WOODWORKING).

PLYWOODS

See WOODS.

POINTILLISM

See NEOIMPRESSIONISM.

POP ART

A visual representation of something in the commercial world which, in the rendering, has become vulgar in distortion or scale, for example, a sculpture of a hamburger.

POPLAR (YELLOW)

See WOODS.

PORTRAITURE

Relates to the drawing or painting of the face (see also DRAWING).

POSITIVE SPACE

See DESIGN ELEMENTS and SILK SCREENING.

POSTER BOARD

See PAPERS.

POSTER PAINT

See PAINTING and PAINTS.

POSTER PAPER

Alternate term for tonal paper (see also PAPERS).

POSTERS

The most effective posters are rendered in a bold and simple manner, as the one in Fig. P-14, which attracts attention through contrast and simplicity. It is possible in a given culture to convey a message with one pictorial symbol or word. Posters were never intended to be literary tomes. People who view posters do not have time to read many lines of small print.

Posters are essentially attention-attracting devices: first, to attract the attention of the passerby; and second, to hold that attention until a given message is communicated. Attraction may be achieved through color and contrast. In poster rendering, it is best to limit color to choices of two or possibly three, as illustrated in the concept of counterchange (see also COUNTERCHANGE). The message itself should be simple. Avoid cluttered messages which neutralize the eye and negate attraction. When the lettering is rendered, it should be exacting and clear both in execution and content. Leave the "unusual" lettering effects for the art sophisticate who has a feeling for design as it relates to distortion in lettering. It is always preferable to render

lettering from left to right. Vertical and diagonal lettering can be confusing and difficult to read [see also ALPHABET, LETTERING, and LETTERING (CUT-PAPER)].

Use poster board as a ground for poster work. Use lettering pens, lettering brushes, and steel brushes for basic tool. An inexpensive T-square ruler is a valuable tool in the rendering of straight guidelines [see also BRUSHES, BRUSHES (STEEL), and RULERS]. Cut-paper work lends itself well to poster rendering, particularly cut-paper letters

Fig. P-14

and paper sculpture [see also LETTERING (CUT-PAPER) and PAPER SCULPTURE]. The collage and montage techniques are often employed in poster work, and the silk screen process is often used in mass-produced poster work (see also SERIGRAPHY and SILK SCREENING). As an example of classic poster making, see some of the posters of Toulouse-Lautrec.

POSTIMPRESSIONISM

An outgrowth of Impressionism in 1880, this movement was essentially a reaction against the Impressionistic dogma which laid emphasis on light, impressions, and colors of the spectrum. The Postimpressionists, who deplored the formlessness of Impressionism, put subjective emphasis on form. Adherents included: Cézanne, Gauguin, Toulouse-Lautrec, and Van Gogh (see also IMPRESSIONISM and NEOIMPRESSIONISM). Postimpressionism laid the ground work for Cubism which followed (see also CUBISM).

POT

See CERAMICS.

POTTERY MAKING

See CERAMICS.

POTTING

See CERAMICS.

PRE-HELLENIC ART

One of the arts of antiquity (see also ANTIQUITY and AEGEAN ART). Pre-Hellenic art was developed in the islands and coastal regions of the Aegean Sea. The Pre-Hellenic-Aegean or Cretan culture, which is associated with it, lasted from circa 4500 B.C. to 1200 B.C. [see also GREEK ART and HISTORY (ART)].

PREHISTORIC ART

Beginning some 20,000 years ago, the prehistoric periods include the Paleolithic (Old Stone Age), the Mesolithic (Transition), and Neolithic (New Stone Age) [see also ALTIMIRA, HISTORY (ART), LASCAUX, NEOLITHIC PERIOD, and PALEOLITHIC PERIOD].

PRESERVATIVES

Tempera paint, pulp papier-mâché, and some of the other modeling materials tend to take on a rancid odor when kept over a period of time. If preservatives are added to these mixtures, the paints will be kept smelling fresh, and mildew will be retarded in modeling materials.

For tempera paint: Add a dash of salt to tempera mixtures.

For modeling materials: Add a few drops of oil of pep-

permint, oil of cloves, or oil of wintergreen to modeling materials such as pulp papier-mâché, sawdust, and wheat paste, or asbestos and wheat paste. For an alternate preservative, add a teaspoon of boric acid to every pint of water used in preparing these mixtures (see also MODELING MATERIALS and PAINTS).

PRESERVING FLOWERS

There exists an old Victorian method of dipping flowers, or floral bouquets, into melted wax for preservation. When doing this, make sure that the melted wax is not excessively hot and the flowers are not wet. Years ago, wedding bouquets were preserved in this manner and displayed in dome-shaped glass cases. An alternate way of preserving flowers is illustrated with the pressing method and subsequent lamination technique (see also DECORATIVE PAPERS, DRYING WEEDS, LAMINATED, and PRESSING FLOWERS AND LEAVES).

PRESERVING LEAVES

See PRESSING FLOWERS AND LEAVES.

PRESERVING WEEDS

See DRYING WEEDS.

PRESS

See DRY-MOUNT PRESS.

PRESSING FLOWERS AND LEAVES

Flatten flowers or leaves on a piece of waxed paper and place another piece of waxed paper on top. Weight this with five or six heavy books. The longer the leaves or flowers are weighted, the drier and flatter they become. Smaller flowers and leaves may be used in the paper lamination techniques (see also DECORATIVE PAPERS, DRYING WEEDS, LAMINATED, and PRESERVING FLOWERS).

PRE-SURE-STICK PAPER

See PAPERS.

PRIMARY COLORS

See COLOR.

PRIMITIVE ART

Relates to art forms of prehistoric man, particularly those at Altamira and at Lascaux. It also includes the creative expressions of the Australian aborigines and the rock portraits as well as the stone carvings of the Eskimos, for example.

A secondary meaning relates to contemporary artists, as well as those in the past, whose paintings indicate that they lack classic training [see also HISTORY (ART)].

EXAMPLE: Paintings of Grandma Moses.

PRINTING INKS

See INKS and PRINTING INK SUBSTITUTES.

PRINTING INK SUBSTITUTES

Oil-Base Printing Ink: Mix 5 parts powdered paint with 1 part clear varnish and ½ part linseed oil. Take a little of this mixture and roll it out with a brayer on a piece of plate glass. When the printing ink begins to crackle in sound, it is ready to be applied with a brayer to a printing surface, such as a linoleum block (see also INKS and PRINTMAKING).

Spatter Ink: Mix 1 part powdered tempera with 4 parts water. Put mixture into a household spray can or brush it over a piece of screening with a scrub brush for spatter prints (see also HAND PRINTS, INK, and PRINTMAKING).

Water-Base Printing Ink: Mix powdered paint with glycerine. Put a little of this mixture on a piece of plate glass and roll it out with a brayer. When the printing ink begins to crackle in sound, it is ready to be applied with the brayer to a printing surface such as a linoleum block (see also INKS and PRINTMAKING).

Water-Base Silk Screen Ink: Use a detergent, such as Tide, with powdered tempera paint; add enough water to create a thick creamy mixture and beat with a fork (see also PRINTMAKING, SERIGRAPHY, and SILK SCREENING).

PRINTMAKING

This section deals specifically with classroom printmaking processes and in no way relates to professional printmaking such as the intaglio, planographic, relief, and stencil processes. For a more complete definition of terms and categories relating to these processes [see also PRINTMAKING (PROFESSIONAL)].

In all of the classroom printmaking experiences, variations may be achieved through both color and texture changes. The same printing plate may be dramatically altered in appearance through a change in the texture of the paper on which the print is taken, or by a change in the color (see also COLOR and PAPERS). Printing inks are available in a wide range of colors and have either water or oil bases (see also INKS). Variations of paper for a printing ground would include paper toweling, tissue, foil, alphatone paper, blotting paper, rice paper, classified newspaper sections, or construction paper (see also PAPERS).

Methods of applying paint or printing inks: Unless otherwise indicated in the foregoing processes, basically there will be two ways of applying ink to a surface which is to be printed: the stamp pad method and the brayer method.

Stamp pad method: Make a stamping pad for printing by folding several squares of paper toweling and place them in a saucer. Wet the paper toweling with water until the toweling is flat on the saucer. Sprinkle some powdered tempera over the wet paper toweling. Work this powdered tempera down into the toweling until the paper is thoroughly saturated with color. It may be necessary to add a little water. Onto the stamp pad, drop a little liquid glycerine. Work this around the top of the stamp pad. The glycerine will help to retard drying. Flat, cellulose sponges may substitute for folded paper towels.

NOTE: Commercial colored stamp pads may be used, and ink pads can be made more intense in color by brushing on some stamp pad ink (see also INKS).

The Brayer method: The brayer method involves the inking of a plate with a rubber brayer which is rolled across its surface and thereby charges the plate with ink. It is necessary to put a little of either water-base or oil-base printing ink on a piece of plate glass with the approximate measurements of 9″ x 12″ (see also BRAYER).

The ink is rolled out on the glass plate with the rubber brayer. The idea is to "prime" the ink so that it is of an even consistency. The ink is rolled over the glass with the rubber roller until a crackling sound occurs. This is usually an indication that the ink is evenly spread on the glass and is sufficiently well distributed on the rubber brayer roller so that when the brayer is rolled over a printing plate, it will spread the ink evenly. This method of "inking the plate" requires rolling the rubber brayer over the printing surface until all of the areas which will be printed are thoroughly and evenly charged with ink.

Method of establishing surface on which to do printing: Prints will be more effective when they are stamped or pressed on a surface which has some padding. Lay a Sunday newspaper on the table where the printing will be done. For example, if a potato print were to be rendered, the paper ground on which the print would be taken would be laid on top of the pack of Sunday newspaper. Thereafter, each print would be pressed down on this surface. The elasticity and "bounce" of a soft surface will produce a print of high quality.

Block Prints (Linoleum Block Prints): Incise, or cut away, a design on a linoleum block with linoleum cutters (see also LINOLEUM BLOCKS, LINOLEUM CUTTERS, and RELIEF). Use the brayer method of applying printing ink to the surface of the linoleum block. Place the block face down on the printing paper. Apply pressure to the back of the block—stepping on it is most effective. An example of a linoleum-block print is shown in Fig. P-15. You may also use one of the commercial block printing presses.

NOTE: Using the same technique as indicated in the linoleum block, incise a design on a rectangle of soft apple wood with linoleum tools. The resulting print would be called a woodcut [see also PRINTMAKING (PROFESSIONAL), PRINTS, and RELIEF].

Bottle Print: Paint a design on a tall wine or oil bottle with tempera paint to which a little glycerine has been added. Roll the bottle over the print paper for a bottle print. See Fig. P-16.

Brayer Print: On two or three pieces of plate glass, put different hues of printing inks. Roll out the ink with a brayer on each plate, using a separate brayer for each color.

Fig. P-15

Fig. P-16

On another piece of plate glass, roll out free areas of color with different brayers and different inks. Try to change line and direction, overlapping colors and taking advantage of textural possibilities. Place the print paper over the surface of the inked glass. Gently apply pressure to the back of the paper with the palm of the hand. Lift up the paper for the brayer print. See Fig. P-17.

NOTE: It is possible to print two or three of the same design from the glass plate.

Brayer Relief Print: On a piece of chipboard with the approximate dimensions of 7″ x 12″, glue some textured areas for a design. These textured areas might include sandpaper, lace, chicken wire, corrugated paper, and tacks. Place print paper—rice paper is excellent for this one—

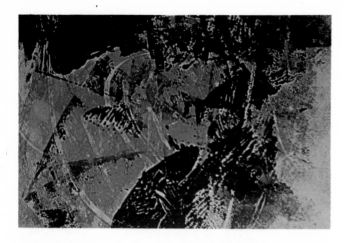

Finger Paint Print: Method of taking up a print from the indirect process of finger painting (see also DECORATIVE PAPERS).

Fish Print (Direct Process): Wash fish with soap and water, dry it, rinse it, and dry it again. Brush black drawing ink over the fish, sweeping the brush over all of the areas including eyes, head, fins, and tail. Daub off the excess ink with a sponge. Place a sheet of Japanese rice paper over the fish. Press lightly with the finger tips. Lift up the rice paper for the fish print. See Fig. P-20.

Fish Print (Indirect Process): Wash fish and dry it as described previously. Sponge a little water over the fish, leaving the fish moist. Place Japanese rice paper over it and press the paper down. Charge a soft sponge with black drawing ink. It is better in this step not to apply too

over the textured area of the design (see also PAPERS). Roll an inked brayer over the paper. The print will appear through the paper as the brayer defines the textured areas through pressure. See Fig. P-18. For an alternate method, ink the plate, apply rice paper over the plate, and roll a clean brayer over the paper for printing pressure.

Fig. P-18

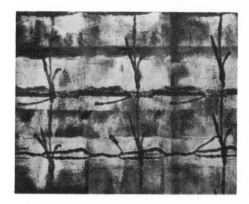

Fig. P-19

Brayer String Print: Tie string, thread, and/or cord around the rubber portion of a brayer. Charge it by rolling it over printing ink on a piece of plate glass (see also CHARGE). Then, roll the brayer which has the string and cord tied to it over a piece of print paper. The string which has been tied to the rubber brayer will produce an interesting linear design. Since the linear design is consistent, a sweep of the brayer can produce a border or a plaid. See Fig. P-19.

Fig. P-20

much ink. A sponge which is moist-dry will produce the best effects (see also CHARGE). Gently rub the sponge over the paper which has been placed on top of the fish. Rub the sponge over all areas so that all details will be taken up. Take the paper off for the fish print.

Gadget Print: Gadgets make interesting shapes for printing. Such things as nut forks, bottle tops, forks, lipstick tops, and rubber erasers make excellent gadget printing tools. Stamp these gadgets into the tempera-paint stamp pad which was described in the introductory paragraph on printmaking, and then stamp them on the print paper. Allover or repeat patterns are rendered effectively with gadget printing (Fig. P-21) (see also PATTERNS).

Fig. P-22

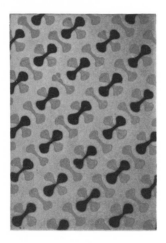

Fig. P-21

Fig. P-23

Gum Eraser Print: Incise a linear design into the end or side of an art gum eraser (see also ERASERS and INCISED). Use a tempera-paint stamp pad for printing gum eraser prints. Allover or repeat patterns are rendered equally well with gum eraser prints (Fig. P-22) (see also PATTERNS).

Hand Prints: See HAND PRINTS.

Leaf Prints: To obtain an interesting leaf print, simply stamp the leaf into a tempera-paint stamp pad as described previously. Print the leaf on paper. See Fig. P-23. Several leaves of different sizes and shapes may be combined into an integrated design motif for repetitive printing on paper. More permanent leaf prints can be made on fabric by

pinning the leaf pattern to a fabric which has been secured to a flat board with tacks or pins. Spray the leaves with a pressurized can of enamel paint (see also SPRAYS). Hold the spray can about 1½″ away from the leaves being sprayed. When the leaves are taken away, they will appear on the fabric as a silhouette form.

Linoleum Print: See Block Print in this listing.

Monoprint:

Type 1: Put some water-soluble printer's ink on a piece of plate glass and roll it out with a brayer until it is smooth and tacky. With a tool such as a rubber eraser on the end of a pencil, draw a design directly on the inked plate of glass. Place a sheet of newsprint or rice paper over the design. Gently press the paper down on the inked plate with the palm of the hand. Lift up the paper for the monoprint (Fig. P-24).

As many as three prints can be taken from the same design. When the design becomes too light for transfer onto a sheet of print paper, apply more printers ink, roll with a brayer, draw a design, and try another.

Type 2: Render a design on a sheet of acetate or a piece of plate glass with Duco cement (see also ADHESIVES). Allow the cement to dry thoroughly. When the cement has dried, roll a brayer which has been charged with printers ink over the surface of the acetate sheet or plate glass which carries the Duco cement design. Place a piece of print paper over the surface of the design on the print plate. Press the paper down on the plate with the palm of the hand. Lift the paper up for the monoprint. One

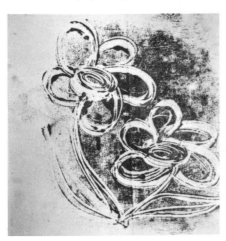

Fig. P-24

may take as many prints as desired from this type of monoprint. The only limiting factor is the durability of the Duco cement as related to adherence to the plate.

Ozalid and/or Blueprint Paper Prints: Ozalid and blueprint paper may be obtained from stationery stores as well as from art supply houses.

Ozalid prints: Arrange interesting shapes and textured areas over a sheet of sensitized ozalid paper. Put a piece of plate glass over the arrangement. Place a desk lamp with a large globe over the design in order to expose the paper to intense light for 20 minutes. Cut the top off a 5-gallon

oil can and place a small container of liquid ammonia at the bottom of the can. Insert the ozalid paper into the can and place a piece of chipboard on top of the can to keep the ammonia fumes within. Allow the paper to remain in the can for 5 to 10 minutes, or until it is "developed."

Blueprint paper prints: Arrange interesting shapes and textured areas over a sheet of sensitized blueprint paper. Put a piece of plate glass over the arrangement. Place in the sun for approximately 1 minute. Wash in water for 3 minutes and, dry the blueprint paper in a darkened enclosure such as a box.

NOTE: The two aforementioned experiences in sensitized paper prints are offered as suggestions. One should not feel limited to using a light globe with ozalid paper any more than one should feel limited to using sunlight with blueprint paper. Try sun lamps with blueprint paper and sunlight with ozalid. Try shorter and longer exposure times, depending wholly upon the intensity of the light used. The forms and textures used offer limitless possibilities. A transparent form of acetate sheeting will provide one kind of printed area, while a solid form of nontransparent material will provide another. String, hemp rope, wire screening, cellophane, and wire are materials worth considering for interesting textural effects and patterns.

Potato Print: Cut a potato in half and incise or excise a design on the flat half of the potato's surface (see also

Fig. P-25

EXCISED and INCISED). Place the potato printing surface on a tempera-paint stamp pad, as described previously, and print an allover pattern on paper (Fig. P-25) (see also PATTERNS).

NOTE: Try stamping a potato design over a sheet of colored tissue [see also TISSUE (COLORED)]. The wet surface of the potato design (without an ink or paint application) will bleach out a design on the tissue. A variation of this process would be to place a white paper ground under a sheet of colored tissue, and then stamp the potato design down. The color will transfer onto the white paper ground (see also GROUND and PAPERS).

Rubber Tube Print: Cut a design from an ordinary rubber tire tube. Glue the design on a piece of plywood or chipboard, using white resin glue as an adhesive (see also ADHESIVES and PAPERS). Roll an inked brayer over the rubber-tube printing plate. Lay the printing plate down on paper and apply pressure to print. See Fig. P-26.

Fig. P-26

Sandpaper Print: On a piece of fine sandpaper, render a crayon design. Apply the crayon heavily to those areas which would appear dark and lightly to those areas which would appear lighter when printed. Roll an inked brayer over the surface of the crayon-designed sandpaper and place it face down on a piece of print paper. Using the back of a tablespoon, apply a great deal of pressure to the back of the sandpaper. See Fig. P-27.

NOTE: An alternate method of applying pressure would be to send the print and print paper through an ordinary clothes-type wringer.

Silk Screen Print: This is not an authentic silk screen

Fig. P-27

print, but a simplification of the process of serigraphy (see also SERIGRAPHY, SILK SCREENING and STENCIL). Put a piece of organdy into an embroidery hoop. Cut a stencil from a piece of newsprint. For this process, the paper can be folded in half for a symmetrically cut design (see also PAPER SCULPTURE and STENCIL). Place the newsprint stencil underneath the embroidery hoop. The stencil should be small enough to be contained within the area of the embroidery hoop, but the newsprint itself, which encompasses the cutout stencil, should be larger than the hoop, overlapping it by about 2″ all the way around. Use a cardboard squeegee, or a small rectangle of chipboard, to push the printing ink from the top of the inside of the embroidery hoop to the bottom of the inside of the hoop (see also PRINTING INK SUBSTITUTES and SQUEEGEE).

When the printing ink has passed from the top to the bottom of the inside of the embroidery hoop, with the stencil underneath, the printing ink will act as an adhesive and will affix the stencil to the organdy. Thereafter, it will be a simple matter to apply more of the printing ink to the inside of the embroidery hoop and to pass the ink with the squeegee from the top to the bottom. As many prints as desired can be printed. See Fig. P-28.

NOTE: Cardboard box tops may be used instead of embroidery hoops. Cut a "window" from the box top, and tape the organdy to the inside of the box with brown kraft tape (see also TAPES). Instead of using a paper stencil, try blocking out areas of the organdy, or screen, with crayon. Better still, use lithographic crayons.

Fig. P-28

Spatter Print: Method of putting a positive shape such as a leaf or a cutout design down on paper and spraying over it (see also HAND PRINTS). The resulting effect is like a reverse silhouette (Fig. P-29) (see also SILHOUETTES). Spatter paint, as well as spatter guns which spray the paint, may be purchased commercially. However, tempera and water produce a suitable spatter paint (see also PAINT SUBSTITUTES). Paint may be put into household spray cans or may be spattered over the positive shape by rubbing a stiff scrub brush over some wire screening. A more simplified method of application is to use one of the pressurized spray cans of paint (see also SPRAYS). If spatter painting

Fig. P-29

on fabric, use an oil-base enamel pressurized spray can for permanency.

Stencil Print: Plan a design on paper, preferably using a limit of three colors. Place a sheet of transparent stencil paper over the design, using separate sheets of stencil paper for each color used in the design (see also PAPERS). With an X-Acto knife, or stencil knife, cut out three separate stencils, one for each color which is represented in the design. Put the paper down on a drawing board or piece of cork tile; tack it or pin it to the board.

Place the first stencil on the paper in the desired area. Using a thick, prepared mixture of tempera paint, begin to stipple in the first area of color (see also BRUSH STROKES and STIPPLE). The second stencil is then placed on top of the stippled area, making sure that the stencil will register the second color in the desired area. The second color is stippled in, and so on for the third color and the third area of paint. Avoid heavy application of paint; build up the color with several light applications. See Fig. P-30.

NOTE: Water-base as well as oil-base printing inks may be used instead of the tempera paint mixture (see also INKS, and for additional techniques in stencil designs, see STENCIL and TEXTILE DESIGN).

Cutout stencils which feature circles and similar forms require bridges as indicated in illustration Fig. P-31.

String Print: Dip a length of string approximately 18" long into a mixture of tempera paint with a cream-like consistency. Lay the string down on the print paper allowing it to fall into what appears to be an interesting design. Allow one end of the string to extend about 4" over and off the edge of the paper. Lay another piece of paper over the string design, and place a book on top of the paper. Apply pressure with the hand to the top of the book and, at the same time, grasp the extended piece of string at the margin and pull it out. Lift up the book and the papers for the string prints (Fig. P-32). Try laying a second piece of string dipped in a contrasting color over the first string print design. Proceed as before for a "double exposure" string print.

Tagboard Print: Cut a design out of a piece of tagboard with either an X-Acto knife or a scissors and glue it to a piece of chipboard (see also KNIVES and PAPERS).

(a)

(b)

Fig P-30

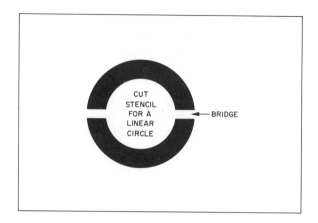

Fig. P-31

Roll a brayer which has been charged with printer's ink over the face of the tagboard design. Lay the design face down on the print paper, applying pressure to print. Stepping on this one is effective. See Fig. P-33.

Vegetable and Fruit Prints: Cut carrots in half, or use celery, onions, or heads of cabbage. Either paint over the surface of the vegetables or press them into a tempera-paint stamp pad as previously described. Print face down on paper. See Fig. P-34 for an onion print.

Incorporate with an allover or repeat pattern idea. Try overlapping, rotating, and inverting the forms. Cut fruit in half and proceed as directed above for fruit prints. Use oranges, lemons, or grapefruit.

PRINTMAKING (PROFESSIONAL)

Relates to *intaglio,* which includes etching, dry-point etching, engraving, aquatint, and mezzotint; to *planographic,* which includes lithography on either limestone, zinc, or aluminum plates; to *relief* printing, which includes woodcuts and wood engravings; and to *stencil,* which includes serigraphy or silk screen printing (see also INTAGLIO, PLANOGRAPHIC, RELIEF, SILK SCREENING, and STENCIL).

PRINTS

The product of all printmaking processes in the fine arts or, more specifically, the graphic arts (see also FINE ARTS and GRAPHIC ARTS). These prints are called etchings, dry-point etchings, engravings, aquatints, mezzotints (see also INTAGLIO), lithographs (see also PLANOGRAPHIC), woodcuts (see Fig. P-35), wood engravings (see also RELIEF), or serigraphs (see also SILK SCREENING and STENCIL), depending upon the process used.

PRINTS (HANDS)

See HAND PRINTS.

(a)

Fig. P-33

Fig. P-34

(b)

(c)

Fig. P-32

Fig. P-35

P

PRISMS

Solid elongated triangular glass forms, the two ends of which are equal triangles, and the three sides of which are parallelograms.

Two prisms are needed for a demonstration of the light theory in color (see also COLOR).

PROCESS FILM

Also called Pro-film, and stencil film; a gelatine film which is used in the silk screening processes (see also SERIGRAPHY, SILK SCREENING, and STENCIL).

PRO-FILM

See PROCESS FILM.

PROPORTION

See DESIGN ELEMENTS.

PRO-TEC

See HAND PROTECTING CREAM.

PUMICE POWDER

See ABRASIVES.

PUNCHES

Ticket Punch: Single punch with ¼″ diameter punch holes and a ¾″ punching reach; used for paper.

Triumph Eyelet Punch: Combination paper and eyelet punch which uses a ⁵⁄₃₂″ size medium eyelet. This punch will not only punch the hole for the eyelet but will affix the eyelet permanently into a cardboard or fabric ground. It is particularly useful in booklet making (see also BOOKLET MAKING and EYELETS).

PUPPETS

The most common method of making puppets is with the papier-mâché process (see also PAPIER-MÂCHÉ). There are, however, other methods of making puppets which are less time-consuming than the papier-mâché process. In most puppet making, it is necessary to model the head and neck on a wooden dowel stand. This stand consists of a length of ½″ doweling which is 10″ high and is placed on a wooden stand with the approximate dimensions of 6″ x 6″ (see also DOWELING and PAPIER-MÂCHÉ).

Use asbestos and wheat paste, or sawdust and wheat paste, to model the head over the wooden dowel stand (see also MODELING MATERIALS). The advantage of using these modeling materials in fashioning the puppet head is that paint may be applied directly to the material. It can be shellacked and decorative details may be added. Wait until the modeling material is thoroughly dry before attempting to paint it, however, and certainly before attempting to take it from the dowel stand.

Styrofoam puppets are made from blocks of styrofoam which have been cut into egg shapes with the added appendage of the neck which has been hollowed out for finger placement (see also STYROFOAM). Features are built up with plastic clay which will adhere to the styrofoam without the use of adhesives [see also CLAY (PLASTIC)]. After all the features are pressed into shape, dip the puppet head into a mixture of plaster of paris (see also PLASTER OF PARIS). The puppet head can then be painted and decorative details such as hair can be glued on with white resin glue (see also ADHESIVES). This is an interesting puppet to try!

In addition, there are paper bag puppets, wooden spoon puppets, stocking puppets, stick puppets, and tennis ball puppets. Do a little in the way of experimentation and exploration to find ways of making puppets which are unique and different. For additional information relative to puppetry (see also PAPIER-MÂCHÉ).

QUADRO

Four-sided or rectangular ground on which a painting is rendered (see also GROUND, KAKEMONO, MAKIMONO, and TONDO).

QUIRE

Vendor's term relating to quantities of paper; a quire is 24 sheets (see also PAPERS).

RABBIT SKIN GLUE

See ADHESIVES.

RAFFIA

Soft, flexible, strawlike material which is used primarily to create decorative effects used in puppetry, masks, and animals (see also PAPIER-MÂCHÉ). It is also used to create textural effects in weaving, and it is used in stitchery (see also STITCHERY and WEAVING). Raffia is available in blue, green, orange, purple, red, yellow, brown, black, and natural.

RAFFIA NEEDLES

See NEEDLES.

RAILROAD BOARD

See PAPERS.

RASP

See CARVING MATERIALS and WOODWORKING.

RAZOR BLADES

Versatile tool for professional artists, not children. They can be used to scrape paint and cement from glass and as a cutting instrument in scoring paper in the paper sculpture process. They can be used to achieve textural effects in watercolor painting, such as cutting into the paper ground for bark texture on tree trunks (see also PAINTING and PAPER SCULPTURE).

REALISM

Sometimes called naturalism; a portrayal of nature, people, and objects as they appear to the artist, without a conscious effort on his part to distort, modify, or rearrange the elements.
EXAMPLE: "A Real Allegory," by Gustave Courbet.

REAM

See PAPERS.

RECEDING COLOR

See COLOR.

RED CEDAR

See WOODS.

RED GUM

See WOODS.

RED OAK

See WOODS.

RELIEF

Relates to two areas: sculpture (plastic arts) and printmaking (graphic arts) [see also HISTORY (ART)].

R

Sculpture:

Low relief or bas-relief: The rounding and cutting of figures and designs so that they appear a little higher than the flat background. It is often seen in frieze work and in ornamental carving on furniture and vases [see also HISTORY (ART)].

High relief or half-round: The cutting or hewing of stone or wood so that the figure or design is halfway out of the flat background. This is seen in frieze work and in decorative detail on cathedral constructions.

Full round or sculpture-in-the-round: A full, three-dimensional form around which one might walk to observe from all angles; no background exists (see also SCULPTURE).

EXAMPLES: "David," by Michelangelo; and "Recumbent Figure," by Henry Moore.

Printmaking: The term *relief* (also known as cameo), relates to a category of processes in printmaking along with intaglio, planographic, and stencil. Relief work relates to woodcuts where areas are carved away on the printing plate, leaving other areas high and in relief. Such areas, when printed, will register as positive areas of form. Relief work relates also to wood engraving where lines are incised into the wood plate. Such lines, when printed, would register as white lines, leaving other areas in bold areas of form. Albrecht Dürer was the greatest of all wood engravers. Relief work also relates to linoleum block printing, using methods both of carving away areas and of incising lines [see also PRINTMAKING (PROFESSIONAL) and PRINTS].

RENAISSANCE

Considered to be the first step toward modern European art; began in Florence in the fourteenth century with Giotto and lasted until the seventeenth century. This was the time when collective thought and traditions of the past were cast off. Artists became more personalistic in their approach and made individual, as well as individualized, contributions. The period of the Renaissance has been called the "rebirth"; it followed the period of the Middle Ages or Medieval Art (see also MEDIEVAL ART). High Renaissance refers to that time during the Renaissance period when the art forms had reached their apex of development and beauty; it is usually associated with the time of Michelangelo, Raphael, and Leonardo da Vinci [see also HISTORY (ART)].

REPEAT PATTERNS

See PATTERNS.

REPOUSSE

Metal technique wherein designs are rendered in relief through a hammering process from the back of the metal sheet. Repoussé may be employed in low relief (bas-relief), high relief (half-round), or in full round (sculpture-in-the-round) (see also RELIEF).

REPRODUCTIONS (ART)

Every school district, as well as every school, should build up a collection of good reproductions with high fidelity of color. The following partial list of sources is offered for reference:

Artex Prints, Inc., Westport, Connecticut.

Commerford Gallery, 117 East 57th Street, New York 22, New York.

Museum of Modern Art, 11 West 53rd Street, New York 19, New York.

Prothmann, Dr. Konrad, 2378 Soper Avenue, Baldwin, Long Island, New York.

Society for Visual Education, Inc., 1345 Diversey Parkway, Chicago 14, Illinois.

University Prints, 15 Brattle Street, Cambridge 38, Massachusetts.

NOTE: For travel posters, write to travel bureaus or to the consulate of the nation in which you are interested.

RESIN DYES

See DYES.

RESIN (EPOXY)

See ADHESIVES.

RESIN (LAMINATING)

See LAMINATED RESIN.

REZ-N-GLUE CEMENT

See ADHESIVES.

RHYTHM

See DESIGN ELEMENTS.

RICE PAPER

See PAPERS.

ROASTING PAN

Used for marbling paper in the decorative paper processes (see also DECORATIVE PAPERS).

ROCOCO PERIOD

Eighteenth century art period which followed the Baroque period and preceded the period of Classic Revival or Neoclassicism. The Rococo period was characterized by its elaborate interiors which emphasized the curved line and gold embellishments. The excesses of the Rococo period brought about a revival of the classic form in art under the leadership of Jacques David [see also CLASSICISM and HISTORY (ART)].

ROMAN ART

One of the arts of antiquity; (300 B.C. to A.D. 400) influenced by Etruscan and Greek arts. Centuries later it achieved a character of its own [see also ETRUSCAN ART, GREEK ART, and HISTORY (ART)]. Typical of Roman art are sculptured forms in relief and in sculpture-in-the-round.

EXAMPLES (architecture): Colosseum (amphitheater of Vespasian and Titus) and the Pantheon, both in Rome.

ROMANESQUE ART

Style which flourished in western Europe in the eleventh and twelfth centuries, beginning about 800 and lasting until 1200. Architecture was characterized by its rounded arches, as opposed to the pointed arch of the Gothic period [see also GOTHIC and HISTORY (ART)]. Painting was characterized by its religious themes and its storytelling qualities.

EXAMPLE: "Building the Tower of Babel", (Romanesque painting); The Cathedral and Bell Tower in Pisa (Romanesque architecture).

ROMANTICISM

This was an era in art expression which followed the period of Classicism or Neoclassicism [see also CLASSICISM and HISTORY (ART)]. In essence, it was a reaction against the somewhat stoic qualities of the period which preceded it. Romanticism exemplified freedom both in feeling and in expression.

EXAMPLE: "Mounted Officer of the Imperial Guard," by Jean Louis Theodore Géricault.

ROUND-NOSE PLIERS

See WOODWORKING.

ROVING

See COTTON ROVING and YARNS AND STRINGS.

RUBBER CEMENT

See ADHESIVES.

RUBBER CEMENT THINNER

See SOLVENTS.

RUBBINGS

Essentially, this is an introduction into the realm of the collage through experiences in visual texture rubbings. Once an awareness of textural qualities is established, students can then go on with a readiness for the tactile textures which are used extensively in the collage (see also COLLAGE and DESIGN ELEMENTS).

Rubbings may be produced by placing some squares of newsprint over some textured areas and rubbing over them with the side of a crayon. Textures for rubbings may be found on the covers of books, the fabrics of purses, wallets, floors, walls, grains of wood, and veins of leaves. The beauty of texture can be observed when a rubbing from rough burlap is compared with one from a finer woven fabric. The relativity of texture can be observed when burlap is compared with the rougher texture of concrete.

Follow-up experiences with this area of rubbings could be in the form of a rubbing collage. The rubbings could be cut into interesting shapes and pasted down on a stiff ground. If the rubbings were taken with different colors of crayons, the collage would have another dimension of interest. Examples of rubbings can be seen in Fig. R-1.

RUG BACKING

See STITCHERY.

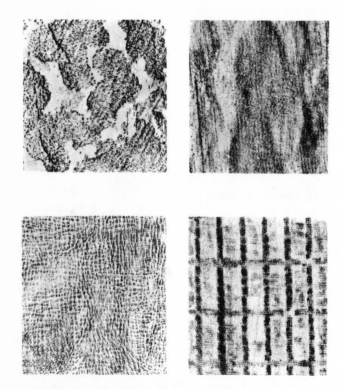

Fig. R-1

SALT

The uses of household salt in an art program are numerous.

Cut Flowers: In the demonstration of flower arrangements, a dash of salt in the water will insure continued freshness.

Fabrics: To prevent new fabrics from running, put ⅛ cup of salt in the rinse water. Salt is also used in the dyeing processes as a mordant (see also MORDANTS).

Furniture Stains: To remove stains from furniture, make a paste of salad oil and salt. Apply this paste to the stained area on the furniture, and allow it to remain for 1 or 2 hours before wiping it off.

Grease Stains: Mix 4 parts alcohol with 1 part salt and apply to stained areas. Rub gently.

Modeling Dough:

Type 1: Mix together 1 part salt and 1 part flour and enough water to made a modeling material that will hold its shape (see also MODELING MATERIALS).

Type 2: Add 1 part salt to 1 part starch and add enough water to make a modeling material that will hold its shape (see also MODELING MATERIALS). This may also be used as a type of patching plaster (see also SPACKLE).

Sponges: To revitalize old sponges, soak them in a cold, salt-water solution.

Tempera Paint: As a preservative to keep tempera paint fresh smelling, add a dash of salt to the painting medium (see also PRESERVATIVES).

Whitewash: Add salt to whitewash to help it adhere to surfaces.

SALT AND FLOUR

See MODELING MATERIALS.

SAND CASTING

See CASTING (SAND).

SAND PAINTING

Obtain eight jars, such as mustard jars, and fill them half full of tempera paint mixture in the following colors: red, yellow, orange, green, blue, violet, brown, and black. Add filtered sand to the jars of paint, allowing the sand to fill the jars to the top. Stir the mixture and allow it to stand until thoroughly dry. When pictures or designs have been rendered on a ground of chipboard, add white resin glue to those areas which will take the colored sand (see also ADHESIVES). Sprinkle the colored sand on the desired areas. Allow the sand paintings to dry thoroughly and then shake off the excess sand. Spray with Krylon plastic spray (see also KRYLON).

SANDPAPER

See ABRASIVES, CERAMICS, PRINTMAKING, and WOODWORKING.

SARAN WRAP

An interesting new material for experimentation in the art area, available in grocery stores. Cover toothpick constructions with Saran wrap, and paint the wrap with white resin glue. When the glue dries, the Saran wrap takes on a character which resembles a molded, textured, cellulose acetate. Figure S-1 shows such a toothpick sculpture, utilizing Saran wrap and glue (see also ADHESIVES, CELLULOSE ACETATE, and SCULPTURE).

SARCOPHAGUS

Ornamental coffin of stone, clay, wood, or metal; often associated with Etruscan sarcophagi [see also ETRUSCAN and HISTORY (ART)].

SAWS

See WOODWORKING.

Fig. S-1

SCHOOL PASTE

See ADHESIVES.

SCISSORS

Blunt Point: For kindergarten-primary grades; 4″ in length; available with or without rubber-lined handles.

Clip Point: For intermediate grades; 5″ in length; available with or without rubber-lined handles.

Sharp Point: For upper grades; 5″ in length; available with or without rubber-lined handles [see also CUTTING, PAPER CUTTERS, PAPER SCULPTURE, SHEARS, and SUPPLIES (CLASSROOM)].

NOTE: Scissors are available which are made specifically for left-handed students. When ordering, ask for left-handed scissors in either 4″ or 5″ lengths.

SCORING

See PAPER SCULPTURE.

SCRAP MATERIALS

Scrap materials are excellent for experiments in construction and design. The utilization of scrap materials such as egg-crate sections, buttons, and yarn develop into animals

S

and other forms. Figure S-2 shows a delightful turtle constructed from egg cartons, newspapers, and other scrap materials. Scrap materials are excellent for the rendering of the collage, as well as adding needed decorative details to papier-mâché animals, masks, or puppets (see also COL-LAGE, PAPIER-MÂCHÉ, and PUPPETS).

Fig. S-2

Use tile, broken ceramics, broken glass, buttons, earrings, beads, seeds, shells, and pebbles for mosaic projects (see also MOSAICS). Use coat hangers and odd bits of wire for wire sculpture and mobiles (see also MOBILES, SCULPTURE, and WIRE SCULPTURE). Use old automobile gears for creating impressions in wet sand in the sand casting process [see also CASTING (SAND)]. Use leaves, string, yarn, wheat, and gift wrapping for laminated papers (see also DECORATIVE PAPERS and LAMINATED). Use tongue depressors, medical swab sticks, bamboo sticks, balsa wood, ice-cream sticks, toothpicks, cocktail picks, and doweling for sculpture, mobiles, and stablies (see also MOBILES, SCULPTURE, and STABILES). Use velvet ribbon, string, gift-wrapping ribbon, grained ribbon, hemp rope, twine, cotton roving, wool, raffia, braiding, and cord for additional textures in weaving (see also WEAVING). Scrap materials can be kept in a large grape box and stored on a shelf in a classroom. No class should be without a sizable scrap box.

SCRATCHBOARD

See DRAWING (SCRATCHBOARD) and PAPERS.

SCRATCHBOARD DRAWING

See DRAWING (SCRATCHBOARD).

SCREEN FILLER

See SILK SCREENING.

SCREW DRIVER

See WOODWORKING.

SCULPTURE

Art of creating three-dimensional forms in *relief*, as in sand casting; *in-the-round*, as with carving materials; or in *moving sculpture*, as in the mobile. Sculpture is one of the plastic arts [see also CARVING MATERIALS, CASTING (SAND), DIMENSION, MOBILES, and RELIEF].

For classroom sculpturing experiences, students may work with carving or modeling materials [see also CARVING MATERIALS, CERAMICS, CLAY (KITCHEN-OVEN), CLAY (NON-FIRING), CLAY (PLASTIC), MODELING MATERIALS, and PAPIER-MÂCHÉ]. Combining scrap materials into sculpture can provide an interesting experience (see also CONSTRUCTIVISM, DADA, EXCELSIOR, LAMINATED RESIN, SCRAP MATERIALS, and STABILES). Sculptured forms can also be created with laminated paper (see Fig. S-3) (see also LAMINATED PAPER). Use pipe cleaners as a "warm-up" for creating sculpture with wire (see also PIPE CLEANERS, WIRE, and WIRE TOOLS).

Fig. S-3

SEALING WAX

See WAX.

SEASCAPE

Relates to drawings or paintings of the sea, ships, or harbors, as opposed to the landscape which is concerned primarily with land (see also LANDSCAPE).

SECONDARY COLORS

See COLOR.

SELVAGE

See WEAVING.

SERIGRAPHY

Alternate terms for the silk screen process and for the stencil process in printmaking. Silk screen printing is used extensively for fabric design, posters, and fine prints [see also PRINTS, PRINTMAKING, PRINTMAKING (PROFESSIONAL), SILK SCREENING, and STENCIL].

SGRAFFITO

Decoration produced by scratching through a surface layer to reveal a different colored ground (see also CERAMICS and DECORATIVE PAPERS).

SHADING SHEETS

These are commercially made, visually textured patterns which are printed on transparent film with a waxed backing; they are used extensively in advertising layout work. The pattern is placed over the area that the artist wishes to have shaded, and it is cut to size to fit that area. The shading sheet is burnished down on the area until it is adhered permanently to the drawing.

As halftones are made through this process, a form of line engraving is possible (see also HALFTONES and INTAGLIO). There are over 100 different, visual-textured patterns from which to choose, including 17 transparent colors; black and white are opaque.

NOTE: Pattern charts are available from Para-Tone Incorporated, 512 West Burlington Avenue, La Grange, Illinois.

SHEARS

Relates to scissors of a large size or any mechanical cutting instrument such as the paper cutter (see also PAPER CUTTER and SCISSORS).

SHED

See WEAVING.

SHELF PAPER

See PAPERS.

SHELLAC

Shellac is available in its characteristic high-gloss finish in either white (bleached) or orange (unbleached). White shellac is used to give surfaces a protective covering, while the orange is used to achieve certain antique effects on furniture. Never use orange shellac on colored surfaces unless you wish to neutralize or change the color of the surface. Shellac dries rapidly, usually in 1 or 2 hours, and it does not raise the grain of the wood as does varnish.

Wood Finishing: The first coat of shellac should be thinned with denatured alcohol using 4 parts alcohol to 1 part shellac. The purpose of thinning the first coat is to allow for penetration into the wood. The second and third coats may be applied full strength. Between each coat of shellac, rub the wood surface with fine steel wool. The gauge of the steel wool should become finer as each succeeding coat of shellac is applied. Before another coat of shellac is applied, make certain the previous coat is thoroughly dry. If the next coat is applied on a tacky surface, the succeeding coats will be tacky, and will never dry thoroughly (see also LACQUER, LINSEED OIL, and VARNISH).

SHELLAC SUBSTITUTE

See SODIUM SILICATE.

S

SHIP LOG

See PARCHMENT.

SHOT

See WEAVING.

SHOWCARD BOARD

See PAPERS.

SILHOUETTE PAPER

See PAPERS.

SILHOUETTES

A silhouette is essentially a profile portrait, which is cut out of black paper and glued to a white ground. Figure S-4 shows an example of a free-hand miniature silhouette

Fig. S-4

rendered by a professional artist. Faithful likenesses of children can be rendered in about 60 seconds. For younger children, it is best if the teacher does the drawing; older children may take turns "sitting" and drawing for one another.

Procedure: One needs a sharp, direct light for silhouette drawing so that a sharp shadow can be thrown on the wall. Use either a 150-watt electric bulb or a slide projector

for light. Tack a sheet of newsprint 12″ x 18″ to a piece of chipboard or plywood. Rest the chipboard or plywood on the chalk tray. Seat the student in front of the board and close to it. Turn the light directly on the child so that his profile is centered on the paper.

Working quickly, begin to outline the profile on the paper with a pencil. Start at the forehead, and then draw the features of the face. Come back to the top of the head and draw the hairline, the head, and the back of the neck. Clip this white newsprint drawing to a sheet of black paper of equal size. Holding the two sheets of paper together and cutting along the outline of the profile drawing, a black silhouette will result. Glue this black silhouette to a piece of white drawing paper with rubber cement (see also ADHESIVES and PAPERS).

SILK SCREENING

Serigraphy, or the process of using silk screens for multipurpose prints and posters, was first conceived by sign painters as a low-cost, fast, and versatile medium, but it is now listed among the printmaking processes under the general heading of the stencil process. An example of a silk screen print is shown in Fig. S-5. Silk screening has

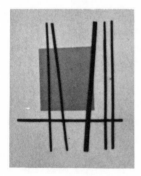

Fig. S-5

achieved a niche of its own as one of the fine arts, and is illustrated most dramatically by the serigraphs of Sister Mary Corita [see also POSTERS, PRINTMAKING, PRINTMAKING (PROFESSIONAL), and PRINTS].

The process has been simplified and modified for elementary school experiences by using paper positive cutouts which are adhered to organdy screens in embroidery hoops (see also PRINTMAKING). The art of silk screening is practiced extensively in secondary school art programs, particularly in the area of multiple poster making (see also POSTERS).

There are many silk screening methods including: block-out, stencil film, tusche stencil, paper stencil, and the photographic stencil in both the direct and indirect processes. All of these employ the one basic concept of the stencil process which states that areas will be blocked out where color is not to register, and will be left exposed where color is to register. This applies, whether a paper or a fabric ground is used.

In paper stenciling, the stencil paper is cut away to allow the color or ink to be stippled on a ground. In the *block-out method* of silk screening, it is quite the reverse. A block-out solution is applied to all positive areas of the design on the silk screen where the color or ink is expected to register in color (see also POSITIVE SPACE). The background, on the other hand, where the negative areas exist and no color or ink is expected to register, is then covered with a negative solution (see also NEGATIVE SPACE). Eventually, before any printing is done, the block-out solution which covered the positive areas of the design is washed away, leaving a fabric stencil through which color or ink may be passed with pressure from a squeegee (see also SQUEEGEE). In the stencil-film method, the stencil is cut from a laminated paper consisting of a layer of lacquer film and a layer of transparent white backing. This lacquer film is then adhered to the screen. The paper backing is peeled away, and another type of fabric stencil is formed for silk screening. The block-out method and the stencil-film method are those most popularly used in secondary school art programs and are described in the following sections.

Block-Out Method:

Materials needed: Silk screen, squeegee, black drawing ink, drawing pen with fine bead point, sponge, screen-filler powder, soft sable brushes, block-out solution, negative solution, length of 14-ply cardboard, gum paper tape, silk screening inks or textile colors, solvent thinner or reducer, kerosene, and negative solution solvent.

Silk screens: May be ordered in any size from 4″ to 42″, depending entirely upon the size of the design that is to be printed. A rule of thumb in selecting silk screens for specific designs is to allow approximately a 3″ border of silk around the design after it has been centered in the silk screen. Silk screens may be purchased already assembled, or with assembled frames and yardage in either silk, cotton organdy, or silk screen nylon. Fabric for home assembled kits should be washed before being stretched and nailed to the frame. The washing removes the sizing from the fabric and will produce a high quality print without pinhole imperfections. Screens may be used over and over again provided that they are cleaned with the proper solvent (see also SOLVENTS). Figures S-6 and S-7 show the two sides of a silk screen, each of which is important in the preparation of the master stencil screen. In discussing both the block-out method and the stencil film method, the back of the screen will be referred to as *side "A",* and the front of the screen as *side "B."*

Squeegee: Rubber-edged tool with a wooden handle which is used at a 45° angle to move silk screen ink or

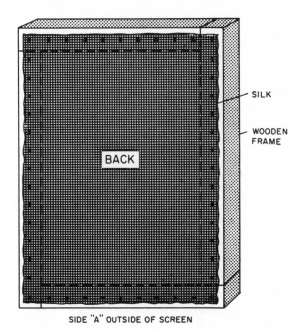

SILK

WOODEN FRAME

BACK

SIDE "A" OUTSIDE OF SCREEN

Fig. S-6

S

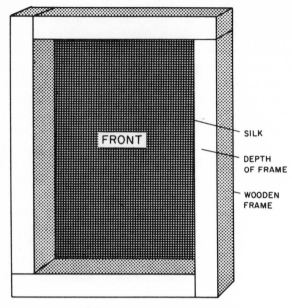

SILK

DEPTH
OF FRAME

WOODEN
FRAME

SIDE "B" INSIDE OF SCREEN

Fig. S-7

color from one end of the screen to the other, or from top to bottom (see also SQUEEGEE).

Black drawing ink: For tracing the master design to the silk screen.

Drawing pen and holder: For use with drawing ink in the tracing process. Recommended brand and size: Gillott Artists Pens, #404 bead point.

Screen filler: Powder filler which must be mixed with water to a creamy consistency before being applied with a damp sponge to the screen. Screen-filler is used to fill up the pin-point openings between warp and weft silk threads, and to allow ease of application in painting with the block-out solution.

Block-out solution: That solution which is painted on the screen with a soft sable brush to those areas of the design which will be blocked out. Eventually this solution is washed out of the fabric, after the negative areas have been sealed, and will create the openings necessary for a fabric stencil opening on the screen.

Negative solution: Also called fill-in lacquer; that solu-

tion which is applied to the negative background of the design or to those areas which will not take color.

14-ply cardboard: Strip of cardboard approximately 4″ wide, with a length which will be determined by the width of the silk screen. This stiff cardboard is used as a type of squeegee to apply the negative solution to the screen.

Gum paper tape: Folded in half lengthwise and taped inside the screen along the sides, from screen to frame. Taped corners and edges will prevent the color or ink from seeping through and will also preserve the screen.

Silk screen inks or colors: All coloring agents used in printing processes are called inks; while coloring agents used for fabrics are generally referred to as being colors.

Inks: Available in both water-soluble and oil-base ink; sold in cans or jars. Inks come in a concentrated pastelike consistency and must be thinned down. When thinning, it is best to remember that the consistency of the ink must resemble thick honey. For oil-base inks, mix two parts of color to one part of solvent reducer. For water-base inks, mix with water to a thick-honey consistency. Substitutes for water-base silk screening inks exist (see also PRINTING INK SUBSTITUTES).

Textile colors: A proper consistency for textile colors can be obtained by mixing 1 part of color to 3 parts of slow-drying extender (see also EXTENDERS and FABRIC DESIGN).

Solvent thinner or reducer: Mineral spirit solvent used to thin oil-base inks.

Extender: Increases the volume of color without disturbing the intensity. When ordering, ask for *regular* extender.

Kerosene: Used to clean silk screen between working periods, on the same design project.

Negative solution solvent: Used to clean screen of negative solution and excess inks when project is completed and the silk screen is to be either stored or used for another design (see SOLVENTS).

Procedure:

1. Render a design on paper. For the first experience, limit the design to only one color.

2. Place silk screen, side "A" down and side "B" up, on the design so that the design may be seen through the silk screen fabric. Center the design on the silk screen.

3. Trace the design onto the silk fabric with a bead point drawing pen and black drawing ink.

4. After mixing screen filler to a creamy consistency as described earlier, apply the filler lightly with a damp sponge to side "A" of the silk screen. Make sure that all pinholes are covered. Allow to dry.

5. Turn the screen over to side "B" and prop it up with a small block of wood so that the screen tilts toward you. With a soft sable brush paint the block-out solution on those areas of the design which will be rendered in color, or the positive areas. Allow to dry.

6. Pour some of the negative solution to the top of the screen, on side "B", tilting the screen up and away from you so that the negative solution may collect at the top ridge. Again, place the screen on a wood block to create a tilted angle toward you and use the stiff cardboard squeegee to bring the negative solution down so that the entire screen (including the block-out solution) is covered evenly. Allow to dry thoroughly and repeat, applying another coat of negative solution.

7. When the negative solution is thoroughly dry, turn the screen over to side "A" and with a wet sponge and cold water begin to carefully wash out the block-out solution from the screen fabric. Do this with a gentle motion and with caution. Then turn the screen over to side "B" and allow the tap water to wash out the remaining block-out solution. All of the block-out solution will have to be removed in order to insure a design with sharpness and clarity of line. Allow the screen to dry thoroughly.

8. On side "B", apply gummed tape to the inside corners of the screen. Fold the tape in half lengthwise and tape down the length and width of the screen on all four sides. Put additional bracers of tape at the corners. The tape is applied properly if half of it rests on the silk and half on the wooden frame.

9. The preparation of the screen is now completed and you are ready to apply the ink or color and begin to print.

NOTE: It is a generally accepted practice to attach metal hinges to the top of the wooden screen, and then to attach them again to a wood base underneath. To do this, obtain two small silk screen hinges and attach half of the hinge sections to the top of the screen at the wooden base, with side "B" up and side "A" down. Attach the second half of the hinge sections to a board slightly larger than the screen which is used as a base. A hinged screen will insure a sharp print as it greatly reduces the possibility of moving it while running the rubber squeegee up and down with the color.

10. Place one or two desk blotters cut to the size of the screen on the baseboard.

11. Place the paper or fabric ground on top of the blotter. You may tape these down for more control.

12. Bring the silk screen down and apply some of the silk screen ink or color to the top of the screen. Distribute it evenly so that all parts of the design will be covered.

13. Place the rubber squeegee at the top of the silk screen and in back of the ink or color and bring the color down with the squeegee, holding the squeegee at about a 45° angle and applying firm pressure.

14. Lift up the screen. The print will have registered on the ground and the process is completed.

Cleaning the screen between printings: In the event that you wish to stop printing but still wish to use the same design for another day, clean the silk screen thoroughly in the following manner:

Oil-base inks or colors: Apply kerosene to two small cloths and begin to clean the screen from both sides at the same time. This will prevent applying too much pressure to the face of the screen and will mitigate against the loosening or altering of the tension of the silk which is stretched across the wooden frame. As soon as one section of the screen is cleaned, dry it with a clean cloth. Continue in this manner until the entire screen is cleaned.

Water-base printing inks: Clean the screen with water instead of kerosene solvent in the manner described for oil-base inks above.

Cleaning the screen and removing of design: When the project in printing has been completed and the screen is to be stored or used for another design, the final screen cleaning is accomplished in the following manner.

1. Place the screen, side "B" up, side "A" down, on a pad of newspapers with a desk blotter on top.

2. Pour some of the negative solvent into the inside of the screen, allowing it to soak for approximately 15 to 20 seconds.

3. Tilt the screen up from the blotter and working both sides at the same time, as described in cleaning "Oil-base inks or colors," using two cloths soaked in solvent. Continue rubbing with these cloths and drying with clean ones until a greater portion of the negative solution and excess ink or color has been removed.

4. The final cleaning is done with a medium-sized, flat bristle, stencil brush which has been dipped into the negative removing solvent. Clean the screen on both sides with this brush (see also BRUSHES).

5. Dry the screen with a soft cloth.

NOTE: There are alternate cleaning solvents for the negative removing solvent such as lacquer thinner, acetone, and silk screening adhering solution (see also SOLVENTS).

Stencil Film Method:

Materials needed: Silk screen, squeegee, stencil film, film line cutter, X-Acto knife, adhering solution, negative solution, size 3″ x 3″ of 14-ply stiff cardboard, gum tape, chipboard which is the size of the silk screen, and silk-screening inks or textile colors.

Silk screen, and squeegee: See description listed previously under block-out method.

Stencil film: Also called process film and lacquer film; a sheet of laminated paper with lacquer on the top and a transparent white coating on the bottom, available in sheets 30″ x 40″ and in rolls 300″ x 40″. The stencil film is transparent and therefore the intended design can be easily copied onto the film with a special tool, eliminating the need for pen and ink tracing used in the block-out method.

Film line cutter: A metal tool with a plastic handle which is available in small, medium, and large sizes. The medium tool is a good all-purpose tool if the choice must be made in favor of one. Film line cutters are used to copy the master design directly onto the stencil film. An easy pressure is used, for it is important that one does not cut into the white paper backing. As the line is cut, a type of lacquer burr will curl and appear on the surface of the film. This burr can be removed by pulling it toward you or by cutting the tip with an X-Acto knife (see also BURR). To cut large areas out of the stencil film, outline the area with the film line cutter, then lift up the area with the edge of a knife and cut out small sections at a time.

Adhering solution: Adheres the stencil film and stencil film backing to the back (side "A") of the silk screen. The stencil film is adhered when the design has been completed on the film (through tracing) from the master design. Those areas in the stencil which have been cut out will produce the positive areas for screening; and those areas which would be considered negative space would be completely blocked out by the remaining stencil film (see also NEGATIVE SPACE and POSITIVE SPACE).

Negative solution: Is used around the borders of silk which do not contain the stencil film. In other words, the stencil film is cut smaller than the entire screen, leaving an approximate silk margin of 2½″ to 3″ all around. The negative solution will seal those exposed areas on the screen, thus preventing ink or color from seeping through on the desired ground. A small 3″ x 3″ square 14-ply stiff cardboard squeegee is used to pass the negative solution around the borders of the silk screen on side "A".

NOTE: A type of waterproof cloth tape can be substituted for the negative solution. It is a faster method of blocking out the border areas. Available in rolls: 2″ x 180′ and 3″ x 180′.

Gum tape: Used in same manner as described in block-out method.

Chipboard: The chipboard is cut to exactly the size of the silk screen and is placed underneath the stencil film when the stencil film is being adhered to the silk screen on side "A". The backing of chipboard provides a firm backing for this process.

Inks: See material on inks which was presented earlier in describing the block-out method.

Procedure:

1. Render a design on paper. For the first experience limit the design to only one color.

2. Place a piece of stencil film directly on top of the design with the lacquerd side up and the white paper backing down.

3. With a film line cutter begin to trace the design directly onto the stencil film lacquered surface. Use an X-Acto knife to cut away larger areas as described earlier.

4. Place the completed stencil film design on top of the piece of chipboard which is the exact size of the silk screen. As you place the stencil film on the chipboard, center it. Make sure that the lacquer side is up and the paper side is down on the chipboard.

5. Now, place the silk screen down on the stencil film which is resting on the chipboard underneath. The silk screen should be placed down on side "A", with side "B" up.

6. You are now ready to adhere the stencil film to the silk screen. In this step the lacquer sheet will bond itself to the silk screen with the application of adhering solution, and the paper backing will be peeled off. Dampen a cloth with adhering solution. Begin to apply the adhering solution to a small area of the silk. Dry this firmly and immediately, then proceed again to apply the adhering solution with a cloth to another area of the screen. Dry again. Repeat this process until the entire screen has been treated. When finished allow the screen to dry for approximately 10 to 15 minutes.

7. Turn the screen over to side "A" and begin to peel off the white paper backing. Lift a corner and pull it back in a gentle manner. The white paper backing is of no further use and may be discarded.

8. Now you are ready to apply the negative solution to the exposed silk margin around the stencil film which is now adhered to the screen. On the corner of side "A" apply a little of the negative solution and with the small square of cardboard which will act as a squeegee, begin to pull the negative solution down and around all sides until the exposed area is completely covered. Allow to dry completely and then repeat the process giving the borders on side "A" another application of the negative solution. Allow to dry.

NOTE: Fabric tape will substitute for this step.

9. Turn the screen over to side "B" and apply the gummed tape to the inside corners as described earlier in the block-out method.

10. Repeat steps 9 through 14 as described in the block-out method.

Cleaning the screen between printings: Same as described earlier in block-out method.

Cleaning the screen and removing of design on stencil film:

1. Place the screen, side "A" down, on a blotter with a padding of newspapers underneath.

2. Put some of the adhering solution on the screen and allow to penetrate the stencil film for approximately 15 to 20 seconds. Begin to rub the screen with a cloth and lift it from the pad of newspapers at the same time. Wipe with a clean cloth.

3. Put more adhering solution onto the screen and allow it to set again for 10 or 15 seconds. Begin to rub the screen again with a cloth and dry it with another clean cloth.

4. Using a stencil brush for the final cleaning, dip it into some of the adhering solution and begin to work out the remaining particles of stencil film and ink from the screen. Do this on both sides of the screen. Dry with a clean cloth.

NOTE: There are solvents other than adhering solution (see also SOLVENTS).

SILVER PAPER

See PAPERS.

SKETCH

Direct and quick line rendering of a subject (see also DRAWING).

SLAB

See CERAMICS.

SLIP

See CERAMICS.

SMOCKS (ART)

Discarded men's shirts make excellent smocks for students during art periods. Shirts are worn backwards and are buttoned down the back. Sleeves may be cut off or rolled up.

S

SOAPSUDS CRAFT

The utilization of soapsuds craft is a handy aid in manufacturing "snow" for stagecraft, dioramas, peep shows and Christmas decorations (see also DIORAMAS, HOLIDAYS AND SPECIAL EVENTS, and PEEP SHOWS).

Procedure: Pour several cups of packaged soap or detergent into a mixing bowl. Add a minimum of water and mix with an electric beater. Color may be added, if desired, by using a few drops of food coloring. When the soapsuds are the consistency of whipped cream, they may be spooned on surfaces for decorative "snow" effects. The soapsuds may be painted on windows for Halloween and Christmas decorations. Soapsuds may also be used for textural effects on papier-mâché animals. Try a white French Poodle with a soapsuds coat. Allow soapsuds to dry for 24 hours.

SODIUM SILICATE

Sodium silicate is also known as Egg-Keep, a clear liquid egg preservative which is put on the shells of eggs to ensure freshness. Sodium silicate is used in the classroom as a water-soluble substitute for shellac, varnish, and clear lacquer. It is available in pint bottles in drug stores for the cost of under a dollar. It is especially effective for high-gloss finishes on painted papier-mâché animals, and puppet heads; also gives high-gloss finishes to boxes, wastepaper baskets, and booklets which have been covered with decorative papers. It is not recommended as a finish for flat two-dimensional work as it tends to warp the paper. Sodium silicate is economical and functional. It needs no thinner and brushes may be cleaned with clear water.

When mixed to a paste with pulverized dry ceramic clay, it acts as an adhesive in mending broken greenware in ceramic programs (see also CERAMICS).

SOFT EDGE

Nondefinitive edges in painting; blended (see also HARD EDGE).

SOLVENTS

Solvents for paints, textile colors, printing inks, and adhesive cements can be used to clean working tools or to thin down the medium. The only exception would be the solvent for paraffin wax and beeswax which could not be used to thin down the wax. Thus, it may be generally stated that the solvent is also the thinner.

Solvents and thinners:

The following is a list of solvents and thinners, along with the medium or media with which they are used (see also ADHESIVES, EXTENDERS, LACQUER, PAINTS, SHELLAC, VARNISH, and WAX).

Water: Water-base paints (casein, gouache, poster paint, tempera, calcimine, acetate colors, watercolors) and water-base printing inks.

Turpentine: Oil-base paint, enamel, oil stain, varnish, beeswax, and paraffin wax.

Benzine or turpetine: Oil-base printing inks.

Denatured alcohol: Shellac and alcohol stain.

Lacquer thinner: Lacquer.

Textile thinner: Textile colors.

Acetone: Duco cement.

Rubber cement thinner: Rubber cement.

Silk Screening Solvents: Adhering solution, negative solution solvent, lacquer thinner, and acetone may be used as solvents for lacquer film or process film, fill-in lacquer, or negative solution. Kerosene may be used for tusche (hardened), silk screen oil-base colors or inks, and silk screen oil-base textile inks or paints. Water is a solvent for tusche (unhardened), silk screen water-base paints or inks, and water-soluble filler. Use hot water for glue.

SPACE

See DESIGN ELEMENTS.

SPACKLE

Commercial trade name for patching plaster; used in artwork for finishing papier-mâché, three-dimensional maps and globes (see also MAPMAKING and PAPIER-MÂCHÉ). The use of spackle over strip or pulp papier-mâché will create a much smoother surface and enhance the treatment of detail.

Students have used spackle effectively in the construction of adobe brick models of early California missions (see also ADOBE). It was also used to simulate the effect of the limestone coverings on the adobe constructions. Spackle is available in small boxes in powder form. It should be mixed with water until it is the consistency of heavy putty. It can be thinned down with water and may be applied with a brush if desired.

SPATTER GUN

To be used with spatter inks (see also INKS). The spatter gun can be adjusted to produce a large spatter effect, a mist, or a spray (see also HAND PRINTS and PRINTMAKING).

SPATTER PRINTS

See HAND PRINTS and PRINTMAKING.

SPINE

See BOOKLET MAKING.

SPRAY CANS

Household spray cans are effectively used as atomizers with fixatives (see also ATOMIZERS, FIXATIVES, and FIXATIVE SUBSTITUTES). They are also used in the rendering of spatter prints in printmaking (see also HAND PRINTS and PRINTMAKING).

SPRAYS

Pressurized spray cans of paint are available for almost every conceivable type of paint or wood covering, including enamels, varnishes, shellacs, lacquers, and fluorescents (see also LACQUERS, PAINTS, SHELLAC, and VARNISH). There are spray cans of fixative, of plastic, and of glue (see also ADHESIVES and KRYLON). There are also spray cans of liquid starch which can be used as fixatives (see also FIXATIVES and FIXATIVE SUBSTITUTES).

SQUEEGEE

Rubber-edged tool with a wooden handle (see Fig. S-8), which is used in silk screen printing, or serigraphy, for the purpose of carrying or pushing the silk screen ink from the top of the screen to the bottom. The squeegee enables the ink to be uniformly carried with equal pres-

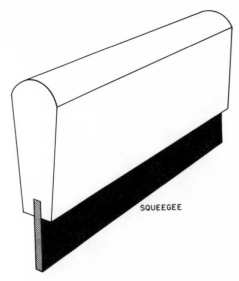

SQUEEGEE

Fig. S-8

sure through a silk screen which has on it a blocked-out design (see also SERIGRAPHY, SILK SCREENING, and STENCIL). The design is usually blocked out with either tusche or process film (see also PROCESS FILM). The ink seeps through the exposed areas of the screen, registering a print on the paper or fabric underneath.

Younger students can use a simplified method of silk screen printing (see also PRINTMAKING). In this simplified process, a rectangular piece of chipboard serves as a substitute for the squeegee.

STABILE

Form of sculpture which has the quality of being light in feeling, yet firm in placement (Fig. S-9), as opposed to the mobile which is light in feeling, yet not firm in placement (see also MOBILE and SCULPTURE). Stabiles may be fashioned from scrap material such as balsa wood, swab sticks, bamboo sticks, or toothpicks (see also SCRAP MATERIALS). Duco cement is used as an adhesive to glue the sticks together. In stabile construction, it is well to start with a firm base of either triangular or rectangular formations. Sometimes color is added to stabiles in the form of panels of gelatine paper or colored tissue [see also JELLS, PAPERS, and TISSUE (COLORED)].

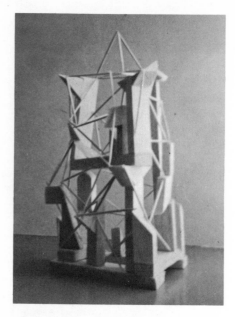

Fig. S-9

STAINED GLASS WINDOWS

Stained glass windows are considered to be Byzantine in origin. They are held together with strips of lead and are seen traditionally in cathedrals, particularly of the Gothic period, such as the Cologne cathedral. Classroom experiences in "stained glass windows" are as follows:

Stained Glass Windows (Glass):

Materials needed: Small broken piececs of colored glass, or Venetian tile tesserae, which may be purchased commercially, tile nippers, white resin glue, and an old frame with the glass in it.

Procedure: Arrange the colored glass or tile into a design on the frame glass, leaving about 1″ margin around the glass so that it may be fitted back into the frame when the project is completed. Arrange the colored glass on the outside of the frame, not on the inside. The colored glass may necessitate cutting with a tile nipper in order to achieve the desired design patterns. If so, cut the glass or tessera in a paper bag to avoid the possibility of shattering glass and danger to the eyes. Glue the pieces of colored glass down on the frame glass with white resin glue (see also

ADHESIVES). When the glue has dried thoroughly, place the colored, designed, frame glass back into the frame and secure it there with the small nail catches in the back. Put wire hangers in back of the frame and hang these stained glass frames in areas through which light may filter. Hang them at different lengths in classroom windows or on doors. The variety of the designs whether pictorial or abstract, as well as the variety of the sizes of the frames will enhance the interest of the display. An example of a stained glass window is shown in Fig. S-10.

Fig. S-10

Frames may be painted gold, white, or a variety of colors. If they are painted white, they may be "antiqued" with orange shellac or some thinned-down burnt umber (see also SHELLAC). The shellac or thinned-down burnt umber is applied to the frame, allowed to stay for a couple of minutes, and then wiped off with a cloth (see also LAMINATED RESIN).

Stained Glass Windows (Paper): Render the design on white drawing paper with crayons which have been applied heavily to the ground (see also GROUND). Apply linseed oil to the back of the paper to achieve the look of transparency. Hang these on window panes for effective lighting.

Stained Glass Windows (Tissue Paper): Method of adhering colored tissue to windows with liquid starch or Mazola oil as an adhesive [see also ADHESIVES, PAPERS, and TISSUE (COLORED)].

Indirect Method: Create a design on paper which is of the same size as the window on which the "stained glass" is to be rendered. Block in color with either paint or crayon. Lay tissue over the design and trace individual areas of color which will correspond to the range of colors represented in the tissue. Lay these on a flat surface, creating and building the design section by section in a jigsaw fashion. Starting from the bottom of the window, brush the liquid starch adhesive directly on the pane of glass. Begin to lay the tissue on the glass, piece by piece.

Direct Method: Apply abstract, free-form colored tissue shapes to the window in a direct method with the liquid starch as an adhesive. Overlap the colored tissue with other hues in order to achieve interesting color arrangements.

NOTE: Do not apply adhesives of either liquid starch or Mazola oil to the back of colored tissue and then attempt to transfer colored tissue to a window. Tissue is fragile, and it will be impossible to lift after adhesive is applied. A more successful method would be to place the tissue flush against the windowpane, and then begin to brush on the adhesive. The tissue is highly absorbent and will allow the adhesive to penetrate and make immediate contact with the window. Additional overlays may be applied in the same manner.

STANDARD COLORS

See COLORS (STANDARD) and SUPPLIES (CLASSROOM).

STAPLE GUN

Automatically drives heavy-gauge 5/16″ staples into wood, plastic, or board. While the staple gun (Fig. S-11)

Fig. S-11

is considered a handy tool for bulletin-board and general display work where staples can take the place of tacks and pins, it is a dangerous tool for children to handle without supervision. The staple gun should always be pointed downward and kept in a locked position when not in use (see also BULLETIN BOARD).

STAPLES

See STAPLE GUN.

STARCH

Liquid starch is used as a base for finger painting (see also DECORATIVE PAPERS). It is used as an adhesive for collage techniques with colored tissue paper (see also COLLAGE, PAPERS, and STAINED GLASS WINDOWS). It is used as a stiffening agent for cotton roving and yarn (see also BALLOONS and COTTON-ROVING MOBILES). It is used as a vehicle agent in mixing powdered paint or tempera in order to achieve interesting, transparent color (see also PAINTING). It is also used as a fixative (see also FIXATIVES, FIXATIVE SUBSTITUTES, and SPRAYS).

STARCH PAINTING

See DECORATIVE PAPERS.

STEEL BRUSHES

See BRUSHES (STEEL).

STEEL EDGE

See RULERS.

STEEL WIRE

See WIRES.

STEEL WOOL

See ABRASIVES.

STENCIL

A sheet of paper or other material in which a design has been cut so that the design can be reproduced on other surfaces by applying ink or paint to the open areas. This printmaking process is used in serigraphy or silk screening. A simplified stencil technique can be used in the lower grades [see also PRINTMAKING, PRINTMAKING (PROFESSIONAL), PRINTS, SERIGRAPHY, and SILK SCREENING].

STENCIL FILM

See PROCESS FILM and SILK SCREENING.

STENCIL KNIVES

See KNIVES.

STENCIL PAPER

See PAPERS.

STENCIL PROCESS

See PRINTMAKING, PRINTMAKING (PROFESSIONAL), PRINTS, and SERIGRAPHY.

STICKS

See BAMBOO STICKS, MOBILES, SCRAP MATERIALS, SCULPTURE, and STABILES.

STILL LIFE

Arrangement of inanimate objects in the creation of a subject for drawing, painting, or photography.

STIPPLE

Rapid up-and-down motion with a brush; associated with the stencil process (see also BRUSHES, BRUSH STROKES, PRINTMAKING, and TEXTILE DESIGN).

STITCHERY

An exciting and highly popular simplification of the tapestry idea for wall hangings. See Fig. S-12. Stitchery can be imaginative with free, nonobjective areas of colored yarn or appliqué cloth, or there can be panels which are planned in detail and transferred to the fabric ground with white or yellow carbon paper (see also APPLIQUÉ, GROUND, NONOBJECTIVE ART, PAPERS, and TRACING AND TRANSFER).

Materials needed: Burlap or other suitable ground such as canvas or felt, crewel needles for embroidery, tapestry needles, embroidery floss, yarn, cotton roving, thimbles, and a variety of patterned and textured cloth for work in appliqué.

Procedure: Construct a frame of wood which will be identical in size to the stitchery ground on which you will work. Old picture frames and curtain stretchers make excellent substitute frames for working on panels. Tack the fabric ground to the frame using either burlap, rug backing, fiberglass wire screening, canvas, or felt. Use onion or apple bags for smaller panels. Either stitch directly on the fabric ground or work from a planned cartoon (see also CARTOON). Use one of the colored carbon papers when transferring a planned design onto a fabric ground (see also TRACING AND TRANSFER). Use any number of stitches, such as the outline stitch, cross-stitch, chain stitch, French knot, or satin stitch.

Appliqué materials to the fabric ground using either areas of colored felt or patterned cloth, or both. Sew ropes or cotton roving to the fabric ground. Add buttons or beads, or both. When finished, take the fabric ground or stitchery panel off the frame. Stitch up the sides, but at the top and bottom, stitch a double edge so that a length of wood

Fig. S-12

doweling may be inserted. The doweling at the top will permit hanging with a cord tied to both ends; and at the bottom, the doweling will act as a weight.

NOTE: There is an excellent source book for stitchery which explains in detail the following stitches: lazy-daisy, herringbone, feather, blanket, outline, cross-stitch, and others. This booklet comes with individual charts illustrating the stitches: *The Gingham Book of Embroidery* (New York: The Educational Bureau of Coats and Clark, Inc.).

STONE AGE

Included the Paleolithic, Mesolithic, and Neolithic periods when stone was used extensively for dwellings, weapons, tools, and other implements [see also BRONZE AGE, HISTORY (ART), IRON AGE, NEOLITHIC PERIOD, and PALEOLITHIC PERIOD].

STONES

See LAPIDARY.

STOVE PIPE WIRE

See WIRES.

STRING

See YARNS AND STRINGS.

STRUCTOLITE

See CARVING MATERIALS.

STUMPS (GRAY PAPER)

A short thick roll of paper cut to a point and used to rub down lines; used in charcoal sketching and drawing as a tool for shading and blending (see also CHARCOAL, DRAWING, and PASTELS).

STYROFOAM

Extremely lightweight material which offers possibilities for sculpture, carving, mobiles, and puppetry (see also CARVING MATERIALS, MOBILES, and PUPPETS). Commercial styrofoam weighs 1.6 pounds per cubic foot and can be shaped by rubbing one piece against another. It may be cut with a knife or coping saw (see also KNIVES and WOODWORKING). It will act as a base for a stabile or a dried-flower or weed arrangement (see also DRYING WEEDS and STABILES).

Styrofoam is available in colors of red, dark green, light green, light blue, and white. It comes in sizes: ½″ x 12″ x 36″, 1″ x 1″ x 36″, and 2″ x 12″ x 36″ and is available at art supply, plastic supply, and surplus houses. The adhesive which is used for styrofoam is called Rez-N-Glue; and will adhere styrofoam to itself or other surfaces. A good source of plastic materials and styrofoam is Cope Plastics, Highway 100, Godfrey, Illinois (see also PLASTICS).

SUBORDINATE

Relates to the structure of design and composition; when one area is dominant, the other areas become subordinate. Subordinance denotes a lack of prominence or emphasis (see also DESIGN ELEMENTS).

SUGAR PINE

See WOODS.

SUPPLIES (CLASSROOM)

The following list is offered as a basic inventory for a one-year art program in the kindergarten-primary grades or kindergarten through grade 3; the intermediates, or grades 4 through 6; the upper grades including junior high, or grades 7 through 9; and high school, or grades 10 through 12. Adjustments may be made relative to whether or not school districts prescribe to the 6-3-3 or the 8-4 plan for grade distribution.

Teachers and administrators may use this list as a reference in ordering supplies for a one-year program based upon a class enrollment of 30 students. By necessity, secondary schools will multiply quantities by the number of special art classes taught. Further adjustments can be made relative to supplies on hand, substitution of materials, and numbers of children in the classrooms. If school districts order on a six-months basis, instead of the year's basis

S

which is described, cut quantities in half. Throughout the list of materials, standard colors both in paints and papers include red, orange, yellow, blue, green, violet, brown, and black.

Item	Kinder-garten to Grade 3	Grades 4-6	Junior High	High School
Abrasives:				
Sandpaper (packages)	4	4	4	4
Steel wool (packages)	1	1	1	1
Adhesives:				
Duco cement, 1¾-oz. tubes, (dozen)		2½	2½	2½
Higgins vegetable glue, 8-oz. can	1	2	2	2
Rubber cement, 4-oz. jar, (dozen)	½	½	2½	2½
School paste, pint jar	6	6	2	2
Wheat paste, 5-lb. sack	4	4	2	2
White resin glue, 1¼ oz.	4	12	18	18
Brayers:				
4″ rubber roller		4	2	2
8″ rubber roller			2	2
Brushes:				
Easel, flat, ⅞″	30	12	8	6
Easel, round, ½″	30	12	8	6
Lettering, flat, ¼″			6	6
Lettering, flat, ½″			6	6
Oil, round, No. 1				5
Oil, round, No. 10				5
Oil, brights, No. 3				5
Oil, brights, No. 9				5
Oil, flats, No. 5				5
Oil, flats, No. 12				5
Paste, ½″ (dozen)	2½	2½	2½	2½
Stencil, ¼″ (dozen)		1½	½	½
Stencil, ⅜″ (dozen)		1½	½	½

Item	Kinder-garten to Grade 3	Grades 4-6	Junior High	High School
Brushes (Continued):				
Varnish or enamel, ½″ width	2		2	2
Varnish or enamel, 1½″ width	2		2	2
Varnish or enamel, 3″ width	2		2	2
Watercolor, sable, 7⁄16″, (dozen)			2½	2½
Watercolor, sable, 11⁄16″, (dozen)			2½	2½
Watercolor, sable, 13⁄16″, (dozen)			2½	2½
Canvas boards:				
Rectangle, 16″ x 20″ (dozen)				2½
Charcoal:				
Black vine, box of 12		3	3	3
Clay:				
Low-firing moist, 25-lb sack	3	3	3	3
Plastic clay, 1-lb box (dozen)	4	2	1½	1½
Colored chalks:				
Assortment, large, box of 12	2			
Assortment, medium, box of 48		2		
Assortment, small, box of 144			1	1
Crayons:				
Assortment, large, box of 8 (dozen)	2½			
Assortment, small, box of 8 (dozen)		2½	2½	2½

Item	Kindergarten to Grade 3	Grades 4-6	Junior High	High School
Drawing boards:				
Wooden, 18″ x 24″ (dozen)		2½	2½	2½
Easels:				
Double panel, 26″ x 20″, 50″ high	2	1		
Erasers:				
Gum, 2″ x 1″ x 1″	1	1	30	30
Kneaded, soft (dozen)		2½	2½	2½
Pink pearl soft (dozen)		2½	2½	2½
Glass:				
Plate glass, 9″ x 12″		6	3	3
Glazes:				
Low-firing, 1 pint				
Green	1	1	1	1
Yellow	1	1	1	1
Brown	1	1	1	1
Blue	1	1	1	1
Orange	1	1	1	1
Black		1	1	1
Clear glaze		1	2	2
Engobes, standard colors		1	1	1
Inks:				
Black drawing ink, 1-oz bottle (dozen)			2½	2½
Block printing, oil-base, ¼-lb tube				
Red			1	1
Blue			1	1
Orange			1	1
Green			1	1
Yellow			1	1
Inks (Continued):				
Violet			1	1
Brown			1	1
Black			1	1
White			1	1
Block printing, water-soluble, ¼-lb tube				
Red	4		2	2
Blue	4		2	2
Orange			2	2
Green			2	2
Yellow			2	2
Brown			2	2
Black	4		2	2
White			2	2
Colored drawing inks, 1-oz bottle				
Red	2		1	1
Blue	2		1	1
Orange	2		1	1
Green			1	1
Yellow			1	1
Brown			1	1
White			1	1
Knives:				
Mat knife	1	1	1	1
Palette knife				5
Stencil knife		4	5	5
Linoleum blocks:				
Mounted, 4″ x 6″ (dozen)		2½	2½	2½
Mounted, 8″ x 10″ (dozen)			2½	2½
Linoleum cutters and handles:				
Set of 1 handle and 6 cutters, No. 1, 2, 3, 4, 5, and 6		6	5	5

S

ITEM	AMOUNT PER 30 STUDENTS			
	Kindergarten to Grade 3	Grades 4-6	Junior High	High School

Paint:

Tempera, powdered, 1-lb can

Extender	6	4	2	2
Red	8	5	2	2
Blue	6	4	2	2
Orange	6	4	2	2
Green	6	4	2	2
Yellow	8	5	2	2
Violet	6	4	2	2
Brown	6	4	2	2
Black	6	4	2	2
White	8	5	2	2
Flesh	4	3	1	1
Watercolors, pans of 8 colors (dozen)		2½	2½	2½

Paints:

Oil, tubes, 1" x 4"

Zinc white				16
Ivory black				8
Burnt umber				8
Raw sienna				8
Ultramarine blue				8
Yellow ochre				8
Cadmium light yellow				8
Cadmium medium red				8
Alizarin crimson				8
Viridian green				8

Poster colors, pint jars

Red			2	2
Blue			2	2
Orange			2	2
Green			2	2
Yellow			2	2
Violet			2	2
Brown			2	2

ITEM	AMOUNT PER 30 STUDENTS			
	Kindergarten to Grade 3	Grades 4-6	Junior High	High School

Paints (Continued):

Black			4	4
White			4	4

Palettes:

Wooden, (dozen)				2½

Paper cutter:

1 cutter per 4 classrooms on elementary school level and 1 cutter per classroom on secondary level

Bogus, 12" x 18" (ream)	1	1	1	1

Butcher paper, roll 30" x 450'

1 roll per 8 classrooms or per 240 students

Charcoal paper, 19" x 25"			30	30
Chipboard. No. 70 weight, thin	15	15	15	15
Chipboard, No. 40 weight, thick	15	15	15	15
Construction, standard colors, 9" x 12", 100-sheet packages, (per color)	1	1	1	1
Construction, standard colors, 12" x 18", 100-sheet packages, (per color)	2	2	2	2
Drawing, manila, 12" x 18" (ream)	1	1	1	1
Drawing, white, 9" x 12" (ream)	3	3	1	1
Drawing, white, 12" x 18" (ream)	4	4	1	1
Finger paint papers, 100 sheets, (packages)	4	2	1	1

Item	Amount Per 30 Students			
	Kindergarten to Grade 3	Grades 4-6	Junior High	High School

Papers (Continued):

Kraft paper, roll,				
30″ x 450′	1 roll per 8 classrooms or per 240 students			
30″ x 450′	1 roll per 8 classrooms or per 240 students			
Mat board, 30″ x 40″	5	5	30	30
Newsprint, colored,				
18″ x 24″, (ream)				
Blue	½	¼		
Yellow	½	¼		
Pink	½	¼		
Newsprint, plain,				
18″ x 24″, (ream)	2	2	½	½
Oak tagboard, plain,				
12″ x 18″	30	30	30	30
Poster board, 22″ x 28″			30	30
Stencil paper, 9″ x 12″,				
20-sheet packages		4	4	4
Tonal or poster paper, 9″ x 12″, standard colors, 100-sheet packages, (per color)	2	2	1	1
Tracing paper or onion skin, 8½″ x 11″, (ream)		¼	½	½

Pencils:

Type 4-H or No. 2, (dozen)		2½	2½	2½

Pens and holders:

Esterbrook, (set)				
Round, No. 0, 2, 5	1	1	5	5
Square, No. 6, 8, 10	1	1	5	5
Shading, No. 11, 13, 15, 17, 19	1	1	5	5
Speedball, (set)				
Square, A-5, A-3, A-0	1	1	5	5
Round, B-5, B-3, B-1	1	1	5	5
Oblong, C-5, C-3, C-0	1	1	5	5
Oval, D-5, D-00	1	1	5	5

Item	Amount Per 30 Students			
	Kindergarten to Grade 3	Grades 4-6	Junior High	High School

Scissors:

Blunt point, 4″ (dozen)	2½			
Clip point, 5″ (dozen)		2½		
Sharp point, 5″ (dozen)			2½	2½

Starch (liquid):

Household	8	4	1	1

Tape:

Cellophane, roll, ½″	2	2	1	1
Masking, roll, ½″	1	1	1	1

Turpentine and linseed oil:

8-oz bottle			15	15

Watercolor pans:

Metal (dozen)		2½	2½	2½

SUPPLIES (VENDORS)

The following list of vendors, as well as the supplies and materials they carry for schools and artists, is skeletal and not exhaustive. It is presented as a quick reference for materials described in this book. Other vendors exist and deserve the consideration of the reader in making his own selection in terms of specific need and geographical location.

American Handicrafts Company, 33 East 14th Street, New York, New York: General craft materials such as copper enameling, copper tooling, basketry, honeycomb candles, wicking, silk screen supplies, mosaics, papers, etc.

Branch offices are located in Atlanta, Chicago, Columbus, Denver, Detroit, Fort Worth, Houston, Minneapolis, Philadelphia, San Antonio, St. Louis, Seattle, Inglewood, San Francisco, and Los Angeles.

American Seating Company, 701 Bayshore Boulevard, San Francisco, California and 800 Supulveda Boulevard, El Segundo, California: General school supplies and equipment, etc.

S

Arthur Brown and Bros., Inc., 2 West 46th Street, New York 36, New York: Drawing and drafting supplies such as silk screen, papers, school art supplies, airbrushes and compressors, picture frames, hobby crafts, studio furniture and equipment, plastics, etc.

Austen Display, 133 West 19th Street, New York 11, New York: Imported Belgian colored tissue in 42 colors, flint paper in 18 colors, and foils in 12 colors.

Brodhead Garrett Company, 4560 East 71st Street, Cleveland 5, Ohio: Lumber, benches, machinery, hand tools, automotive equipment, hardware, paints, electrical and electronic supplies, metalworking arts, plastics, arts and crafts, mechanical drawing materials, papers, etc.

Chesapeake Picture Frame Company, 414-SA East Baltimore Street, Baltimore 2, Maryland: Artists' frames, moldings, and general art supplies.

Cope Plastics, Highway 100, Godfrey Illinois: General plastic supplies such as plexiglass, cellulose acetate, styrofoam, jewelry findings, laminates, cements, fiberglass, hot pack ovens and heaters, etc.

Craftools Incorporated, Department SA2, Wood Ridge, New Jersey: Lapidary equipment, including units, trim and faceting saws, tumblers, etc.

Drakenfeld, B. F., and Company, 45 Park Place, New York 7, New York: General Pottery supplies.

The Pacific coast agents are Braun Corporation, Los Angeles, California, and Braun Knecht Heimann Company, San Francisco 19, California.

Hammetts, Kendall Square, Cambridge, Massachusetts: Industrial arts and occupational therapy supplies such as large and small looms, basketry, metal crafts, yarns and strings, etc.

Immerman and Sons, 1924 Euclid Avenue, Cleveland 15, Ohio: General craft supplies for copper enameling, mosaics, marquetry, metal etching, metal tooling, etc., also paper and veneer woods.

Larson, J. C., 820 South Tripp Avenue, Chicago 24, Illinois: General craft supplies for leathercraft, metal craft, woodcraft, mosaics, burlap, basketry, etc.

La Clair Silk Screen and Craft Supplies, Corner 21st Avenue and Taraval, San Francisco, California: Silk screening supplies and general arts and crafts materials.

Lorraine Fibre Mills Incorporated, 430 Bond Street, Brooklyn 31, New York: Dyed burlap of all colors.

Milton Bradley Company, Springfield, Massachusetts: Art supplies, nursery and kindergarten materials, games, arithmetic aids, reading aids, school furniture, etc.

Paasche Airbrush Company, Department 18, Chicago 14, Illinois: Airpainting equipment.

Sculpture House, 38 East 30th Street, New York 16, New York: Natural stone, pink alabaster, ebony, translucent crystal; stones that can be cut with a pocket knife.

Stanley Tools, Education Department, New Britain, Connecticut: Tools for general shop, woodworking, electrical and sheet metal work, etc.

Western Ceramics Supply Company, 1601 Howard Street, San Francisco 3, California: General pottery supplies.

SURREALISM

An outgrowth of Dadaism (see also DADA). Surrealism was influenced by the writings of Sigmund Freud; in content, it puts emphasis on fantasy and the unconscious.

EXAMPLE: "Giraffe on Fire," by Salvadore Dali.

SYMBOLIC

Use of symbols in design and composition (see also ICONOGRAPHY).

SYMBOLISM

The use of symbols in painting, as illustrated by the late nineteenth century paintings of Odilon Redon (see also ICONOGRAPHY and SYMBOLIC).

EXAMPLE: "Mystery," by Odilon Redon.

SYMMETRICAL

See BALANCE.

SYMMETRY

See BALANCE.

TABBY WEAVE

See WEAVING.

TACHISME

See ABSTRACT-EXPRESSIONISM.

TACTILE

See DESIGN ELEMENTS.

TAGBOARD

See PAPERS.

TALLOW

Animal fat or suet which is used as a base for candles (see also CANDLEMAKING).

TAPA CLOTH

See DECORATIVE PAPERS.

TAPES

Cellophane: A clear transparent tape with either a gloss or matte finish. The matte finish is transparent but does not have a shining surface when pressed down and used. Matte-finished cellophane tape is particularly good for binding reproductions with a protective covering along the edges; it is available in ¾″ size under the commercial trade name of Scotch tape, among others. Gloss-finished tape is available in sizes: ½″, ¾″, and 1″.

Gummed Kraft Paper Tape: This tape is brown kraft paper, gummed on one side (see also PAPERS and SILK SCREENING). It is used in the simplified silk screen process to adhere organdy to box tops (see also PRINTMAKING). It is available in sizes: 1″, 1½″, and 2″.

Masking Tape: This is a nontransparent contact tape which is used in painting to "mask-off" areas such as around windows and in washes in watercolor painting. It is available in sizes: ½″, ¾″, and 1″.

Miracle Tape: Made of foam rubber with an adhesive contact back and front. It will adhere to walls, bricks, and cement and will hold art displays as well as light, three-dimensional materials (see also BULLETIN BOARDS and WAX).

NOTE: A vendor of miracle tape is Sunset House, 118 Sunset Building, Beverley Hills, California.

Mystic Tape: Colored, fabric-textured contact tape; used in booklet making (see also BOOKLET MAKING). It is available in sizes: ¾″, 1½″, 2″, and 3″ and in colors: green, red, wine, blue, yellow, white, and black.

TATLINISM

See CONSTRUCTIVISM.

TEMPERA

See PAINTING and PAINTS.

TEMPLATE

Half profile of a ceramic pot which is used in hand-built pottery to achieve perfect symmetry of form (Fig. T-1) (see also CERAMICS).

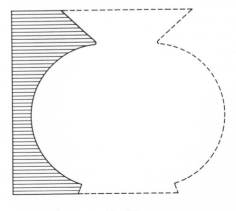

Fig. T-1

T

TENSION

Relates to oblique lines in drawing and painting (see also DRAWING and PAINTING). A secondary meaning relates to degree of tightness of the warp thread in weaving (see also WEAVING and YARNS AND STRINGS).

TERRA COTTA

See CERAMICS.

TERTIARY COLORS

See COLOR.

TESSERA

See MOSAICS.

TESSERAE

Plural of tessera (see also MOSAICS).

TEST (GOODENOUGH)

See GOODENOUGH TEST.

TESTOR'S CEMENT FOR PLASTICS

See ADHESIVES.

TEXTILE COLORS

For textile designs including stencil and painting. Colors are available in sets as well as in individual color containers including cleaner, extender (to mix with colors to make them lighter), and penetrator-thinner. Wide ranges of colors are available in ¾-ounce, 2-ounce, 8-ounce, 16-ounce, and gallon containers (see also SILK SCREENING and TEXTILE DESIGN).

TEXTILE DESIGN

The creation of a design on fabric with media such as crayon, oil-base spray paint, and, most generally, textile colors (see also SILK SCREENING).

Crayon Design: Fabric should be washed and ironed in order to remove sizing or stiffening agent from new mate-

rial. Smaller children may draw directly on the fabric. After the design is rendered, the fabric is placed between two sheets of white newsprint and is ironed with a warm iron (250°F) for 3 minutes in order to set the crayon design in the fabric.

Primary grade children may use crayon in the stencil process. A design may be cut from a piece of tagboard by folding it in half and cutting a symmetrical form. The fabric is then tacked to a drawing board and the stencil is tacked over it. Short crayon strokes are applied from the edge of the stencil inward toward the middle. The crayon design is set with an iron as described previously (see also PRINTMAKING).

Textile Color Design: The stencil process employed with textile colors requires specific instructions (see PRINTMAKING). As was indicated in the crayon design process, wash new material before using; this will remove the sizing from the cloth and will insure greater permanency of color. The fabric is tacked to a drawing board with a blotter underneath the fabric to catch the excess color. The stencil is placed over the fabric and either tacked to the board or held securely in place.

The textile color is worked into the brush and the excess color is stippled off on paper toweling. Remember for all stencil work, *very little* of the medium used for color is necessary. It is always preferable to build up color with several light applications than to employ one heavy one. A stipling motion is used in the stencil process, or one might employ sweeping brush strokes (as long as the strokes begin at the edge of the stencil and sweep toward the middle of the open area of the stencil design). Good stencil work has sharp edges; this is achieved through light application of color with particular emphasis to building up the color along the edges of the stencil. If the textile color is too thick, it may be thinned down with penetrator-thinner. If it is too dark, lighten it with extender. In lightening a color, pour a little extender into a container and add color to it; never the reverse. Allow textile color designs to dry for 24 hours. Set with a hot iron at 350°F using a pressing cloth over the design which is set face up on the ironing board. Turn the fabric over and iron on the other side. Iron each side for approximately 3 minutes (see also BATIK and TIE-DYE).

NOTE: For another type of textile design experience which is particularly applicable in the primary grades, use colored felt pens, either in freehand decorative rendering or with stencils (see also PENS and PRINTMAKING).

TEXTURE

See COLLAGE, DESIGN ELEMENTS, and RUBBINGS.

TEXTURE BOX

The collection of interesting and contrasting textures which are contained in a small box. This experience in collecting is particularly applicable in kindergarten-primary grades where the collecting instinct of children is high. Children should be encouraged to prepare a box with things that "feel different;" to explore their homes for such things as velvet, tin, burlap, rice paper, mirrors, or plastic.

Children might be encouraged to be aware not only of differences in roughness and smoothness of materials but also of differences in tactile temperatures. For example, a mirror would be cold in feeling, while a piece of wool would be warm. Textures also have degrees of sound. For example, cellophane paper crackles to the touch, while velvet is quiet. Children not only enjoy this initial experience in awareness of textural qualities of materials, but they enjoy trading their texture boxes with other children. Half the fun of feeling textures is to close one's eyes and try to guess what the material is that one is feeling (see also COLLAGE, DESIGN ELEMENTS, and RUBBINGS).

THINNERS

See SOLVENTS.

THREE-DIMENSION

See DIMENSION.

THROWING

See CERAMICS.

THROWN POTS

See CERAMICS.

TIE-DYE

This is a dyeing process wherein areas of fabric are tied off in order to "save" fabric from dye and/or color. After repeated tying and dyeing, informal designs will appear on the fabric which are intense in color and interesting in terms of visual textures.

Materials needed: Six enamel pans; dry dye (Tintex, Rit, Putnam, or others) in the following colors: red, yellow, and blue; cotton sheeting; and string (see also DYES).

Procedure: Mix the dyes according to the description given for the preparation of dyes in the batik process (see also BATIK). Set up a work area for dyeing as described in the batik process. Use a square of old sheeting with the approximate dimensions of 14″ x 14″. If new material is used, wash it and iron it to remove sizing.

1. Dip the square of fabric into cold water.

2. Lift the square from the water at the middle of the fabric. Hold cloth in the hand with the pointed center coming up from the fist.

3. Obtain a length of string about 30″ long and double it. Wind the doubled string around and around the fabric above the fist; finally, loop the string *only once* to make the tie secure. *Do not knot the string.* If the string is knotted, it will be difficult to untie once it is wet.

4. Dip the entire fabric including the tied area into the yellow dye bath. The longer the fabric remains in the dye bath the more intense the colors will become. Allow the fabric to remain in the dye bath for approximately 3 minutes. In this step you are not only dyeing the fabric yellow, but you are "saving" a section of the white fabric from the yellow dye. The tying of the fabric will consistently "save" areas from color.

5. Remove the fabric from the yellow dye bath, allowing the excess dye to run off. Press off the excess dye between the fingers of the hands. *Do not wring the fabric.*

6. Now dip the fabric into a clear water bath which is contained in the second enamel pan, next to the yellow dye. Again allow excess water to run off, patting it off between the hands.

7. Tie off another section of the fabric somewhere underneath the first tied-off section. In this step you will be "saving" some of the yellow color.

8. Dip into a red dye bath. Here you will note that the yellow fabric turns orange (see also COLOR).

9. Repeat steps 5, 6, and 7 and tie off some of the orange fabric color. Then dip into the blue dye bath. Rinse in clear water.

NOTE: The color of the fabric is now brown. A further exploration into the pigment theory of color will promote understandings relative to "what happens when complements are mixed together" (see also COLOR).

10. As the final step, untie all of the string. It should be emphasized that the string remains tied throughout all of the different dye baths. When all of the strings have been untied and the fabric is opened, there will be a series of circles of different colors as shown in Fig. T-2.

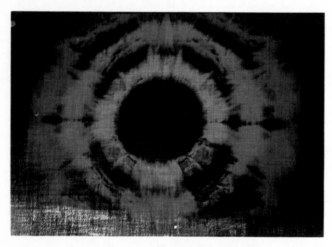

Fig. T-2

The circle nearest the center will be white, the next circle will be yellow, and the final circle will be orange. The background will be brown. This represents only the classic technique in tying and dyeing. There are, of course, many, many more. The most exciting designs come from pure experimentation.

Try folding the material and dyeing it. Try pleating the material in an accordion fashion and then tying it at both ends for a serape. Try pleating the material in an accordion fashion and tying it at both ends and at the middle for a series of straight lines. If you want a plaid, pleat the material in an accordion fashion, going in the opposite direction, and tie it as before, at the ends and in the middle. Try tying marbles in the cloth for a series of tiny circles. Try twisting the corners of the fabric and tying these in knots for an interesting marbled effect.

Additional pointers: The basic rule to remember is that in the dyeing process one must dye with the light dyes first and then go on to the darker dyes. Never dye from the darker to the lighter; you will only muddy the dyes and the effect will be much less intense in color. You may skip dyes or use only one. The choice is up to the individual.

Whatever one does with this process and however it is used, whether as an experience unto itself or as a related one in the designing of scarves, tablecloths, curtains, or ties, familiarity with the process will promote further understandings, and understandings will bring about further experimentation with the tie-dye process. One thing is certain, there are no failures in the tie-dye process! Dyed articles should be put in a mordant solution to insure permanency of color (see also MORDANTS). For additional fabric decorative processes (see also BATIK and TEXTILE DESIGN).

TIME LINE

Horizontal representation of historical facts usually accompanied by dates and pictures; used extensivey in social studies correlated art activities. Students of kindergarten-primary grades use only pictures for time lines; older students, usually beyond the fourth grade, accompany pictures with significant dates.

TIN CRAFT

Use tin cans and tin cutters for tin-craft projects. Make ornaments for Christmas trees and punch holes for hanging with an awl (see also HOLIDAYS AND SPECIAL EVENTS and WOODWORKING). Cut free forms for mobiles from tin (see also MOBILES). Try some tin sculpture (see also SCULPTURE).

NOTE: When cutting tin, wear gloves. The sharp edges of tin are rather dangerous and for this reason tin-craft is not suitable for the lower elementary grades.

TINT

See COLOR.

TISSUE (COLORED)

Imported Belgian tissue, specifically a brilliant high intensity paper which is available in 42 tints, shades, tones, and hues (including blacks, grays, and browns). The size of the tissue sheet is 20″ x 30″, and it may be purchased by the single sheet, by the quire, or by the ream [see also COLOR, REAM, QUIRE, PAPERS, and SUPPLIES (VENDORS)].

This high quality colored tissue is used extensively for color inserts or overlays in the collage, mobile, stabile, and laminated-paper processes (see also COLLAGE, LAMINATED PAPERS, MOBILES, and STABILES). It is also adhered to windows with either Mazola oil or liquid starch, in one of the stained glass window processes (see also ADHESIVES and STAINED GLASS WINDOWS). Tissue of this type can be soaked in water and the ensuing liquid may be used as a painting medium (see also MEDIUM and PAINT SUBSTITUTES).

NOTE: This imported Belgian tissue is not to be confused with the more common type of colored wrapping papers of the tissue type. In all instances when reference is made to *colored tissue*, in this book, it will relate specifically to imported Belgian tissue [see also SUPPLIES (VENDORS)].

TJANTING

See BATIK.

TONAL PAPER

Alternate term for poster paper (see also PAPERS).

TONDO

Round or circular painting. Tondos were popularized in Italy in the mid-fifteenth century (see also KAKEMONO, MAKIMONO, and QUADRA).

TONE

See COLOR.

TONGUE DEPRESSORS

See SCRAP MATERIALS.

TOOLING

See LEATHER.

TOOLS

See WIRE TOOLS and WOODWORKING.

TOOTHPICKS

See SCRAP MATERIALS and SCULPTURE.

TORN PAPER

In making a collage, this interesting technique utilizes the pasting of torn colored papers to a paper ground (see Fig. T-3), rather than using the conventional paper forms.

Fig. T-3

Control can be achieved with this technique by rendering the form desired with brush and water on the papers which will be torn. Try using magazine illustrations or advertisements instead of colored construction paper with the torn-paper technique. Try making a mosaic by using small pieces of torn colored paper (see also COLLAGE and MOSAICS).

T

TOTEM POLES

Build totem poles with boxes of various sizes by laying the larger ones on the bottom and the smaller ones on top. Use large soup boxes, small hatboxes and smaller shoeboxes. Fasten them together with staples and masking tape. For details such as eyes, beaks, wings, and hands, crush newspaper and either tie it or tape it into place. Cover entire totem pole with several layers of strip papier-mâché (see also PAPIER-MACHE). Paint the totem pole with tempera and give it a final finishing coat of shellac. Add decorative details using scrap materials, raffia, and feathers. Smaller totem poles may be fashioned by using match boxes with the same technique. Features can be built up with plastic clay and then covered with strip papier-mâché [see also CLAY (PLASTIC)]. As an experience in carving, totem poles can also be made of balsa wood (see also BALSA WOOD and CARVING MATERIALS).

TRACING AND TRANSFER

Sometimes called ichnography; essentially the tracing of a design and transferring it to another ground; a duplication.

Tracing and Transfer of a Design:

Type 1:

1. Place onion-skin tracing paper over the design.
2. Trace the design on the onion skin paper.
3. Blacken the back of the onion skin paper with heavy black pencil.
4. Place the traced design on the desired ground and go over the contour of the design, or the lines of the design, with a pencil, applying enough pressure so that the blackened back will transfer the design.

Type 2:

1. Repeat steps 1 and 2 of type 1.
2. Place onion-skin tracing paper over carbon or graphite paper (see also PAPERS).
3. Place carbon and onion-skin tracing paper over desired ground and go over the contour of the design with pencil, applying enough pressure so that the carboned back will transfer the design.

Type 3:

1. Blacken the back of the design with pencil.
2. Place the design on the desired ground and go over the contour of the design with pencil, applying enough pressure so that the blackened back of the design paper will transfer the design.

Type 4:

1. Put typing paper over the design and hold both to a window through which light is filtering.
2. Trace the design on the typing paper.
3. Blacken the back of the typing paper with heavy black pencil.
4. Place the design on the desired ground, and go over the contour of the design with pencil, applying enough pressure so that the blackened back will transfer the design.

A small design or cartoon can be transferred to a larger panel (see also ENLARGING).

TRACING PAPER

See PAPERS.

TRANSITIONAL

Semiabstract; halfway between realism and abstract (see also ABSTRACT and REALISM).

TRANSPARENT

Quality of not being opaque (see also OPAQUE). In paints and painting, watercolor has the quality of being a transparent medium, that is, one can see through watercolor to the ground underneath. On the other hand, tempera has the quality of being an opaque or nontransparent medium. Transparent relates to papers, paints, glazes, tesserae, and enamels.

TRIAD

See COLOR.

TRIADIC

Color harmony using three colors such as a triad (see also COLOR).

TRIPOLI

See ABRASIVES.

TRIPTYCH

Painting on three folding panels (see DIPTYCH).

TRI-SQUARE

See WOODWORKING.

TRU-TONE COLORED PAPER

See PAPERS.

T-SQUARE RULER

See RULERS.

TUSCHE

Block-out solution used in the tusche stencil silk-screening process (see also SILK SCREENING).

TWILL

Diagonal-patterned weave (see also WEAVING).

TWO-DIMENSION

See DIMENSION.

ULTRAVIOLET LIGHT

Light at the extreme end of the color spectrum in the light theory; used in X-radiography to study paintings and to detect forgeries (see also COLOR).

UMBER

Also called burnt umber; an oil pigment used in oil painting [see also PAINTING and SUPPLIES (CLASSROOM)]. Burnt umber is also used to achieve certain antiqued finishes on white picture frames (see also STAINED GLASS).

UNDERCUTS

An outward or convex curve with an inward hook. Undercuts (Fig. U-1) in modeling and relief work will prevent the use of a plaster mold and duplication of form. Plaster molds must be lifted straight up from the form, and the use of undercuts would prevent it (see also CERAMICS, MOLDS, and PAPIER-MÂCHÉ).

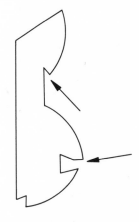

Fig. U-1

UNDERGLAZE

See CERAMICS.

UNDERGLAZE CRAYONS

See CERAMICS.

UNDERGLAZE PENCILS

See CERAMICS.

UNITY

See DESIGN ELEMENTS.

UPPER-CASE LETTERS

See ALPHABET.

VALENTINE BOXES

Use hatboxes trimmed with crepe paper for the conventional type of valentine box (see also HOLIDAYS AND SPECIAL EVENTS and PAPERS). The old-fashioned type of valentine box makes up in tradition what it lacks in function. The chore of passing out valentines on this special day seems almost endless, particularly when the job falls upon a teacher in a primary classroom. Valentines have been dropped into boxes with no names; and this is always a pleasant surprise! The chore of passing out valentines is easily negated with individual valentine mail boxes. These may be fashioned out of brown or white paper bags and decorated by the students with crayon, cut paper, or paint. Students attach these to their desks or to the backs of their chairs with tape.

Valentine mail is always more happily and readily distributed when the distribution "comes with the mailing." Beyond that, it brings a sense of relief to that child who worries that he will receive no valentines at all. It is reassuring to look into his box and see them collecting; and if they do not collect an empty mail box should motivate the teacher to do something positive about it.

VALUE

See COLOR and DESIGN ELEMENTS.

VANILLA

Add a teaspoon of vanilla to a gallon of enamel paint to cut down the paint odor (see also PAINTS).

VANISHING POINT

See PERSPECTIVE.

VARNISH

Available in gloss, semigloss, and flat finishes. Varnish will take from 8 to 12 hours to dry. Some paint manufacturers, however, add drying agents to speed up the drying time. Varnish "raises" the surface of the wood and thereby provides a hard protective finish. It may be thinned down with petroleum spirits such as turpentine (see also SOLVENTS). In applying varnish to a given surface, one should be extremely careful to note whether one coat is dry before another is added. If a second coat is applied to a tacky surface, the succeeding coats will remain permanently tacky.

Using Retouch Varnish: The oil painter often finishes his painting with a coating of retouch varnish. This is applied to achieve high lights of color and to eliminate dull spots which often appear when oil paintings dry. When retouch varnish is used, a more permanent varnish must be applied to the surface of the canvas in about a year (see also PAINTING).

Wood Finishing: Clean and sand the surface which will be varnished. Thin the first coat of varnish slightly to allow for penetration and easy application. The second coat can be applied full strength. Rub the surface lightly with 0000-gauge steel wool when the varnish has dried. Finish with a coating of paste wax.

VARNISH SUBSTITUTE

See SODIUM SILICATE.

VAULTING

Architectural structure as an arched roof or dome in a cathedral which allows maximum distance between walls (see also BUTTRESS and GOTHIC).

EXAMPLE: Vaulting in Gothic architecture.

VEHICLE

The vehicle in paints is that substance which makes the binder and pigment flow into a painting medium. In water-base paints, the vehicle is water; in oil paints, it is oil (see also BINDER, PAINT, and PIGMENT).

VENDORS (ART)

See SUPPLIES (VENDORS).

VENEER WOODS

See MARQUETRY and SUPPLIES (VENDORS).

VERMICULITE

Animal formation; white, porous material which is used as a grog to achieve lightweight and textural effects in carving materials such as aggregate mixtures (see also CARVING MATERIALS). It can be mixed with wheat paste to achieve a modeling material (see also MODELING MATERIALS). Commonly in all carving and modeling mixtures necessitating the use of vermiculite, zonolite may be used. Both are available at building supply houses (see also GROG and ZONOLITE).

VISUAL ARTS

Those arts which can be seen, as opposed to forms of art which rely on other senses.

VISUAL TEXTURE

See DESIGN ELEMENTS and RUBBINGS.

WARM COLORS

See COLOR.

WARP

See WEAVING and YARNS AND STRINGS.

WASH

Watery mixture of watercolor or tempera which is laid down on grounds (see also GROUND and PAINTS). Detail is often rendered over washes with darker paint and brush or with pen and ink.

EXAMPLE: "The Paddock," by Raoul Dufy.

WATER-BASE INKS

See INKS and SILK SCREENING.

WATER-BASE PAINTS

See PAINTS.

WATERCOLOR BRUSHES

See BRUSHES.

WATERCOLOR PAPER

See PAPERS.

WATERCOLORS

See PAINTING and PAINTS.

WAX

Beeswax: Sticky, sweet-smelling, brownish wax; literally the wax of bees. It is available in small disk shapes or in larger quantities of five, ten, or more pounds. It is used by professional batik artists and in candlemaking (see also BATIK and CANDLEMAKING).

NOTE: Beeswax is available from Braun Knecht Heimann Company, San Francisco 19, California. Other offices are located in Denver and Salt Lake City [see also SUPPLIES (VENDORS)].

Bulletin-Board Wax: Used as an adhering agent in creating three-dimensional bulletin-board displays. It is colorless, odorless, and stainless and can be used to attach solid objects of almost any size, weight, or shape to flat bulletin-board areas. It will adhere to glass, blackboards, woodwork, or other similar surfaces. Bulletin-board wax retains its adhesive quality, and articles attached to boards will remain almost indefinitely. It is available in individually-wrapped sticks, in packages of approximately 20.

NOTE: Vending supply houses: Teaching Materials Service, 285 Herbert Drive, Beloit, Wisconsin; and Palfreys School Supply Company, 7715 East Garvey Avenue, South San Gabriel, California [see also BULLETIN BOARD and SUPPLIES (VENDORS)].

Paraffin Wax: Used as a substitute material for beeswax in classroom art programs relating to the batik process and candlemaking (see also BATIK and CANDLEMAKING). Paraffin is available in individual packages of ¼ pound, 4 to a box. It may be obtained from grocery stores for the approximate cost of twenty-five cents.

Paste Wax: Household paste wax is used for wood finishes, for driftwood sculpture, and in finishing dried clay carvings (see also CARVING MATERIALS, DRIFTWOOD, ENCAUSTIC, LACQUER, LINSEED OIL, SHELLAC, and VARNISH).

Picture Wax: For the protection and preservation of art work where glass is not desired for framing and display; used most commonly for gouache paintings (see also PAINTING). Picture wax should be used sparingly, in small areas at a time, using a soft cloth for application.

Sealing Wax: Old-fashioned sealing wax is used to seal letters and packages and is available from stationery stores in colored sticks such as magenta, gold, blue, and silver. Sealing wax generally comes with a wick which will support a flame and allow the wax to melt onto a given surface. Approximately 6 drops of wax are required for an adequate seal. If a metal seal is available, it should be moistened before it is stamped into the sealing wax.

WAXED PAPER

See PAPERS.

WAX-PLASTER MIXTURE

See CARVING MATERIALS.

WEATHER BALLOONS

See PAPIER-MÂCHÉ.

WEAVER

One who weaves. Term is also applied to the long strand of reed which is used in basket weaving (see also BASKET REED and BASKETRY).

WEAVING

Vocabulary:

Heddle: Horizontal bar across a large loom which changes the position of the warp threads for desired kinds of weaving.

Loom: Any type of commercial or improvised device which will permit warp threading and allow for weaving.

1. Large looms may be purchased at any supply house which specializes in weaving equipment and supplies. These looms are available in extremely large sizes up to 9' x 12', table sizes, and small sizes which are portable. Some of the looms available are heddle bar looms, inkle looms, rug looms, muff looms, cap looms, mat looms, belt looms, and purse wall hanging looms among others [see also SUPPLIES (VENDORS)]. A woven wall hanging is shown in Fig. W-1.

Fig. W-1

2. Apple box looms are most readily available and most easily utilized for classroom experiences. Nails are hammered into the width strips of the apple box as shown in Fig. W-2. The spacing of the nails will need to be uniform; for kindergarten-primary grades, the spacing should be wider, approximately 1″ apart. Upper-grade students may space the nails at ½″ or ¼″ markings. The warp thread is tied to one end nail and brought down and around two nails, and up and around two nails, and so on until the loom is threaded with the warp thread. It is finally tied to the end nail on the other side (see also YARNS AND STRINGS).

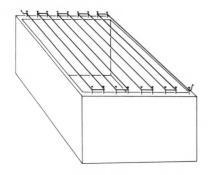

Fig. W-2

3. Wooden frame looms may be constructed from soft pine in square or rectangular shapes. Wooden picture frames may also be used as looms. Nails may be hammered into the top and bottom of the frame and the warp thread may be threaded as described previously.

4. Chipboard looms are made of squares, rectangles, and circles of chipboard (see also PAPERS). Notches are cut out with scissors or with knives. Another method of constructing a chipboard loom is to tape the edges with mystic or brown kraft tape and insert pins at the top and bottom to hold the warp thread (see also TAPES).

Selvage: The outer edge of the woven article.

Shed: The opening which is created in the warp thread when a heddle is used; generally found in larger looms.

Shot: One horizontal passing of the weft thread across and through the warp threading.

Shuttle: An implement which is made of wood or notched chipboard and carries the weft thread. It can be unwound as it is passed through the warp thus providing a continual supply of weaver thread.

Tension: The relative tightness or looseness of the warp thread on a loom. For good weaving, the tension of the warp and weft should be uniform throughout.

Warp: The vertical threading of a loom; the threads through which the weft is woven.

Weaver: May use a shuttle or tapestry needle for a weaving implement (see also NEEDLES). Weaving needles may be improvised with paper clips or taped bobby pins.

Weft: The thread, yarn, or cotton roving which is either carried in a shuttle or strung through a weaving implement or needle and is woven back and forth across the warp thread.

Weaving Process: There are many weaving patterns among which are the tabby weave, the twill, basket, and herringbone, among others. For initial weaving experiences, the plain weave is suggested. This consists of weaving the weft thread over one and under one across the warp and back again. As experience is gained in this craft, one may vary weft patterns and try an over-two, under-two weave, or an over-one, under-two weave, etc. The process of elementary weaving on simple looms is as follows:

1. Select a loom of your choice and thread it with warp thread.

2. Utilizing the plain weave of over one, under one, weave approximately 1″ or less across the warp thread. This will afford a firm base for weaving and will be repeated at the end of the woven article.

3. When the weft thread ends, either tie it to the end of another weft length or begin weaving with it where the other weft thread ended *in back* of the last warp thread.

4. In pulling the weft thread through the warp in one shot and returning with the weft thread to the other side of the loom, avoid pulling or tightening the selvage edge. Pulling the weft thread across too tightly will result in an unsightly hourglass weaving product.

5. As you weave back and forth, push the weft thread up with a comb or similar tool.

6. When the weaving is almost completed, finish it off with the plain weave of over one, under one as was done in the beginning.

7. Take the finished woven piece off the loom by lifting the warp thread off the notches, pins, or nails which hold the woven piece to the loom.

NOTE: For plaids, alternate the colors of the warp thread; then, as you weave back and forth, alternate the colors of the weft thread (see also STITCHERY and YARNS AND STRINGS).

WEDGING

See CERAMICS.

WEEDS (DRYING)

See DRYING WEEDS.

WEFT

See WEAVING.

WESTERN ART

Art of the Western world would include: Aegean-Cretan or Minoan (Pre-Hellenic), Etruscan, Inca, Greek-Hellenic, Mayan, Roman, Early Christian, Byzantine, Romanesque, Gothic, Aztec, Renaissance, Baroque, Rococo, Classicism or Neoclassicism, Romanticism, Impressionism, Postimpressionism, Abstract, and Abstract-Impressionism [see also HISTORY (ART) and EASTERN ART].

WHEAT PASTE

Dry powdered material which when mixed with water becomes a highly utilitarian adhesive for classroom art projects; may be purchased at hardware or paint stores.

Method for mixing: Gradually add 1 pound of wheat paste flour to 10 pints of water. Stir until thoroughly mixed. If a thinner paste is desired, add 1 or 2 more pints of water. Always use a clean container, and if lumps develop, strain the paste through a piece of cheesecloth (see also ADHESIVES, CHEESECLOTH, MODELING MATERIALS, and PAPIER-MÂCHÉ).

WHITE OAK

See WOODS.

WHITE PINE

See WOODS.

WHITE RESIN GLUE

See ADHESIVES.

WICK

See WICKING.

WICKING

Relates to the linen or cotton threads which support the flame in candles. Commercial candle wicking can be purchased for candlemaking projects in 30′ lengths from American Handicrafts Company, 33 East 14th Street, New York, New York [see also CANDLEMAKING and SUPPLIES (VENDORS)].

WILLOW (BLACK)

See WOODS.

WIRES

Aluminum Wire: For wire sculpture and armatures; available in diameters of ⅛″, ¼″, and ⅟₁₆″ (see also ARMATURES, SCULPTURE, and WIRE TOOLS).

Clothes Hangers: Used for mobiles and armatures (see also ARMATURES, MOBILES, and SCULPTURE).

Steel Wire: Use soft No. 13 gauge for wire sculpture and armatures (see also ARMATURES and SCULPTURE).

Stove Pipe Wire: For mobiles and armatures (see also ARMATURES, MOBILES, SCULPTURE, and WIRE TOOLS).

Note: Aluminum wire is the softest and most pliable of the wires listed and therefore is most suited to elementary school art experiences.

WIRE SCULPTURE

Try some sculpture in wire using wires and wire tools. Figures, animals, or abstract forms may be fashioned from wire and attached to wooden bases with metal brads (see also SCULPTURE, WIRES, and WIRE TOOLS).

WIRE TOOLS

Needle-Nose Pliers: For bending, twisting, curling, and shaping detailed work in wire.

Nippers: For cutting and trimming ends of wire.

Round-Nose Pliers: For general bending and shaping of wire (see also SCULPTURE, WIRES, and WIRE SCULPTURE).

WOODCUTS AND WOOD ENGRAVINGS

See PRINTMAKING (PROFESSIONAL), PRINTS, and RELIEF.

WOODGRAIN PAPER

See PAPERS.

WOODS

The following woods are available from Brodhead Garrett Company, 4560 East 71st Street, Cleveland 5, Ohio, which specializes in serving the school shop programs [see also SUPPLIES (VENDORS)]. Woods are available in varied thicknesses and are sold by the 100 board feet. All woods are of the highest grade as defined by the National Hardware Lumber Association.

Ash: Tough, elastic wood; used for woodenware, furniture, and shipbuilding.

Banak: Lightweight hardwood; pinkish-brown to brownish-gray.

Basswood: White, soft hardwood; used for drawing boards, boxes, furniture, baskets, and patterns.

Birch: Heavy, hard, and strong; used for dowels and spools.

Cedar (Aromatic Red): Light softwood.

Cherry: Satin-textured; used for furniture and cabinetwork.

Cypress: Light, soft, durable wood; pale brown to red in color; used for chests, furniture, and fine cabinetwork.

Doweling: Dowel rods are available in 36″ lengths in the following diameters: ⅛″, 3⁄16″, ¼″, 5⁄16″, ⅜″, 7⁄16″, ½″, ⅝″, ¾″, ⅞″, 1″, and 3″ (see also BRAYERS, CERAMICS, and PAPIER-MÂCHÉ).

Gum (Red): Hardwood; pinkish cast to deep reddish brown; used for furniture.

Limba: Hardwood; light-colored.

Mahogany (Genuine): Reddish brown color; used for furniture and cabinets.

Mahogany (Philippine): Used for furniture and cabinetwork.

Maple (Hard): Heavy hardwood; used for furniture, woodenware, and workbenches.

Oak (Red): Heavy and strong; used for furniture.

Oak (White): Strong wood; used for furniture.

Pine (Antique White): Knotty pine.

Pine (Sugar): Light-colored, softwood; used extensively in elementary school programs (see also WOODWORKING). It is also used in model making and pattern making.

Plywood Panels: Available in ¼″ 3 ply and ¾″ 7 ply in birch, cherry, gum, limba, mahogany, oak, pine, and walnut.

Poplar (Yellow): Light softwood; used for furniture, exterior work, patterns, toys, and woodenware.

Walnut (Black): Hardwood; used for furniture and cabinet making.

Willow (Black): Light, soft-textured hardwood; used for furniture and woodenware.

WOODS (FINISHING)

See LACQUER, LINSEED OIL, SHELLAC, and VARNISH.

WOODS (VENEER)

See MARQUETRY.

WOODWORKING

Woodworking should begin in the kindergarten and should be carried on throughout the remaining grades. Students need only to have supplies and woodworking tools which have been carefully selected for their age and grade level. The following tools and equipment are suggested for a minimal, general woodworking program.

Awl: For making holes; hit with a hammer.

Bit and Brace: For boring holes; bits: ½″, ¾″, and 1″; brace: 1½-pound type.

Chisel: ¾″, 6-ounce type; for chipping or cutting wood. Hit with a hammer.

W

Clamps: For securing wood into position for sawing; sizes: 2″, 3″, 4″, 5″, and 6″ mouths.

Hammers: Claw hammer; 13-ounce hammers for kindergarten-primary grades and 16-ounce for intermediate-upper grades.

Hand Drill and Drills: For boring small holes; hand drill: 1-pound type; drill sizes: ⅟₁₆″, ⅛″, ³⁄₁₆″, and ¼″.

Hinges: An assortment of varied sizes needed.

Nails: Varied lengths of 15, 16, and 17 gauge nails.

Pincers: Several pair.

Pliers: Several pair.

Rasp: For smoothing rough-textured wood; 8″ flat.

Sandpaper: Assortment packages with grits from fine to coarse.

Saws:

Crosscut: 12″ for kindergarten-primary, 16″ for intermediate, and 20″ for upper grades.

Keyhole: Used for cutting larger holes in wood after initial hole has been bored with a brace and bit.

Coping: For cutting around curves; secure several saw handles and enough blades to insure an adequate supply.

Screw Drivers: Several; 8 ounce.

Steel Wool: Assortment packages with varied gauges.

Tri-Square: Measuring tool; 8 ounce, metal.

Wood: Keep a supply of apple, orange, and liquor boxes on hand for an economical woodworking program. Soft pine wood is best suited for a beginning woodworking experience and can be ordered in the following sizes: ½″ x ½″ x 36″, 1″ x 1″ x 36″, 2″ x 2″ x 36″, 1″ x ½″ x 36″, 4″ x ½″ x 36″, 8″ x ½″ x 36″, and 10″ x ½″ x 36″ (see also WOODS). Assortments of different sizes of wood doweling is desirable. In the lower grades, wood doweling is used for wheel axles. It is also used in puppetry for stand making (see also PAPIER-MÂCHÉ and PUPPETRY). Specific sizes of wood doweling in 36″ lengths are available (see also WOODS).

Workbenches: Available with either one vise or two vises; use 22″ workbenches for kindergarten-primary grades, 24″ for intermediate grades, and 27″ for upper grades.

WOOF

See WEAVING.

WOOL

See YARNS AND STRINGS.

WORKBENCHES

See WOODWORKING.

WRITING

Term applies to both cursive and manuscript writing, examples of which are shown in Fig. W-3, (see also ALPHABET, CALLIGRAPHY, and LETTERING).

Fig. W-3

X-ACTO KNIVES

See KNIVES.

Y

YARNS AND STRINGS

Carpet Warp: Warp thread for carpet making; sold in ½-pound tubes in colored and white; also available in quantity and sold in 5- and 10-pound lots.

Cotton and Floss: For hand weaving and stitchery; sold in tubes and yards to the pound depending upon weight of cotton and floss; available in natural, white, and colored.

Cotton Chenille: For hand weaving and stitchery; available in white and colored in 4- and 6-ounce skeins.

Cotton Roving: Also called rug filler; used for hand weaving, stitchery, decorative effects on bulletin boards and papier-mâché objects, and cotton roving mobiles. It is available in white, natural, and an assortment of colors; it is sold in 4-ply ½-pound skeins.

Cotton Warp: For general loom weaving using cotton warp thread; sold in 2-ounce tubes and 1-pound cones; available in white, natural, and colors.

Jute: For weaving and stitchery; available in white, natural, and colors; sold by the pound.

Wool: For general loom weaving and stitchery; available in white, natural, and colors. Sold in 1-, 2-, 4-, and 6-ounce skeins (see also CARICATURES, COTTON ROVING, MOBILES, PAPIER-MÂCHÉ, STITCHERY, and WEAVING).

NOTE: All of the yarns and strings described are available from the J. L. Hammett Company, Cambridge, Massachusetts [see also SUPPLIES (VENDORS)].

YELLOW

One of the three primary colors; considered to be the color with the highest visibility, for example, hunting jackets are made of yellow fabric, and road signs and highway dividing lines are painted yellow (see also COLOR).

YELLOW POPLAR

See WOODS.

ZONOLITE

Volcanic earth formation which is brownish-gold in color; used as a grog to achieve lightweight and textural effects in carving materials such as aggregate mixtures (see also CARVING MATERIALS and GROG). It can be mixed with wheat paste and will serve as a modeling material (see also MODELING MATERIALS). Commonly it is used as a substance in which to root young plants and is therefore available at nursery establishments as well as building supply houses. In all carving and modeling mixtures necessitating the use of zonolite, vermiculite may be substituted (see also VERMICULITE).